the About.com guide to

HOME
COOKING

---

225 Family-Friendly Recipes with a Dash of Sophistication

Peggy Trowbridge Filippone with Lynette Rohrer Shirk

Adams Media
Avon, Massachusetts

About.com is a powerful network of more than 600 Guides—smart, passionate, accomplished people who are experts in their fields. About.com Guides live and work in more than twenty countries and celebrate their interests in thousands of topics. They have written books, appeared on national television programs, and won many awards in their fields. Guides are selected for their ability to provide the most interesting information for users, and for their passion for their subject and the Web. The selection process is rigorous—only 2 percent of those who apply actually become Guides. The following are some of the most important criteria by which they are chosen:

- High level of knowledge/passion for their topic
- Appropriate credentials
- Keen understanding of the Web experience
- Commitment to creating informative, actionable features

Each month more than 48 million people visit About.com. Whether you need home-repair and decorating ideas, recipes, movie trailers, or car-buying tips, About.com Guides can offer practical advice and solutions for everyday life. Wherever you land on About.com, you'll always find content that is relevant to your interests. If you're looking for "how to" advice on refinishing your deck, About.com will also show you the tools you need to get the job done. No matter where you are on About.com, or how you got there, you'll always find exactly what you're looking for!

About Your Guide

 Peggy Trowbridge Filippone is a writer and food service industry professional who loves to cook. She has written news columns about cooking as well as hosted various food forums on several services over the past eighteen years. As the eldest of six children, she began cooking at the ripe young age of eight. While pursuing her initial career as an insurance litigation specialist, she began hosting picnics, barbecues, and dinner parties for business associates to show off new culinary creations. Food and cooking soon became her dominant passion, with particular emphasis on food history. After nearly twenty years in the insurance industry, Peggy left the field to concentrate on raising her daughter and began writing guest food articles for small publications. At the same time, she had discovered the online world in the mid-1980s and began sharing her advice and knowledge of food on a national level first as an assistant, then as a host of several online food forums. Peggy has been the About Guide to Home Cooking on the World Wide Web for the past ten years and also works as a consultant for kitchen products and cookbook authors.

Acknowledgments

My greatest thanks go to my husband, Joe, and my daughter, Joelle, both of whom have patiently taste-tested the good, the bad, and the ugly of my recipe experiments and put up with the banging of pots and pans in the kitchen, often into the wee hours of the morning. My gratitude also goes out to my many friends who have been guinea pigs over the years, kind and gentle with criticism when needed and bursting with enthusiasm when I hit the jackpot with a new taste sensation. It is the daily support and feedback from my readers that truly keeps me in the kitchen playing with my food.

ABOUT.COM

CEO & President
Scott Meyer

COO
Andrew Pancer

SVP Content
Michael Daecher

VP Marketing
Lisa Abourezk

Director, About Operations
Chris Murphy

Senior Web Designer
Jason Napolitano

ADAMS MEDIA

Editorial

Publishing Director
Gary M. Krebs

Managing Editor
Laura M. Daly

Executive Editor, Series Books
Brielle K. Matson

Development Editor
Katrina Schroeder

Marketing

Director of Marketing
Karen Cooper

Assistant Art Director
Frank Rivera

Production

Director of Manufacturing
Susan Beale

Production Project Manager
Michelle Roy Kelly

Senior Book Designer
Colleen Cunningham

Published by Adams Media, an F+W Publications Company
57 Littlefield Street
Avon, MA 02322
www.adamsmedia.com

ISBN 10: 1-59869-396-4
ISBN 13: 978-1-59869-396-6

Printed in China.

J I H G F E D C B A

Library of Congress Cataloging-in-Publication Data
is available from the publisher.

This publication is designed to provide accurate and authoritative information with regard to the subject matter covered. It is sold with the understanding that the publisher is not engaged in rendering legal, accounting, or other professional advice. If legal advice or other expert assistance is required, the services of a competent professional person should be sought.
—From a *Declaration of Principles* jointly adopted by a Committee of the American Bar Association and a Committee of Publishers and Associations

Many of the designations used by manufacturers and sellers to distinguish their product are claimed as trademarks. Where those designations appear in this book and Adams Media was aware of a trademark claim, the designations have been printed with initial capital letters.

This book is available at quantity discounts for bulk purchases. For information, please call 1-800-872-5627.

How to Use This Book

Each About.com book is written by an About.com Guide—an expert with experiential knowledge of his or her subject. While the book can stand on its own as a helpful resource, it can also be coupled with the corresponding About.com site for even more tips, tools, and advice. Each book will not only refer you back to About.com, but it will also direct you to other useful Internet locations and print resources.

All About.com books include a special section at the end of each chapter called Get Linked. Here you'll find a few links back to the About.com site for even more great information on the topics discussed in that chapter. Depending on the topic, you could find links to such resources as photos, sheet music, quizzes, recipes, or product reviews.

About.com books also include four types of sidebars:

- **Ask Your Guide:** Detailed information in a question-and-answer format
- **Tools You Need:** Advice about researching, purchasing, and using a variety of tools for your projects
- **What's Hot:** All you need to know about the hottest trends and tips out there
- **Elsewhere on the Web:** References to other useful Internet locations

Each About.com book will take you on a personal tour of a certain topic, give you reliable advice, and leave you with the knowledge you need to achieve your goals.

Contents

Introduction from Your Guide

One could argue that home cooking dates back to the domestication of fire. From the ashes of those first foods, we humans have developed quite a palate, with a taste for everything from the mundane to the bizarre. Sharing a meal in the home is an important invitation to conversation and discussion, a practice that is sadly falling by the wayside in the hustle and bustle of the twenty-first century. Psychologists are highly recommending a return to the custom of at least one shared family meal each day as a means of relieving stress and tension in the home. A good home-cooked meal can soothe the savage beast.

When we think of home cooking, we usually think of comfort foods. These are the foods and dishes we were raised on, the thought of which evokes memories of home. Regional location and ethnic background play a big part in what constitutes a comfort food, but so does age. Great-Grandma's favorite comfort food may have been apple pie and Grandma's may have been ice cream, while yours may be macaroni and cheese and your child's may be McDonald's Chicken McNuggets. We are all products of our time.

In these modern times, there are few foods that cannot be cooked at home. We have so many conveniences in our kitchens these days, including microwaves, food processors, toaster ovens, waffle-makers, pasta machines, deep-fryers, steamers, ice cream machines, and the wondrous, life-saving slow cooker. Our pots and pans are high-tech, our knives supposedly never dull, and we can even buy unbreakable dinnerware.

Home cooks used to grow and can their own foods. Today's commercial crops have been modified for a longer shelf-life and to withstand rigorous transportation, with a seemingly corresponding drop in quality. Yet, the organic food market is also an option—for a price. On the other hand, commercialization of groceries has opened our eyes to a brand new horizon of foods that Grandma would never have dreamed of. Exotic fruits, vegetables, and spices from around the world are now commonly stocked in most major supermarket chains. You can opt for low-fat, fat-free, light, sugar-free, and vegetarian products that were unavailable as recently as thirty years ago. You now have access to irradiated eggs to make homemade mayonnaise without fear of salmonella poisoning from raw eggs. There are tens of thousands of varieties of condiment from which to choose. Flash-frozen fruits, vegetables, and meats can actually be fresher and more nourishing than their raw counterparts.

With so many options available today, it's not difficult to be a good cook at home, if not a gourmet cook. Home cooking doesn't necessarily mean completely from scratch. It's perfectly acceptable to save time during the week by using shortcuts such as pre-cut veggies, cooked rotisserie chicken, or boxed cake mixes. Even if you use a boxed mix, frozen food, or canned product, you can toss in something fresh or an added spice to make it your own.

These recipes cover old and new family favorites, many of which are updated to reflect our modern kitchens and tastes. They range from simple preparations to almost gourmet, but none requires any special kitchen skills or expensive equipment. Even the most inexperienced cook should be able to follow the recipes with ease and produce a delicious result.

Cooking is always more fun when you have help in the kitchen, so encourage your family, friends, and loved ones to join in. If you have the opportunity, teach a child to cook. It's not only a great shared experience, but also an enjoyable math and science lesson.

Keep in mind that help is always just an email away on my Home Cooking site online at http://homecooking.about.com. Enjoy!

Peggy Trowbridge Filippone

Chapter 1

Appetizers and Salads

ASK YOUR GUIDE

What is the best way to cook hard-boiled eggs?
▶ **PAGE 4**

Some recipes call for she-crabs. How can I tell the difference?
▶ **PAGE 6**

What are your suggestions for selecting and storing walnuts?
▶ **PAGE 15**

Bacon-Wrapped Breadsticks
SERVES 8

These are so simple and fast to make, yet they're a huge hit at parties. They are also great for snacks. They may be made a day ahead of time, and then reheated in the microwave about 30 seconds to crisp up.

½ pound thin-sliced bacon
¼ cup Parmesan cheese, grated, divided use
1 tablespoon sesame seeds
1 box (4.4 ounces) breadsticks

1. Preheat oven to 425°F. Place a metal baking rack inside a shallow 10" × 15" baking tray.
2. Slice each bacon strip in half lengthwise and sprinkle one side with grated Parmesan cheese and sesame seeds.
3. Wrap the bacon strips spirally around each breadstick, cheese-side out. Place on the baking rack, horizontal to the wires so they don't fall through.
4. Bake 12 to 15 minutes, until bacon is cooked. Sprinkle hot bacon-wrapped breadsticks with additional Parmesan cheese. Let cool before serving.

TOOLS YOU NEED

▶ The metal baking rack used in this recipe is also useful for cooking bacon by itself. Using it, bacon can be baked in the oven, resulting in amazingly flat slices. Do this: Preheat the oven to 400°F. Place a metal baking rack inside a baking sheet. Lay out the bacon slices and bake for 10 to 15 minutes, depending on desired crispness. Voila— crispy bacon with no curls and no grease-splattered skillet!

Artichoke Dip
SERVES 4

I like the combination of salty and slightly sweet in this baked dip. Serve hot from the oven accompanied by pita triangles, bread sticks, crackers, or French bread.

   1 tablespoon butter, softened
   1 can (14 ounces) artichoke hearts
   2 anchovy filets
   1 tablespoon dried currants
   1 cup Parmesan cheese, grated
   1 cup mayonnaise

1. Preheat oven to 350°F, and butter a casserole dish and set it aside.
2. Chop the artichoke hearts and put in a bowl.
3. Mince the anchovies and add them to the artichokes.
4. Add the currants, Parmesan cheese, and mayonnaise to the artichokes and mix well.
5. Spread the artichoke mixture into the buttered casserole dish.
6. Bake for 25 minutes, until brown and bubbly. Serve hot.

ELSEWHERE ON THE WEB

▶ Every year in Castroville, CA, there is a festival to honor the artichoke. This festival includes a run/walk through the artichoke fields of Castroville (with fresh artichokes for the runners to stop and eat along the way!), cooking demonstrations, an agroart competition, and even an artichoke-eating contest! To learn more about the festival or for more recipe ideas surrounding artichokes, visit www.artichoke-festival.org.

What is the best way to cook hard-boiled eggs?

▶ First, place eggs in a single layer in a saucepan. Cover with at least one inch of water over the tops of the shells. Cover the pot with a lid and bring the water to a boil. As soon as it begins to boil, remove the pan from heat and let stand 15 to 17 minutes. Next, drain off the hot water and immediately cover eggs with cold water until eggs are completely cooled. For more tips, visit http://about.com/homecook ing/cookeggs.

Curried Deviled Eggs
SERVES 6

Far from the bland deviled eggs you find at some parties and family gatherings, these deviled eggs are full of flavor and texture. Do take a few extra minutes to add the garnish so they look as impressive as they taste.

6 hard-boiled eggs
5 tablespoons mayonnaise
1 teaspoon yellow mustard
½ teaspoon curry powder
¼ teaspoon onion powder
⅛ teaspoon cayenne pepper
¼ cup celery, chopped
Parsley, chopped for garnish
Paprika, for garnish
Black olives, quartered lengthwise for garnish

1. Slice hard-boiled eggs in half lengthwise. Remove egg yolks to a bowl, and set egg whites aside. Mash the egg yolks until crumbly.
2. Add the mayonnaise, mustard, curry and onion powders, and cayenne pepper to the yolks and mix well. Fold in the celery.
3. Pipe or spoon yolk filling into egg white halves.
4. Garnish with parsley, paprika, and olive slivers and chill before serving.

Dijon Potato Salad
SERVES 6

I make this potato salad with the skin on the potatoes to complement the color of the mustard seeds and pickles. Adjust the consistency with more mayonnaise if it gets dry after being chilled.

30 baby red potatoes, boiled
3 baby sweet pickles (gherkins)
1 hard-boiled egg, peeled
¼ cup onion, diced
2 tablespoons coarse-ground mustard
2 tablespoons Dijon mustard
¾ cup mayonnaise
¼ teaspoon paprika
½ teaspoon salt
¼ teaspoon pepper
2 tablespoons fresh parsley, chopped

1. Quarter the potatoes and put in a bowl.
2. Dice the pickles and add to the potatoes.
3. Chop the hard-boiled egg and add it to the potatoes.
4. Add the rest of the ingredients to the bowl and stir until well mixed.
5. Chill before serving.

WHAT'S HOT

▶ Try this Mock Potato Salad and see what you think. Crumble 4 sleeves of saltine crackers into a large bowl. Add 1 cup chopped celery, 1 cup chopped onions, 1 cup sweet relish, 1 cup dill relish, 6 chopped hard-boiled eggs, 1 cup chopped pimento-stuffed green olives, 1 cup chopped black olives, 1 cup sliced green onions, and a few dashes of cayenne pepper hot sauce. Toss together. Add enough Miracle Whip or similar salad dressing to the consistency of potato salad you like.

Some recipes call for she-crabs. How can I tell the difference?

▶ Luckily, it is fairly simple to distinguish a female crab from a male—and you won't need a magnifying glass to do it! Turn the whole crab on its back and look at the underside. The female has a broad, triangular-shaped area in the center of the underside, whereas the male has a distinctive, elongated spire in the center.

Crab Muffins
YIELDS 4 DOZEN

These are bursting with flavor, and make perfect party food. Try substituting lobster, shrimp, smoked salmon, or tuna for the crabmeat.

¼ cup sweet onions, minced
¼ cup celery, minced
¼ cup (½ stick) unsalted butter
2 tablespoons red bell pepper, minced
2 cloves garlic, pressed
1-½ cups vegetable broth
1 box (6 ounces) cornmeal stuffing mix
1 cup Swiss cheese, shredded
2 cups pasteurized canned lump crabmeat or fresh
2 tablespoons chives, chopped
3 eggs
¼ cup lemon juice
1 cup milk

1. Sauté sweet onions and celery in butter until onion becomes translucent. Add red bell pepper and pressed garlic and sauté an additional 2 minutes.
2. Add broth and bring to a boil. Remove from heat. Add contents of stuffing mix, gently tossing to combine. Let rest, uncovered, for 15 minutes.
3. Preheat oven to 350°F. Coat mini-muffin tins with vegetable spray.
4. Toss Swiss cheese, crabmeat, and chives with prepared stuffing mix.
5. In another bowl, beat eggs, lemon juice, and milk with a fork until mixed. Let sit for 5 minutes until it appears curdled.
6. Pour egg mixture over crab stuffing mix. Toss gently to combine. Fill mini-muffin tins to the rim. Bake about 30 minutes until puffy and golden.
7. Serve hot or at room temperature.

Roasted Garlic and Almond Spread
YIELDS 2 CUPS

Roasting the garlic mellows it into a mild nutty flavor in this popular party dip. It may be made up to a day in advance.

16 cloves garlic, peeled
3 tablespoons olive oil
¼ cup raw sliced almonds, chopped
8 ounces cream cheese, softened
¼ cup sour cream
2 teaspoons Dijon mustard
1 teaspoon Worcestershire sauce
2 tablespoons fresh parsley, chopped
1 teaspoon fresh rosemary leaves, chopped
2 shallots, chopped
3 tablespoons whipping cream
¼ teaspoon hot sauce

1. Preheat oven to 275°F.
2. Place garlic in a shallow, oven-proof casserole, drizzle with olive oil, and toss to coat. Bake in preheated oven for about 30 minutes. Remove from oven and let cool in the oil for at least 30 minutes.
3. Place almonds on a cookie sheet, then place them in the oven and toast them until they are lightly browned, 10 to 15 minutes. Let cool.
4. Scrape garlic and oil into a food processor and purée until smooth. Add cream cheese, sour cream, mustard, and Worcestershire sauce. Process until well blended. Add the almonds, parsley, rosemary, shallots, whipping cream, and hot sauce. Pulse until incorporated, but not completely smooth.
5. Scrape spread into a glass serving dish and chill for 4 hours. Serve with Melba toast, saltines, matzoh crackers, or pita crisps. Refrigerated leftovers should be used within 1 day.

WHAT'S HOT

▶ Did you know that one raw garlic clove, finely minced or pressed, releases more flavor than a dozen cooked whole cloves? When garlic cloves are cooked or baked whole, the flavor mellows into a sweet, almost nutty flavor. And believe it or not, this nutty flavor makes a surprisingly nice addition to desserts, such as brownies and even ice cream. To find recipes with garlic, along with all kinds of other garlicky information and lore, check out http://about.com/homecooking/garlic.

Crab Shrimp Dip
SERVES 12

I like to serve this chunky dip in a chilled bowl to spoon onto crackers.

4 ounces cream cheese, softened
¼ cup mayonnaise
2 teaspoons lemon juice
¼ teaspoon pepper
⅛ teaspoon salt
¼ teaspoon hot sauce

1 cup frozen, cooked popcorn shrimp, thawed
1 cup canned crabmeat, drained
2 tablespoons onion, minced
1 tablespoon fresh dill, chopped

1. Beat the cream cheese with a wooden spoon or electric mixer until soft and fluffy.
2. Mix the mayonnaise, lemon juice, pepper, salt, and hot sauce into the cream cheese and combine well.
3. Add the shrimp, crabmeat, and onion and fold in thoroughly. Stir the dill in last. Chill for at least 2 hours before serving.

Capri Salad
SERVES 4

This salad is called Caprese in Italy, after the Isle of Capri.

6 ripe red tomatoes
6 ounces fresh mozzarella cheese, in one piece

¼ cup extra-virgin olive oil
10 fresh basil leaves

1. Slice the tomatoes and mozzarella into ¼-inch-thick rounds.
2. Arrange the slices of tomato and mozzarella in alternating rows on a platter.
3. Drizzle the olive oil over the tomatoes and mozzarella.
4. Tear the fresh basil leaves into random pieces and sprinkle them over the tomatoes and mozzarella right before serving.

ELSEWHERE ON THE WEB

▶ You can make this crab shrimp dip as hot or mild as you'd like by varying the amount of hot sauce you put in. At www.hotsauce.com, you can browse hot sauces by country of origin, pepper, and heat. Here you'll also find more hot sauce recipes and gift ideas for people who like to kick it up a notch.

Shrimp Rice Salad
SERVES 6

Serve this salad as a main course along with a side salad of sliced ripe tomatoes and sweet tea or lemonade for an authentic Southern-style lunch.

2 pounds shrimp, cooked and peeled
4 cups water
2 tablespoons crab boil seasoning (page 199)
1 cup white rice, uncooked
½ cup sweet onion, chopped
½ cup black olives, chopped
1 cup mayonnaise
Lemon wedges, for garnish
Parsley, for garnish

1. Chop the shrimp into bite-sized pieces and set aside.
2. Bring 4 cups of water to a boil. Stir in the crab boil seasoning and cook for a few minutes. Turn off the heat.
3. Stir the rice into the spiced water and bring to a boil. Cover, then reduce the heat to low and simmer for 15 to 20 minutes. Drain the rice in a colander and allow it to cool.
4. When rice is cool, stir the onion and olives into it, and then add the mayonnaise and combine well.
5. Fold the shrimp into the rice mixture and spoon the salad into a serving bowl. Garnish with lemon wedges and parsley. Chill before serving.

TOOLS YOU NEED

▶ Although this recipe calls for cooking the rice in a pan, if you're an avid rice-eater, you may want to invest in a rice cooker. These rice cookers, which cook the rice and keep it warm while you fix the rest of your meal, can save you time and clean-up and are available in most kitchen supply stores and Asian restaurant supply stores.

WHAT'S HOT

▶ If commercially made sausage bothers you because of the fat content or the unknown factor of which "scraps" might be used by the manufacturers to make it, try making your own sausage at home. If you don't have your butcher grind the meat, a food processor with a metal blade will also work. Be sure ingredients are well chilled, as the chopping/grinding process creates heat that can emulsify your mixture.

Apple Sausage Balls
YIELDS 30

Two classic combinations—pork and apples, and apples and Cheddar—are merged into these tasty party snacks, perfect for Sunday afternoon football munching.

½ pound ground pork breakfast sausage
1½ cups biscuit mix
2 cups Cheddar cheese, grated
½ cup dried apples, finely chopped
1 teaspoon Dijon mustard
Pepper, to taste

1. Preheat the oven to 375°F. Line a baking sheet with foil and spray the foil with nonstick spray.
2. Combine all ingredients in a large bowl. Mix well with your fingers, squeezing and kneading the ingredients together to make dough.
3. Pinch the dough off into 1-inch clumps and roll them between the palms of your hands to form balls.
4. Place the balls on the prepared baking sheet. Bake for 18 to 20 minutes or until golden brown. Serve warm.

Raspberry Cream Fruit Salad Dressing or Dip
YIELDS 3 CUPS

This light and fluffy dressing can be used in or on fruit salads, or as a dip for fresh fruit. It's very easy to make and packs a lot of flavor. The sweet but tangy taste makes a perfect complement to naturally sweet fruits. Try experimenting with other fruit preserves, such as strawberry, blackberry, or boysenberry, instead of the raspberry preserves.

1 cup heavy whipping cream
¼ teaspoon salt
1 cup mayonnaise
1 tablespoon raspberry vinegar
⅓ cup seedless raspberry preserves
1 tablespoon powdered sugar

1. Beat heavy cream and salt with an electric mixer on medium speed until stiff peaks form.
2. Gently fold in mayonnaise, raspberry vinegar, raspberry preserves, and powdered sugar until thoroughly combined.
3. Pour into a decorative bowl, cover, and refrigerate at least one hour before serving. May be refrigerated up to 3 days.

WHAT'S HOT

▶ Serve fruit salad in an ice bowl! Simply fill a bowl partway with water and drop in fresh berries or edible flowers for decoration. Put a smaller bowl in the big bowl and fill the little bowl with ice cubes for weight. Tie bowls up with string, like a package, to keep them in place as water expands. Freeze overnight. Twenty minutes before serving, remove from freezer, unwrap, and allow to sit at room temperature before separating bowls. Voila!

▶ A marble slab is the perfect surface for rolling out puff pastry because it stays cooler in a hot kitchen than a wooden board or laminate countertop. The coolness helps to keep the butter present in the pastry dough in its solid form. This is good, because you want the butter to stay in sheets between the flour layers so it will create steam and make the pastry rise.

Mini Quiche Lorraines
YIELDS 24

Tiny, bite-sized quiches filled with a classic mixture of bacon and sweet onions are a perfect finger food for parties.

1 sheet frozen **puff pastry**, thawed but unfolded	½ teaspoon salt
	¼ teaspoon pepper
5 slices bacon, diced	2 eggs
1 cup sweet onions, diced	2 tablespoons chives, chopped
4 ounces cream cheese, softened	½ cup Swiss cheese, shredded
⅛ teaspoon ground nutmeg	

1. Preheat oven to 400°F. Grease mini-muffin pans.
2. On a lightly floured board, place unfolded, thawed puff pastry sheet and roll out into a rectangle about 12" × 14" inches and ⅛-inch thick.
3. Cut 24 rounds out of the pastry using a 2½-inch biscuit cutter. Fit rounds into mini-muffin cups. Set aside.
4. Fry the bacon until limp, then add the onions and sauté those with the bacon until onions are tender and bacon is crisp. Drain on paper towels.
5. In a bowl, blend the cream cheese with the nutmeg, salt, and pepper until smooth. Beat the eggs into the cream cheese one at a time until incorporated. Fold the chives into the egg mixture.
6. Put a teaspoon of the bacon/onion mixture into each pastry-lined muffin cup then spoon the egg mixture into each cup over the bacon/onion. Sprinkle each with a pinch of Swiss cheese.
7. Bake 10 minutes until puffed and golden. Serve warm. (May be baked ahead and frozen. Reheat in the oven at 350°F for 15 to 20 minutes.)

Tricolor Coleslaw
SERVES 8

This crunchy salad wears the colors of Mardi Gras—purple, gold (well, orange is close), and green—for a festive look on any plate. You can add a few drops of sesame oil, cooked chicken slices, and sesame seeds to create a main meal salad.

½ cup mayonnaise
1 tablespoon milk
1 teaspoon sugar
1 tablespoon cider vinegar
3 cups cabbage, shredded
¼ cup purple cabbage, shredded
¼ cup carrot, shredded
¼ cup green onion
1 teaspoon celery seed
Salt, to taste
Pepper, to taste

1. Mix the mayonnaise, milk, sugar, and cider vinegar together in a large bowl.
2. Toss the cabbages, carrots, and green onions in the bowl with the mayonnaise mixture.
3. Sprinkle the celery seed, salt, and pepper over the cabbage and mix well.
4. Refrigerate 2 hours before serving.

ELSEWHERE ON THE WEB

▶ For other Mardi Gras recipes and party ideas, as well as Louisiana links and lore, visit the About.com Southern Cooking Guide. This site, http://about.com/southern food/mardigras, can guide you to the best places to find gumbo, jambalaya, and Cajun recipes.

Red, White, and Blue Potato Salad
SERVES 6

The beautiful colors of this red, white, and blue potato salad come from the potatoes themselves. If you can't find blue or purple potatoes, simply use all red and white. This recipe is obviously perfect for the Fourth of July due to the coloring, but you can enjoy it year-round.

½ pound baby red rose potatoes (new potatoes)
½ pound baby white rose potatoes
½ pound small blue potatoes
⅛ cup mayonnaise
⅛ cup ranch dressing
2 tablespoons pickle relish

½ tablespoon white wine vinegar
¼ teaspoon dried dill weed
Pinch of sugar
¼ cup chives, chopped
Salt, to taste
Pepper, to taste
Cherry tomatoes, for garnish

1. Simmer all the potatoes (unpeeled) in salted water until tender but not mushy. Let cool until easy enough to handle, but still warm. Cut them into 1-inch pieces and set aside in a large bowl.
2. Combine mayonnaise, ranch dressing, relish, white wine vinegar, dill weed, and sugar, and pour the mixture over the warm potatoes. Sprinkle the chives over the dressing and potatoes and toss to coat.
3. Season with salt and pepper and refrigerate 2 hours or more to let the flavors meld.
4. To serve, let the potato salad come to room temperature. Garnish with cherry tomatoes.

TOOLS YOU NEED

▶ When using cooked potatoes in recipes such as mashed potatoes or potato gnocchi, it is best to use a potato ricer or a food mill to keep the starchy tubers fluffy. If you use an electric mixer the result will be gummy.

Artichoke Walnut Chicken Salad
SERVES 4

Enjoy this crunchy chicken salad simply with a fork, wrapped up in a velvety butter lettuce cup, or as a sandwich filling served in a buttery croissant. It also makes delicious party hors d'oeuvres when it is spooned into bite-sized pastry shells.

2 cups cooked chicken, diced
1 cup mayonnaise
1 tablespoon lemon juice
½ cup artichoke hearts, chopped
½ cup celery, diced
¼ cup walnuts, chopped
½ teaspoon onion powder
1 teaspoon pepper
Salt, to taste
4 butter lettuce leaves

1. In a large bowl, mix the chicken with the mayonnaise and lemon juice until well combined.
2. Toss the artichoke hearts, celery, and walnuts with the chicken mixture.
3. Season with onion powder, salt, and pepper, and mix well. Chill before serving.
4. To serve, line a platter, serving bowl, or individual bowls with butter lettuce leaves and spoon the chicken salad onto the lettuce.

ASK YOUR GUIDE

What are your suggestions for selecting and storing walnuts?

▶ Shelled nuts should be brittle and snap easily. Nuts can quickly turn rancid due to their high oil content, so for long-term storage it's best to buy unshelled nuts and store them in the refrigerator for two to three months or freeze up to one year. Shelled walnuts should be kept refrigerated in an airtight container and can be frozen up to a year. One pound of walnuts will yield about two cups of nutmeat.

Get Linked

Here are some great links to my About.com site for more appetizer and salad recipes and related information.

APPETIZER RECIPES

Hors d'oeuvres, appetizers, dips, and more are at your fingertips on this page.

 http://about.com/homecooking/appetizers

SALAD RECIPES

From side salads to fruit salads to main meal salads, you'll find inspiration on this page.

 http://about.com/homecooking/salad

SALAD DRESSING

You'll find everything you need to dress and accessorize a salad here.

 http://about.com/homecooking/saladdressing

Chapter 2

Dairy, Cheese, and Eggs

ASK YOUR GUIDE:

What is mozzarella made from?
▸ PAGE 21

What is feta cheese?
▸ PAGE 23

What kind of ham should I use for sandwich rolls?
▸ PAGE 33

Does the brand of non-stick skillet I use matter?
▸ PAGE 34

▶ There are so many different ways to serve Brie as an appetizer. Try cutting the top rind from a round of Brie, microwaving the remaining whole cheese briefly so it is melted, and serving it as a quick fondue with apple slices and crackers for dipping. You could also bake a smaller wedge of Brie in the oven with toasted almonds and a splash of amaretto and serve it with French bread, grapes, and whole almonds. Check out http://about.com/homecooking/brie for more Brie recipes.

Baked Brie in Puff Pastry
SERVES 10 TO 12

The Brie cheese melts inside the puffy crust for an elegant appetizer. Serve with apple slices, toast rounds, crackers, or other raw vegetables.

> 1 sheet puff pastry, thawed in refrigerator
> 1 round Brie cheese, about 1 pound in size
> ¼ cup dried apricots, chopped
> Egg wash (1 egg yolk mixed with 1 teaspoon water)

1. Let puff pastry come to room temperature before beginning (about 20 minutes if still frozen).
2. Preheat oven to 400°F.
3. Lightly flour puff pastry, and roll out to ⅛-inch thickness.
4. Cut the Brie in half horizontally and set the bottom half in the center of the pastry. Scatter the apricots on the Brie bottom. Cover with the top half of the Brie, sandwiching the apricots.
5. Wrap the pastry around the Brie and trim away any excess. (Reserve any excess pastry to cut decorative shapes.) Seal the edges by pressing with your fingers.
6. Place on a baking sheet seam-side down. Attach any decorative pieces of puff pastry in design of your choice with water. (At this point, you may cover it and refrigerate for up to 48 hours.)
7. When ready to bake, brush the puff pastry Brie with the egg wash. Bake 15 to 20 minutes until golden. Remove from oven and let rest for about 20 minutes before serving.

Caviar Cream Pie

SERVES 10 TO 12

It's not really a pie—more like a savory cheesecake. Spread it on Melba toast, baguette slices, or crackers.

1 tablespoon butter, softened
1 large white sweet onion, minced
6 large hard-boiled eggs, chopped
3 tablespoons mayonnaise
2 cups sour cream

1 package (8 ounces) cream cheese, at room temperature
¼ cup smoked salmon, chopped
1 jar caviar (4 ounces; red or black)
Chives and parsley, chopped, for garnish

1. Cut an 8-inch round out of waxed paper and place in the bottom of an 8" springform pan. Butter the inside of the pan.
2. Gently dry the chopped sweet onion in a paper towel.
3. Combine hard-boiled eggs and mayonnaise in a bowl and spread it evenly in the bottom of the lined springform pan. Sprinkle with the sweet onion.
4. Beat the sour cream and cream cheese together until smooth, and then fold in the smoked salmon. Drop the mixture carefully on top of the onion layer by the spoonful, then gently smooth it into an even layer.
5. Cover and refrigerate until firm, 2 hours or overnight.
6. When ready to serve, drain caviar. Run a heated butter knife around the rim of the springform pan and release the sides. Invert the cheese pie onto a decorative plate and remove the waxed paper. Spoon the caviar over the top in a decorative pattern. Sprinkle with chopped chives and place parsley around the base.

ELSEWHERE ON THE WEB

▶ If you're having trouble finding caviar in your local supermarket, there are online resources that you can mail order it from. At www.freshcaviar.com they have a helpful FAQ section and they will overnight many different types of caviar right to your door!

Pineapple Bell Pepper Cheese Ball
SERVES 16

This is a cream cheese and Cheddar–based cheese ball with the refreshing flavor combination of pineapple and red and green bell peppers.

4 ounces (½ of a large block) cream cheese, softened
⅓ cup pineapple, crushed and drained well
½ teaspoon Worcestershire sauce
1 tablespoon fresh parsley, chopped
1¼ cups white Cheddar cheese, shredded
¼ cup red and green bell pepper, chopped
1 cup pecans, chopped

1. Put cream cheese, pineapple, Worcestershire, and parsley in a food processor bowl with the metal blade. Process until blended and smooth.
2. Add the white Cheddar cheese and bell peppers and pulse until well mixed.
3. Scoop the mixture onto a piece of plastic wrap, fold the edges closed, and refrigerate for about 2 hours to firm up.
4. Spread chopped pecans on a sheet of wax paper.
5. Unwrap the plastic wrap from the chilled cheese mixture, dampen hands, and shape the cheese into a ball. Roll the ball in the pecans, pressing them in.
6. Wrap the cheese ball in plastic and chill until ready to serve.

WHAT'S HOT

▶ Pineapple—it has wonderful tenderizing enzymes and goes especially well with pork as well as poultry, seafood, and sweet-and-sour dishes. Christopher Columbus is credited with discovering the pineapple on the island of Guadeloupe in 1493, although the fruit had long been grown in South America. He called it *piña de Indes* meaning "pine of the Indians." When George Washington tasted pineapple in 1751 in Barbados, he declared it his favorite tropical fruit.

Mozzarella Dip

YIELDS 3½ CUPS

Think of this dip as a deconstructed pizza, with the crust being the breadsticks.

2 cups mayonnaise
1 cup (8 ounces) sour cream
1 tablespoon pizza sauce
1 cup (4 ounces) mozzarella cheese, shredded
2 tablespoons Parmesan cheese, grated
¼ cup sun-dried tomatoes, chopped
1 tablespoon dried onion, minced
1 teaspoon sugar
Dash each garlic salt and seasoned salt
½ teaspoon dried oregano, crushed
Breadsticks, for dipping

1. Combine mayonnaise, sour cream, pizza sauce, mozzarella cheese, Parmesan cheese, sun-dried tomatoes, onion, sugar, garlic salt, seasoned salt, and oregano in a bowl.
2. Mix thoroughly. Cover and chill for 2 hours.
3. Serve mozzarella dip with breadsticks.

ASK YOUR GUIDE

What is mozzarella made from?

▶ Originating in Italy, this cheese is not aged like most cheeses and is actually best when eaten within hours of its making. In making mozzarella, the curds are heated in water or whey until they form strings (hence the term "string cheese") and become elastic in texture. The curds are stretched, kneaded until smooth, and then formed into round balls to make fresh mozzarella cheese. Formerly water buffalo milk was used; now cow's milk is common.

Savory Cheesecake
SERVES 18

Four kinds of cheese and savory herbs flavor this cheesecake spread for an elegant appetizer.

CRUST:
- ¾ cup whole wheat crackers
- 1 tablespoon almonds, sliced
- 3 tablespoons extra-virgin olive oil
- ¼ teaspoon dried basil
- ¼ teaspoon dried thyme
- ¼ teaspoon dried oregano

CHEESECAKE:
- 2 packages (16 ounces) cream cheese, at room temperature
- ¼ cup feta cheese, at room temperature and crumbled
- ¼ cup Gorgonzola cheese, at room temperature and crumbled
- ½ cup Parmesan cheese, freshly grated
- ¼ teaspoon salt
- ¼ teaspoon white pepper
- ½ teaspoon Worcestershire sauce
- 1 egg
- 1½ cups heavy whipping cream
- ¼ cup sun-dried tomatoes, chopped
- 1 tablespoon chives

Savory Cheesecake (continued)

1. To make the crust: Place cracker crumbs, almonds, olive oil, basil, thyme, and oregano in a food processor fitted with the metal blade. Pulse until blended and crackers and almonds are finely chopped. Press into the bottom and up the sides of a 9" deep-dish glass pie plate.
2. To make the cheesecake: Whip cream cheese until soft. Add feta, Gorgonzola, Parmesan, salt, pepper, Worcestershire sauce, egg, and heavy cream. Beat on low speed until combined. Fold in the sun-dried tomatoes and pour into crust. Sprinkle chives evenly over the top.
3. Bake cheesecake about 45 minutes, until lightly browned on top and no longer jiggly in the center. Let cool to room temperature, then chill in the refrigerator until ready to serve.
4. Let sit at room temperature 15 minutes before serving. Cut into wedges and place on a serving platter surrounded with herbed crackers and toasted Italian bread rounds.

ASK YOUR GUIDE

What is feta cheese?

▶ Feta cheese is a rich and creamy soft cheese of Greece, traditionally made of whole sheep's milk, although many are now made with goat's milk or a mixture of the two. It's been around for centuries, and hardly a Greek meal does not incorporate feta cheese in some manner. The better fetas are aged (but not ripened) four to six weeks and cured in a salty whey and brine. Known as a pickled cheese, the flavor of feta becomes sharper and saltier with age.

Four Cheese Pizza
SERVES 4

This recipe yields enough pizza dough for 2 pizzas. Any extra dough can be used to make soft breadsticks.

PIZZA DOUGH:
- 1 package yeast
- ⅓ cup warm water
- ½ teaspoon sugar
- 2½ cups flour, divided use
- ½ cup cool water
- 1½ teaspoons salt
- 2 tablespoons olive oil

PIZZA:
- ½ recipe pizza dough
- 1 can (8 ounces) herbed tomato sauce or homemade
- 1 cup mozzarella cheese, shredded
- 1 cup Monterey jack cheese, shredded
- 1 cup provolone cheese, shredded
- ½ teaspoon dried oregano, crushed
- ¼ cup Parmesan cheese, grated

1. For the pizza dough: Combine yeast with the warm water, sugar, and ½ cup flour. Let sit 10 minutes.
2. Add cool water, salt, olive oil, and 1 cup flour, and combine with a wooden spoon or dough hook.
3. Add remaining cup of flour and mix to form dough.
4. Knead dough on a floured board or with dough hook for 5 minutes, adding flour as needed to prevent sticking.

Four Cheese Pizza (continued)

5. Let dough rise covered in an oiled bowl for 1 hour in a warm place. Punch down dough and divide in half. Roll the halves into balls and let one rise in a warm place, covered, for 1 hour. (Wrap the other one and freeze for later use.)
6. For the pizza: Preheat oven to 475°F.
7. Roll the pizza dough out into a 12-inch circle on a lightly floured surface with a rolling pin. Place the circle onto a pizza pan or baking sheet pan.
8. Cover the surface of the dough with the tomato sauce, leaving a one-inch border of dough. Sprinkle the mozzarella, jack, and provolone cheeses evenly over the sauce and top with oregano. Bake for about 15 minutes, until crust is baked and cheese is melted. Sprinkle the finished pie with Parmesan cheese.

ELSEWHERE ON THE WEB

▶ Pizzerias achieve crust that is crisp on the outside and tender and chewy on the inside by putting the pizza directly on the floor of the oven. The floor is made of stone or tile and imparts heat directly to the dough. To mimic this, buy a pizza stone. I've seen round ones and rectangular ones. They're inexpensive, readily available, and worth every penny. Go to www.cooking.com and type "pizza stone" into the search box to find reviews and ordering information.

Breakfast Omelet Casserole
SERVES 12

This is an easy breakfast dish that is assembled the night before and baked fresh in the morning. Wrap any leftovers in individual portions and freeze.

1 tablespoon soft butter
8 slices white bread, cubed
½ cup chopped ham
6 eggs
2 cups milk
1 teaspoon dry mustard
½ teaspoon salt
¼ teaspoon pepper
2 cups Cheddar cheese, shredded

1. Butter a 9" × 13" baking dish. Place the bread cubes on the bottom of the dish. Sprinkle ham over the bread.
2. Whisk together the eggs, milk, mustard, salt, and pepper in a bowl. Pour this mixture over the ham and bread. Sprinkle the Cheddar cheese over the top.
3. Cover and refrigerate overnight.
4. To bake, preheat oven to 350°F. Bake casserole uncovered for 25 minutes.
5. Cut in squares and serve hot.

WHAT'S HOT

▶ The frittata most likely preceded the omelet. What could be easier than mixing vegetables or leftover cooked meats into eggs and scrambling them into a dinner meal? Rather like a savory custard pie, it just made sense to make use of the protein in eggs as a meat substitute to add depth and sustenance to vegetables. According to some historians, the word "omelet" comes from the Roman epicure Apicius, who called his dish, which was made from eggs with honey and pepper, *overmele*.

Cheese Soufflé
SERVES 6

This soufflé is an easier version of the traditional kind, which is a little more delicate. This one won't rise as high, but it is every bit as tasty. It is more of a rustic than a refined soufflé.

7 tablespoons (¾ stick plus 1 tablespoon) unsalted butter
6 tablespoons all-purpose flour
2 cups whole milk, divided use
½ teaspoon salt
½ teaspoon pepper
Pinch of nutmeg
5 extra-large eggs
2⅓ cups Swiss cheese, shredded

1. Preheat the oven to 400°F.
2. Butter a 6-cup baking dish and set it aside.
3. Melt the butter in a saucepan over medium heat, then add the flour and mix it in well with a whisk. Add half of the milk, whisking away lumps, and cook until it becomes thick. Add the rest of the milk and stir with the whisk until it becomes thickened and smooth.
4. Remove from heat and stir in the salt, pepper, and nutmeg. Allow about 10 minutes for the milk mixture to cool.
5. While it is cooling, break the eggs into a bowl and beat them with a whisk.
6. Add the beaten eggs and the cheese to the slightly cooled milk mixture, and mix well to combine. Pour into the buttered baking dish.
7. Bake for 30 to 40 minutes, or until the soufflé is puffy and well browned on top. Serve immediately.

ELSEWHERE ON THE WEB

▶ **For dessert, how about a warm and gooey dark chocolate soufflé? Try this recipe on** www.recipezaar.com/175610. **You can read reviews by other people who have attempted it and then write your own when you're done.**

▶ **You can't have griddle cakes without a griddle. No "griddled" cheese either. Diners and pancake houses have an entire slab of hot metal to cook on, commonly called the "flat top." At home, a flat, heavy, nonstick griddle is the key to happiness in pancake-making. It doesn't matter if it is electric or the kind you put over two burners. If you're lucky, there may even be one incorporated into the middle of your stove.**

Orange Ricotta Pancakes
SERVES 2

These delicious pancakes are like warm breakfast cheesecakes with the bright, sunshine flavor of oranges.

¾ cup all-purpose flour
1 tablespoon baking powder
¼ teaspoon salt
2 tablespoons sugar
1 cup ricotta cheese
2 eggs
⅔ cup milk
1 orange, zested and juiced

1. Preheat a nonstick griddle.
2. Combine flour, baking powder, salt, and sugar in a small bowl.
3. Whisk together the ricotta cheese, eggs, milk, orange zest, and juice in a large bowl.
4. Whisk the dry mixture into the wet mixture until just combined.
5. Oil the hot griddle. Pour ¼ cup of the batter onto the griddle for each pancake and cook on both sides until golden.
6. Serve hot with blackberry syrup.

Bacon Cheddar Cornmeal Waffles
SERVES 6

This is a hearty, savory waffle that isn't only for breakfast. Sometimes I like to top the finished waffle with a sunny-side-up egg for added protein and depth.

1¼ cups all-purpose flour
½ cup yellow cornmeal
1 tablespoon baking powder
1 tablespoon sugar
½ teaspoon salt
3 eggs
4 ounces unsalted butter, melted
1½ cups whole milk
6 slices bacon, cooked and crumbled
½ cup Cheddar cheese, shredded

1. Combine flour, cornmeal, baking powder, sugar, and salt in a bowl using a whisk.
2. Combine eggs, melted butter, and milk in another bowl using whisk.
3. Stir egg mixture into flour mixture to combine, but don't overmix.
4. Fold the bacon and Cheddar cheese into the batter.
5. Pour, ladle, or scoop about ½ cup waffle batter onto preheated and oiled waffle iron and cook according to manufacturer's instructions.
6. Serve warm.

ELSEWHERE ON THE WEB

▶ For more waffle recipes, visit the About.com Guide to Baking at http://baking.about.com. You'll find both the sweet and savory variety listed. While there, check out the other baking recipes that use cheese, such as cheese scones, cheese straws, and an easy cheese Danish.

▶ The *real* Swiss cheese, Emmental, takes its name from the Emmental Valley, where it originated circa 1293. It is considered Switzerland's oldest and most prestigious cheese. This pale yellow cheese is made from part-skim, unpasteurized cow's milk and has a mild, slightly nutty, buttery, almost fruity flavor. American versions use pasteurized milk or follow U.S. law and age the unpasteurized cheese at least sixty days.

Four Cheese Pâté
SERVES 16 TO 20

If you like cheese balls, you will love this savory cheesecake pie. It's no-cook, no-bake, and easy.

3 packages (24 ounces) cream cheese, softened, divided use
2 tablespoons milk
2 tablespoons sour cream
¾ cup pecans, chopped
¼ cup dried pears, chopped

4 ounces Brie or Camembert, rind removed, softened
1 cup Swiss cheese, shredded
4 ounces blue cheese, crumbled
½ cup pecan halves, for garnish
Piece of honeycomb, about 3 inches

1. Beat 8 ounces of the cream cheese with the milk and sour cream until smooth. Line a 9" pie plate with plastic wrap.
2. Spread mixture over the bottom and up the sides of the plastic-lined pie plate. Sprinkle chopped pecans and dried pears evenly across the surface and gently press into the cream-cheese mixture.
3. Beat remaining 16 ounces of cream cheese with the Brie cheese, Swiss cheese, and blue cheese until combined. Scrape into pie plate on top of previous layer and smooth the top. Cover with plastic wrap and refrigerate at least 4 hours.
4. When ready to serve, remove top plastic wrap and invert pâté onto a serving dish. Carefully peel off the remaining plastic wrap. Press pecan halves into the top in a decorative pattern. Break up the honeycomb and place it on top of the pâté in the middle.
5. Let cheese pâté sit at room temperature for 30 minutes before serving with apple slices, vegetable sticks, and crackers.

Green Eggs and Ham
SERVES 4

If your kids love the Dr. Seuss book featuring Sam-I-Am, then they will get a kick out of this version of green eggs and ham.

8 eggs
2 tablespoons milk
¼ teaspoon salt
¼ teaspoon black pepper
¼ cup chives, chopped
⅛ cup fresh parsley, chopped
¼ cup broccoli crowns, chopped
1 tablespoon butter

1 thick slice or chunk (4 ounces) of cooked ham, cut into ¼-inch diced pieces
¼ cup Parmesan cheese, grated
Additional parsley, for garnish

1. Place eggs, milk, salt, black pepper, chives, and parsley in a blender and pulse until herbs reach a minced stage. Add broccoli and blend again until broccoli is puréed.
2. Heat a large nonstick skillet over medium heat until hot. Add butter and swirl to cover bottom of the pan. Add ham and sauté about 30 seconds to heat then lower the heat to medium-low.
3. Pour egg mixture over warmed ham. As the mixture cooks, push cooked portions up the side of the pan with a heat-proof spatula, and tilt pan so the uncooked portion reaches the pan to cook. Remove from heat when eggs are still soft, but not runny. Sprinkle with Parmesan cheese. Cover and let rest for 1 minute before serving to let eggs set and cheese melt a bit.
4. Garnish each serving with a sprig of fresh parsley. Serve with a side of fresh fruit and toast, biscuits, or hot rolls.

WHAT'S HOT

▶ Commercial egg substitutes have many preservative additives, so you might want to try making your own homemade egg substitute. In a small bowl, sprinkle 1 tablespoon of nonfat dry milk powder over 2 large egg whites. Beat with a whisk until smooth. Blend in 4 drops of yellow food coloring and 1 teaspoon of vegetable oil. Store in the refrigerator for up to two days. About ¼ cup equals 1 large egg. For recipes using egg substitutes, check out http://about.com/homecooking/eggsubstitute.

Swiss, Ham, and Spinach Rolls
YIELDS 12 ROLLS

Layers of ham, cheese, and spinach are rolled into bread dough, sliced, and baked cinnamon roll–style into sandwich rolls. These rolls can be enjoyed for breakfast, lunch, or as a snack.

ROLLS:

1 loaf frozen bread dough, thawed
2 tablespoons powdered ranch dressing mix
¼ pound good quality deli ham, sliced thin
⅛ pound deli Swiss cheese, sliced thin
½ cup fresh baby spinach leaves, washed and dried
2 tablespoons roasted red bell peppers, chopped

TOPPING:

2 tablespoons butter, melted
¼ cup Parmesan cheese, grated
¼ teaspoon garlic powder
½ teaspoon onion powder
½ teaspoon basil

1. Line a 9" × 13" baking pan with nonstick foil.
2. Roll bread dough into a rectangle 12 by 14 inches. Sprinkle with ranch dressing powder.
3. Top with ham in a single layer, followed by a layer of Swiss cheese, then the spinach leaves. Sprinkle the roasted red bell pepper over the spinach.
4. Roll the long edge jelly-roll-style into a cylinder. Cut the cylinder into 12 equal slices, placing each slice cut-side down in the baking pan with sides touching.

5. Brush tops of rolls gently with melted butter. Mix together Parmesan cheese, garlic powder, onion powder, and basil. Sprinkle evenly over the tops of the rolls.
6. Let rise in a warm place away from any draft until almost doubled in size, about 1 hour.
7. Preheat oven to 350°F. Bake rolls 25 to 30 minutes, until done in the center and golden on top.

ASK YOUR GUIDE

What kind of ham should I use for sandwich rolls?

▶ It is important to use a good quality deli ham for these sandwich rolls. Cheap sandwich ham has too much water and will make the rolls soggy. The flavored hams like pesto or sun-dried tomato are excellent choices, as are Virginia ham, Black Forest ham, Westphalia ham, Jambon Cru, Serrano ham, and prosciutto. Experiment with other meats and fillings such as pepperoni, smoked turkey, or salami. For alternative flavor options, try olive tapénade or pesto.

Does the brand of non-stick skillet I use matter?

▶ No, but I would use the highest quality that you can afford. The best-quality non-stick skillets have a heavy bottom and I would not recommend using the thin kind that has an equally thin non-stick coating.

Brie and Ham Frittata
SERVES 2 TO 4

Potatoes, ham, and Brie cheese beef up this egg dish. It's great for breakfast, yet hearty enough for dinner.

6 eggs
2 tablespoons milk
½ teaspoon salt
Pepper, to taste
2 tablespoons butter
2 cups uncooked potatoes, diced
¼ cup sweet onion, finely chopped
1 cup ham, diced
¼ cup fresh parsley, chopped
½ cup Brie cheese, cubed, rind cut off

1. In a bowl, whisk together eggs, milk, salt, and pepper. Set aside.
2. Melt the butter in a 10" nonstick skillet and brown the potatoes and onions over medium heat until tender (about 20 minutes). Stir often.
3. Add ham and heat through. Sprinkle with parsley.
4. Pour egg mixture over potatoes, onions, and ham. Reduce heat slightly and cover. Check often while cooking, lifting up cooked eggs to let uncooked eggs reach the pan. Cook until eggs are almost set, about 10 minutes.
5. Scatter the cheese on top, cover, and let heat over low until cheese melts.
6. Cut into wedges to serve.

Croissant French Toast

SERVES 4

French toast is known as "lost bread" in French. It is usually made from stale bread. In this version, I substitute stale croissants for stale bread. Freeze the croissants to make slicing easier.

6 eggs
1½ cups milk
1 teaspoon vanilla extract
4 stale croissants, frozen if possible
¼ cup powdered sugar, for garnish

1. Combine eggs, milk, and vanilla in a shallow, flat bowl and mix well with a fork.
2. Slice croissants horizontally into 3 slices each, using a serrated bread knife.
3. Dip each slice of croissant on both sides into the egg mixture and remove with a fork, draining excess egg mixture back into the bowl.
4. Immediately after dipping each slice, pan fry it in melted butter on both sides.
5. Serve each person one reassembled croissant (in the form of 3 slices fanned out on the plate) sprinkled with powdered sugar. Serve with whipped butter and strawberry jam.

WHAT'S HOT

▶ To make your own vanilla extract, chop four vanilla beans into small pieces, being careful to retain all the seeds and crystals. Put into a clean jar and add ½ cup of brandy liquor. Let steep for one to six months, then strain. The mixture keeps indefinitely, and you can continually add to it. For an alternative to brandy, use one split bean steeped in three-quarters of a cup of vodka, letting it stand at least six months.

Get Linked

Here are some great links to my About.com site for more dairy, cheese, and egg recipes and related information.

DAIRY RECIPES AND INFORMATION

Information on all sorts of dairy products—including milk, cottage cheese, yogurt, cream, and butter—and recipes using dairy products as ingredients, like ice cream, can be found here.

http://about.com/homecooking/dairy

CHEESE RECIPES

If you want recipes with cheese in them, look no further than this page.

http://about.com/homecooking/cheese

EGG INFORMATION

You'll find a wealth of information on this page concerning eggs, including omelets, frittatas, and how to properly make and use hard-boiled eggs.

http://about.com/homecooking/egginformation

Chapter 3

Vegetables and Side Dishes

ASK YOUR GUIDE:

Why should I use russet potatoes in this recipe?
▶**PAGE 38**

How do I clean leeks?
▶**PAGE 44**

Should I wash the mushrooms before using?
▶**PAGE 46**

Is there any way to speed up the cooking process for this onion tart?
▶**PAGE 48**

Why should I use russet potatoes in this recipe?

▶ There are two basic types of potatoes: mealy and waxy. The mealy type includes russet and Idaho potatoes, and is often referred to as "baking potatoes" or "old potatoes." Mealy potatoes have lower moisture content and a mealy texture when cooked, which makes them excellent for baking, mashing, and frying. In this recipe you want larger potatoes since the skin will serve as a container, and russets deliver with both size and thicker skin.

Blue Cheese and Bacon Twice-Baked Potatoes
SERVES 8

I often make this recipe in advance and cook it later.

4 large russet potatoes, scrubbed clean
2 teaspoons olive oil
2 teaspoons kosher salt
6 slices bacon, cooked, drained, and crumbled
1½ cups crumbled blue cheese, divided use

½ cup sour cream
¼ cup chives or green onions, chopped
Kosher salt, to taste
Freshly ground pepper, to taste
¼ cup Parmesan cheese, grated
Sweet Hungarian paprika, to taste

1. Preheat oven to 400°F.
2. Rub potatoes with olive oil and sprinkle with 2 teaspoons kosher salt. Prick in several spots with a fork.
3. Place on a shallow baking pan 6 inches apart and bake until center is soft, 45 minutes to 1 hour.
4. When potatoes are cool enough to handle, slice each one in half lengthwise. Carefully scoop out the soft flesh, leaving ¼-inch rim around the potato skin, and place flesh in a mixing bowl. Set skins aside to stuff later.
5. Mash the potatoes with a fork or masher. No need to try to get them perfectly smooth. Stir in crumbled bacon, 1 cup crumbled blue cheese, sour cream, chives, salt, and pepper.
6. Spoon mashed potato mixture into the potato skins and return to the baking tray. Sprinkle with reserved ½ cup blue cheese, Parmesan cheese, and paprika. (Cover and refrigerate or freeze at this point if making in advance.)
7. Return to the 400°F oven and bake about 30 minutes until potatoes are lightly browned and heated through.

Cranberry Acorn Squash

SERVES 4

I like to make this anytime I'm craving Thanksgiving dinner but don't have the time to make the whole meal. I serve it with sliced turkey from the deli or any poultry dish for a taste of the autumn feast.

2 acorn squash (1 pound each)
¾ cup fresh or frozen cranberries
3 tablespoons orange juice or orange marmalade
3 tablespoons brown sugar
2 tablespoons butter
1 teaspoon lemon juice
½ cup toasted pecans, chopped

1. With a fork, pierce the whole squash on each side. Place on a paper towel in the microwave oven. Microwave 12 to 15 minutes or until fork-tender, turning over after 5 minutes. Let stand 5 to 10 minutes.
2. Meanwhile, in a one-quart casserole, combine cranberries, orange juice, brown sugar, butter, and lemon juice. Cover with waxed paper. Microwave for 3 to 5 minutes or until berries have popped, stirring after 2 minutes.
3. Cut the squash in half. Remove the seeds. Place cut side up on a microwave-proof platter.
4. Spoon cranberry mixture into the hollowed-out squash. Cover with waxed paper and microwave for 1 to 3 minutes to heat through.
5. Sprinkle pecans on top before serving.

WHAT'S HOT

▶ It doesn't have to be November to make the real Thanksgiving meal at home, or at least part of it. Check out http://about.com/home cooking/thanksgiving for recipes and tips. Whether it's your first Bird Day meal or your fifty-first, you'll find all your favorite Thanksgiving foods in one place, including deep-fried turkey, stuffing, cranberries, sweet potatoes, pumpkins, leftovers, and more.

Butternut Squash Pesto Casserole

SERVES 6

I like to serve this colorful and fragrant vegetable side dish with grilled chicken for a complete meal, or as a vegetarian entrée accompanied with a green salad and crusty bread.

2 tablespoons olive oil, divided use
1 butternut squash (3 pounds), peeled, seeded,
   and cut into 1-inch cubes
Salt and black pepper, to taste
¼ cup basil pesto, divided use
½ cup Parmesan cheese, grated, divided use

1. Preheat the oven to 350°F.
2. Oil an 8" baking dish with 1 tablespoon olive oil and set aside.
3. Steam the cubed squash over medium heat for 20 minutes, until tender when poked with a fork or the tip of a knife.
4. Purée the cooked squash in a food processor and then season to taste with the salt and pepper.
5. Spread half of the squash purée on the bottom of the prepared baking dish. Spoon ⅛ cup of the pesto on the squash, and then sprinkle ¼ cup of the Parmesan cheese on top.
6. Make another layer with the rest of the squash, pesto, and cheese. Drizzle 1 tablespoon of the remaining olive oil on top.
7. Bake 40 minutes, until browned. Serve hot.

TOOLS YOU NEED

▶ A food processor is a cook's best friend. If you don't have a food processor, though, you can purée the squash by putting it through an old-fashioned food mill or potato ricer. Alternately you can make a chunky casserole by smashing the cooked squash with a potato masher. For a shortcut, substitute frozen squash purée for fresh.

Mustard-Glazed Carrots

SERVES 4

I love to prepare fresh carrots with this zesty glaze.

2 cups carrots, peeled and cut in ½-inch slices	2 tablespoons Dijon mustard
2 tablespoons butter	1 tablespoon honey
1 tablespoon lemon juice	½ teaspoon pepper
	Salt, to taste

1. Steam carrots until they are tender.
2. Sauté the steamed carrots in butter briefly, then add the lemon juice.
3. Stir in the remaining ingredients over low heat.
4. Cook for a few minutes, and then remove from heat.
5. Adjust seasoning with salt.

Praline Sweet Potatoes

SERVES 4

Serve this sweet and crunchy side dish with beef, pork chops, or ham.

3 pounds sweet potatoes	4 tablespoons butter, melted
1 cup brown sugar	
½ cup pecans, chopped	

1. Preheat the oven to 350°F.
2. Peel sweet potatoes and slice them into ½-inch-thick rounds.
3. Steam sweet potato slices for 10 minutes.
4. Overlap the steamed sweet potato slices in one layer in a baking dish.
5. Sprinkle the sweet potatoes with the brown sugar and pecans. Drizzle with the melted butter and bake them uncovered for 45 minutes. Serve hot.

WHAT'S HOT

▶ Sometimes I like to use a compound butter made with fresh ginger in place of plain butter in this carrot recipe. The spicy ginger complements the sweet carrots. Whip 4 ounces of soft, unsalted butter with 1 tablespoon of lemon juice, 1 tablespoon of grated fresh gingerroot, 1 teaspoon of minced parsley, ¼ teaspoon of salt, and ⅛ teaspoon of white pepper. Roll in a log, wrap in plastic wrap, and chill until firm. Use ¼ of the log for this recipe and save the rest in the freezer for up to three months.

Champagne Sauerkraut

SERVES 6

If you like sauerkraut, then you'll love this sweet and spicy version. You may substitute beer for the champagne and chopped apples for the pineapple and serve it up with polish sausage.

1 can (16 ounces) sauerkraut
1½ cups fresh pineapple, diced
1 cup champagne or dry white wine
1 tablespoon honey
Caraway seeds, to taste
Cayenne pepper, to taste

1. Drain sauerkraut before putting it in an uncovered 2-quart saucepan with water to barely cover. Heat until bubbling, over medium heat, and then simmer 15 minutes over low heat.
2. Add pineapple and bring to a boil. After 3 minutes reduce heat and simmer for 20 minutes, stirring occasionally.
3. Add champagne (or wine) and honey and stir lightly; keep at a low simmer for 15 minutes.
4. Season with caraway seeds and cayenne pepper to your liking.

ELSEWHERE ON THE WEB

▶ Did you know that you're not using true "champagne" if it is not from the Champagne region of France? What most people know as champagne is actually technically sparkling wine. For more information on everything champagne including how to read a label and how to differentiate between types, visit www.champagne.fr/en_indx.html.

Creamed Parsley Potatoes

SERVES 4

This side dish of diced potatoes in a creamy, parsley-flecked sauce is a vacation from the usual mashed or baked potato. I especially like to serve it with baked ham and steamed asparagus.

4 medium red potatoes (about 3 pounds)
2 tablespoons butter
2 tablespoons flour
¾ cup milk
1 teaspoon salt
½ teaspoon pepper
2 tablespoons parsley, chopped

1. Peel and cut the potatoes into eighths. Place in a pot of cold salted water.
2. Bring potatoes and water to a boil and simmer for 10 minutes. Drain.
3. Melt butter in a sauté pan and stir the flour into it. Cook for 5 minutes, stirring with a wooden spoon.
4. Add milk slowly to the butter and flour mixture (**roux**) and stir with a whisk to make a creamy sauce. Cook over medium heat, whisking until sauce thickens, then season it with salt, pepper, and parsley.
5. Add the cooked potatoes to the creamy sauce and stir gently to coat the potatoes. Remove from heat and serve hot.

WHAT'S HOT

▶ For more flavor in this recipe, use half chicken broth and half milk for the sauce. Feel free to experiment with herbs such as basil, chives, and rosemary in place of the parsley. For a special touch, top each hot serving with a sprinkle of fresh Parmesan cheese.

How do I clean leeks?

▶ Leeks are grown in sandy soil. The sand and dirt gets trapped in between the layers of the leek. Cleaning the sand out is easy. First cut off the dark green tops, leaving only the white and pale green parts. Next, split the leek lengthwise almost all the way from root to tip, but leave a good inch at the root end. Rinse the semi-split leek under cold water, separating the layers with your fingers to rinse the dirt away.

Leek Gratin
SERVES 4

I like to serve this rich veggie side dish with a simple roasted chicken and steamed carrot coins for a casual, country-style French meal.

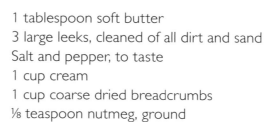

    1 tablespoon soft butter
    3 large leeks, cleaned of all dirt and sand
    Salt and pepper, to taste
    1 cup cream
    1 cup coarse dried breadcrumbs
    ⅛ teaspoon nutmeg, ground

1. Preheat oven to 375°F.
2. Smear the butter around the bottom and sides of a baking dish.
3. Cut the tough root end off of the leeks. This should leave you with the leeks split lengthwise completely.
4. Next, cut the leeks into 2-inch-wide pieces across the grain. Arrange the leeks in the buttered baking dish and season with salt and pepper. Pour the cream over the leeks and then sprinkle the breadcrumbs over them and season with nutmeg.
5. Bake 1 hour, until bubbly and browned and leeks are tender and can be pierced easily with a knife tip. Serve hot.

Shallot Green Beans Almandine
SERVES 4

Green beans sautéed in butter with sweet shallots and toasty almonds come together in this side dish that goes with anything from barbecue to prime rib.

¼ cup almonds, sliced
2 tablespoons butter
2 tablespoons shallots, chopped
2 cups green beans, stems cut
1 teaspoon salt
¼ teaspoon white pepper

1. Sauté the almonds in butter until lightly browned, then remove them from the butter. Set aside almonds and save the butter in the pan.
2. Add the shallots to the pan and **sweat** them over medium heat until tender and translucent. Remove from heat and set aside.
3. Meanwhile, boil the green beans in salted boiling water for 5 to 10 minutes (depending on how crunchy you like them), drain and then add the beans to the pan with the shallots. Sauté over medium heat for 5 minutes then remove from heat.
4. Combine the almonds with the shallots and green beans.
5. Season with salt and pepper and serve hot.

ELSEWHERE ON THE WEB

▶ For a great prime rib recipe to compliment this side dish, visit the About.com Guide to Barbecues and Grilling. This prime rib roast http://about.com/bbq/prime rib is a great summer favorite.

Should I wash the mushrooms before using?

▶ Mushrooms are quite porous, which means they absorb liquid like a sponge so washing them in water is not a good idea. Commercial mushrooms are farm-raised in a sterile medium, so all they need is a dusting with a soft brush to remove any soil residue. Feel free to experiment with any of the numerous varieties of mushrooms available in your local market.

Sautéed Mushrooms
SERVES 4

I like to serve these mushrooms as a topping for grilled steak. You can also cook the mushrooms whole and serve them as a side dish with any meal.

    1 pound mushrooms, sliced
    3 tablespoons olive oil
    2 tablespoons white wine
    ¼ cup chicken broth
    1 teaspoon salt
    ½ teaspoon pepper
    1 tablespoon fresh parsley, chopped

1. Sauté the mushrooms in the olive oil over medium heat for 5 minutes.
2. Add the white wine and chicken broth and simmer over low heat for 5 minutes.
3. Season with salt and pepper.
4. Cook over low heat to **reduce** the liquid by half.
5. Remove from heat and sprinkle mushrooms with parsley. Serve hot.

Herbed Roasted Garlic Mashed Potatoes
SERVES 6

Mashed potatoes rank high on the list of American comfort foods for everyday and special occasions. My favorite is this mixture of potatoes and roasted garlic.

8 to 10 cloves garlic, unpeeled
2 pounds potatoes, peeled and cut into chunks
4 tablespoons butter
⅓ cup sour cream
¼ cup milk
½ cup white Cheddar cheese, grated
1 teaspoon fresh rosemary, chopped
1 teaspoon fresh thyme, chopped
1 teaspoon dried chives
½ teaspoon salt
¼ teaspoon pepper

1. To roast garlic, wrap unpeeled garlic cloves in foil. Bake in a 400°F oven for 25 to 35 minutes or until cloves feel soft when pressed. When cool enough to handle, squeeze garlic paste from peels into a bowl and set aside.
2. Meanwhile, in a covered pot cook potatoes in boiling water for 20 to 25 minutes or until tender. Drain and return to pot. Mash potatoes and garlic paste with a potato masher or press through a ricer. Add butter and mix until melted and incorporated.
3. Add sour cream, milk, cheese, rosemary, thyme, chives, salt, and pepper. Whisk until light and fluffy.
4. Serve hot.

WHAT'S HOT

▶ Lumpy or creamy, smooth, skin-on, or peeled, you can't beat good old mashed spuds. There are seemingly endless variations on the theme of mashed potatoes: Anchovy Mashed Potatoes, Artichoke Mashed Potatoes, Buttermilk Basil Garlic Mashed Potatoes, Cheesy Mashed Potatoes, Horseradish Mashed Potatoes, and even Truffled Mashed Potatoes. Find these at http://about.com/home cooking/mashedpotato. You will also find instructions for cooking potatoes, information about different types of potatoes, and recipes that use leftover mashed potatoes as an ingredient.

Is there any way to speed up the cooking process for this onion tart?

▶ Of course! Sauté the shallots, onions, thyme, salt, and pepper in the butter in a cast iron skillet until tender, about 15 minutes. Put the pastry on in the same manner and then bake at 400°F for 15 to 20 minutes, until pastry is golden brown. You will not be reducing the temperature of the oven, and the shallots and onions will be cooked from the sautéing, making the baking time shorter.

Onion Tart
SERVES 4

I like to serve this upside-down, baked tart with a green salad as a first course for a special occasion or as a light luncheon entrée.

2 tablespoons unsalted butter, softened
3 small sweet onions
3 green onions
1 teaspoon salt
¼ teaspoon pepper
½ teaspoon dried thyme
1 sheet frozen puff pastry, thawed

1. Preheat oven to 400°F.
2. Spread the soft butter over the bottom of a 9" glass pie dish. Slice the sweet and green onions into ¼-inch-thick slices and arrange them in the dish and then sprinkle salt, pepper, and thyme on them.
3. Unfold the puff pastry and cut the four corners off to create a pastry circle. (Discard the corners.) Dock the pastry circle by poking holes all over with a fork.
4. Put pastry on top of onions and tuck the pastry edges in around the perimeter of the bottom of the pan.
5. Bake for 15 minutes, then reduce heat to 325°F and continue baking for 30 minutes.
6. Remove tart from oven and put a cookie sheet over the pie dish. Flip the pie dish over onto the cookie sheet and carefully remove the pie dish. Cut into wedges and serve warm.

Parsnip Purée
SERVES 8

The parsnip is a root vegetable that used to be very common in kitchens, but has fallen by the wayside in recent years. It's delightful mixed with potatoes. You can make this recipe the day before it will be served and then bake it just before serving. It is not your everyday purée.

> 1 pound peeled parsnips, cut in chunks
> 2 pounds peeled potatoes, cut in chunks
> 8 ounces cream cheese, softened
> 4 tablespoons butter, softened
> ½ cup sour cream
> ½ cup milk
> 2 eggs, beaten
> ¼ cup onion, minced
> Salt, to taste
> White pepper, to taste

1. Cook the parsnips and potatoes in salted, boiling water until tender, about 20 minutes. Drain and press the cooked parsnips and potatoes through a ricer and then put them in a mixing bowl.
2. In a separate bowl, beat cream cheese, butter, sour cream, milk, eggs, and onion. Season with salt and white pepper to taste.
3. Whisk cream cheese mixture into the vegetables. Put mixture into a buttered casserole dish. At this point you can cover and refrigerate it overnight if you are preparing it in advance.
4. Bake in a preheated 350°F oven for 45 minutes, until lightly browned. Serve hot.

ELSEWHERE ON THE WEB

▶ Can't get enough of the taste of parsnips? Go to www.epicurious.com and type "parsnip soup" into the recipe search box. You'll find all sorts of parsnip soup recipes right at your fingertips, from the very easy-to-prepare basic to the more adventurous and time consuming.

▶ Refrigeration is the enemy of tomatoes. If you are blessed with an abundance of tomatoes, consider drying them and avoid the cost of commercial sun-dried tomatoes. Read this article for tips: http://about.com/home cooking/sundriedtomatoes. You can also freeze fresh tomatoes whole by placing them in a zip-top bag and sucking out the air with a straw. When you thaw them, the skins slip right off as if they were blanched, and you have the bright flavor of fresh tomatoes.

Broiled Tomato Halves
SERVES 4

I'm a self-confessed tomato freak. My favorite way to enjoy tomatoes is fresh from the garden with a little salt and pepper, but this is a nice alternative for cooked tomatoes. Serve it as a side dish with macaroni and cheese, chicken, or seafood.

2 large ripe tomatoes
½ cup dried bread crumbs
2 tablespoons Parmesan cheese, grated
1 teaspoon dried oregano
1 teaspoon garlic salt
¼ teaspoon pepper
2 tablespoons olive oil

1. Preheat the broiler.
2. Cut each tomato in half through the middle horizontally. Set tomatoes with their cut sides up in a baking dish.
3. Combine bread crumbs with cheese, oregano, garlic salt, and pepper.
4. Top each tomato half with ¼ of the breadcrumb mixture.
5. Drizzle olive oil on top of breadcrumbs.
6. Broil the tomatoes 5 minutes, until crumb topping browns, and then reduce the oven temperature to 350°F and finish baking the tomatoes for about 30 minutes.

Zucchini Tomato Casserole
SERVES 8

For those of you with a bountiful garden, you'll love this one. Even if you don't have a garden, luckily these veggies are available in most markets year-round.

> 2 cups zucchini, sliced ¼ inch thick, divided use
> 2 cups yellow summer squash, sliced ¼ inch thick, divided use
> 1 cup sweet onion, such as Vidalia, thinly sliced, divided use
> 2 medium-large ripe red tomatoes, sliced ¼ inch thick, divided use
> Salt and pepper, to taste
> 1 box (6 ounces) seasoned bread croutons, divided use
> 2 cups Cheddar cheese, shredded, divided use

1. Preheat oven to 350°F.
2. In a 3-quart baking dish, layer half of each of the zucchini, yellow squash, onion, and tomatoes. Season the vegetables with salt and pepper.
3. Scatter half of the croutons over the seasoned vegetables then half of the cheese over the croutons.
4. Repeat the layering with the remaining vegetables, season them with salt and pepper and sprinkle the remaining croutons and cheese on top.
5. Cover with lid or aluminum foil and bake for 1 hour. Serve hot.

ELSEWHERE ON THE WEB

▶ For other main-dish casserole recipe ideas, it's worth taking a trip to the About. com Southern Food Web site. At http://about.com/southernfood/casseroles you'll find casseroles made from almost every ingredient imaginable.

Get Linked

Here are some great links to my About.com site for more tasty vegetable and side-dish recipes and related information.

VEGETABLE AND SIDE

From artichokes to zucchini, you'll find a rainbow of recipes in this comprehensive index to suit any occasion.

http://about.com/homecooking/vegetablesidedish

HOW TO COOK VEGETABLES

After you bring bags of tomatoes home from the farmer's market, check out my cooking tips for them and many other vegetables on this page.

http://about.com/homecooking/cookvegetables

TO YOUR HEALTH

You'll find a wealth of health information on this page concerning vegetables and what's good about them for your body.

http://about.com/homecooking/vegetablehealth

Chapter 4

Pasta, Rice, Grains, and Beans

ASK YOUR GUIDE:

What are leeks?
▶**PAGE 57**

Is wild rice really rice?
▶**PAGE 60**

How do you tell the difference between dressing and stuffing?
▶**PAGE 62**

Gnocchi with Blue Cheese and Bacon
SERVES 4

Gnocchi are little pasta dumplings made from potatoes. Here, they are boiled in boiling water like fresh pasta and then sautéed in a silky sauce.

1 large baked potato (about 1 pound)
¾ cup flour
½ teaspoon salt
1 egg, beaten
6 slices bacon, diced and blanched
¾ cup heavy cream
½ cup blue cheese, crumbled
¼ cup Parmesan cheese, grated
⅛ cup fresh parsley, chopped
Black pepper, to taste

1. Scoop the cooked potato flesh out of the skin and put it through a potato ricer or food mill.
2. In a bowl toss the flour and salt lightly together with the riced potatoes.
3. Make a well in the center of the potato mixture and put the egg in it. Gradually incorporate the potato mixture into the egg to make a dough that comes together. Roll dough into one-inch-thick logs and cut one-inch pieces off the logs.
4. Bring a pot of salted water to a boil, carefully throw in the gnocchi, stir and then cook until they float to the top, 5 to 10 minutes. Meanwhile, cook the bacon in a large sauté pan over medium heat, until lightly crisped.
5. Add the cream to the bacon and reduce to the consistency of thin gravy. Add the blue cheese and Parmesan cheese and swirl the pan over low heat.
6. Drain the gnocchi and immediately add it to the pan sauce. Toss the gnocchi around in the sauce to coat. Season it with parsley and pepper. Serve hot.

▶ This simple form of gnocchi is good on its own, but many traditional gnocchi recipes call for an extra step that puts indentations in the pasta. The indentations grab more sauce and do look a bit fancier. There are tools on the market to make indented gnocchi, but why waste the money when a simple fork will do? Gently roll the gnocchi with a slight rocking down-stroke under the backside of a dinner fork, as if the fork were a paint roller.

Mushroom Lasagna

SERVES 12

This is a hearty meal, full of mushrooms and cheese. Leftovers can be wrapped in individual portions and frozen for 1 month.

5 cups tomato sauce, divided use
1 pound box (16 ounces) lasagna noodles, cooked al dente, divided use
2 cups mushrooms, sliced
2 tablespoons olive oil
3 eggs

2 cups ricotta cheese
2 cups mozzarella cheese, shredded, divided use
½ cup fresh parsley, chopped
Salt and pepper, to taste
½ cup Parmesan cheese, grated

1. Preheat oven to 350°F. Spread 1 cup tomato sauce on the bottom of a lasagna baking dish. Put a layer of noodles on top of the tomato sauce. Set aside.
2. Sauté the mushrooms in the olive oil until limp; set aside to cool.
3. In a bowl combine the eggs, ricotta, and 1 cup mozzarella cheese until well blended. Stir in the parsley, salt, and pepper, then fold in the sautéed mushrooms.
4. Spread half of the ricotta mixture over the noodles in the pan, then top the ricotta with a layer of noodles. Ladle 2 cups of the tomato sauce over the noodles then top with another layer of noodles.
5. Spread the remaining ricotta mixture over the noodles then top with another layer of noodles. Ladle the remaining tomato sauce over the noodles.
6. Scatter the remaining mozzarella cheese over the sauce, then sprinkle with the Parmesan cheese. Bake for 1 hour 15 minutes. Serve hot.

ELSEWHERE ON THE WEB

▶ Do cats like lasagna? There's at least one bright orange cat who does: Garfield. To see just how much this feline enjoys his lasagna (and to help him gulp down as many as possible), log onto www.garfield.com/fungames/lasagnafromheaven.

Apricot Scallion Rice Pilaf
SERVES 4

This recipe is great for when you want more than plain rice for a side dish. The fruit and scallion flavors go well with meat, poultry, or seafood.

4 tablespoons (½ stick) unsalted butter
½ cup scallions, sliced
1 cup long-grain white rice, uncooked
1¾ cups chicken or vegetable broth (1 14-ounce can or homemade)
½ teaspoon salt
¼ teaspoon white pepper
1 bay leaf
½ cup dried apricots, chopped

1. Preheat oven to 350°F.
2. Melt butter in a sauce pan and sauté the scallions in it until tender.
3. Add rice and sauté for 3 to 5 minutes with the scallions.
4. Pour rice mixture into a baking dish. Add chicken broth, salt, pepper, bay leaf, and apricots. Stir to incorporate.
5. Cover and bake for 45 minutes. Remove bay leaf before serving.

Penne with Caramelized Leeks
SERVES 2

This quick and simple dish is amazingly full of flavor. Feel free to add grilled chicken chunks for a one-dish meal.

2 medium leeks, trimmed of tough darker green part
½ tablespoon olive oil
1 tablespoon butter
½ tablespoon brown sugar
2 cups penne pasta
2 tablespoons fresh parsley, chopped
1 teaspoon extra-virgin olive oil
Salt and black pepper, to taste

1. Split the leeks lengthwise and wash each layer thoroughly. Slice across into thin strips, including the light green part.
2. Heat the olive oil and butter together over low heat. When the butter has melted, add the leeks and toss well. Cook leeks over medium-low heat for about 10 minutes or until the leeks start to soften.
3. Sprinkle the brown sugar over the softened leeks. Stir and then continue to cook over medium low heat for 15 to 30 minutes. Add water if necessary.
4. While the leeks are cooking, boil and drain the pasta.
5. When the leeks are done, add the parsley, extra-virgin olive oil, cooked pasta, and seasoning to taste. Toss well and serve.

ASK YOUR GUIDE

What are leeks?

▶ Leeks are a member of the onion family. They look like giant green onions (scallions) on steroids! Leeks have an illustrious history full of legend and lore. They have been cultivated for more than 3,000 years and are even mentioned in the Bible. Dirt tends to collect between the oniony layers of the leek, so it is important to clean them well. See page 44 for cleaning tips.

Boston Baked Beans
SERVES 6

This is the real, slow-cooked version of baked beans. You need to plan ahead and soak the dried beans overnight before making this recipe.

2 cups dried navy beans, soaked overnight then drained
1 cup onion, sliced
4 slices bacon, chopped
1 teaspoon brown mustard
½ cup brown sugar
¼ cup molasses
¼ cup maple syrup
2 tablespoons ketchup
½ teaspoon salt
1 teaspoon pepper
1½ cups water
Apple cider, as needed

1. Preheat oven to 250°F.
2. Cover the beans with water in a pot and then cook them over medium to medium-low heat until tender, about one hour. Drain beans.
3. Combine the remaining ingredients with the beans in a bean pot or baking dish, cover and bake for 4 hours.
4. Add apple cider if the tops of the beans become exposed during baking so they stay submerged.

ELSEWHERE ON THE WEB

▶ Have you ever seen the candy called Boston Baked Beans and wondered why anyone would make bean-flavored candy? The answer is simple: They're not actually beans. Ferrara Pan's Boston Baked Beans are actually candy-coated peanuts. To learn more and take a virtual tour of this candy-making process, visit www.ferrarapan.com/html/beans.html.

Queso Bean Dip
SERVES 6

This is a combination of two Tex-Mex dip favorites: Chili con Queso and Bean Dip. Serve it hot with tortilla chips.

⅓ cup heavy cream
½ package (4 ounces) cream cheese, cut in chunks
2 cups Monterey jack cheese, shredded
½ cup Anaheim chili peppers, chopped (may use canned)
1 cup refried pinto beans
½ cup sour cream
½ cup salsa
¼ cup green onions, chopped
¼ cup black olives, chopped
¼ cup banana peppers, chopped
1 cup Cheddar cheese, shredded

1. Heat the cream in a pan. Stir in the cream cheese piece by piece until it all melts.
2. Add jack cheese over low heat and stir until creamy and melted.
3. Stir in Anaheim chilies, remove from heat. Set aside.
4. Mix the refried beans, sour cream, salsa, green onions, black olives, and banana peppers together and put the mixture in a deep baking dish. Pour the jack cheese mixture on top, sprinkle the Cheddar cheese on top and bake at 350°F for 20 minutes. Serve hot or warm.

WHAT'S HOT

▶ How hot are the different varieties of chilies? Although the heat level can vary even within the same variety of chili, there are technical standards based on Scoville units. Scoville units are a method developed by Wilbur Scoville in 1912. The original method used human tasters to evaluate how many parts of sugar water it takes to neutralize the heat. Find out how hot your favorite chili peppers are at http://about.com/homecooking/chiles.

Is wild rice really rice?

▶ No. Technically wild rice, also called Indian rice, is not a rice, but a marsh-grass seed. Wild rice should be thoroughly rinsed before using to remove any extraneous debris. Wild rice takes longer to cook than white rice, but overcooking produces a starchy result. For recipes using wild rice as an ingredient check out http://about.com/homecooking/wildrice.

Wild Rice Sausage Stuffing

SERVES 12

The use of sausage in the stuffing perks up the normally bland flavor of poultry. This recipe yields 12 to 14 cups, enough to stuff a 12- to-14 pound turkey. You may also stuff other poultry with this, such as duck, Cornish hens, or chicken.

1¼ cups wild rice, uncooked
1¼ cups long-grain white rice, uncooked
1 pound (16 ounces) bulk sausage
2 tablespoons butter
1½ cups celery, sliced
1 cup fresh mushrooms, sliced
2 cups onion, diced
Salt, to taste
Black pepper, to taste
1 cup chestnuts, chopped

1. Cook wild rice and long-grain rice according to package directions. Toss together in large bowl and set aside.
2. In a 12-inch skillet over high heat, cook sausage, stirring frequently until well browned.
3. With a slotted spoon, remove sausage to bowl with rice. Add butter to drippings remaining in skillet and melt over medium heat.
4. Add celery, mushrooms, onion, salt, and pepper. Cook 10 minutes, stirring occasionally until vegetables are tender. Remove from heat and add vegetable mixture to rice mixture in bowl along with chestnuts. Toss well to mix.
5. Cool stuffing before filling the turkey or other poultry.

Herbed Rice

SERVES 8

It's simple but flavorful, thanks to the variety of fresh herbs. You can use any herbs you like and omit any you don't. Use half as many dried herbs if fresh are not available.

2 cups water
1 tablespoon butter
½ teaspoon salt
1 cup long-grain white rice, uncooked
¼ cup mixed fresh herbs, chopped (thyme, chives, basil, tarragon, and parsley)

1. Combine everything in a saucepan and bring to a boil.
2. Stir, cover, and reduce the heat to low.
3. Set timer for 20 minutes and do not lift the lid before 20 minutes.
4. Turn heat off and let rice sit with the lid on for 10 minutes.
5. Serve hot.

ELSEWHERE ON THE WEB

▶ Tired of trekking to the grocery store to buy herbs that are less than par? Why not grow your own in the comfort of your own home? For more information, including helpful growing tips, visit www.backyardgardener.com/herb/.

Oyster and Rice Dressing

SERVES 12

Oysters are an old-fashioned ingredient in dressings and stuffings. They add richness and texture. This side dish can be kept warm, covered, in a 250°F oven for up to 1 hour. It can also be refrigerated for up to 2 days and reheated before serving.

2¼ cups long-grain white rice, uncooked
3¾ cups low-sodium chicken broth
⅓ cup dark rum
2 teaspoons dried basil
2 teaspoons dried thyme
1 tablespoon olive oil
6 shallots, peeled and chopped
2 medium onions, chopped

1 large stalk celery, chopped
3 cloves garlic, minced
2 cups fresh spinach leaves, washed and torn into small pieces
2 tins (3¾ ounces each) smoked oysters, drained and sliced
Salt and black pepper, to taste

1. Preheat oven to 450°F.
2. Place rice in a 9" × 13" casserole. In a saucepan, combine chicken broth, rum, basil, and thyme. Bring to a boil and pour over rice. Cover tightly with foil and bake for 30 minutes, or until rice is tender.
3. Meanwhile, in a Dutch oven, heat olive oil over medium heat. Add shallots, onions, and celery. Cook stirring occasionally until tender, about 10 minutes. Add garlic and cook, stirring, for 1 minute more.
4. Add spinach and oysters; cook, stirring, until spinach is just wilted, about 3 minutes. Stir into rice and season with salt and pepper. Serve hot or warm.

ASK YOUR GUIDE

How do you tell the difference between dressing and stuffing?

▶ The term "stuffing" first appeared in English print in 1538. After 1880, it seemed the word "stuffing" did not appeal to the propriety of the Victorian upper crust, which began referring to it as "dressing." Nowadays, the terms "stuffing" and "dressing" are used interchangeably, with "stuffing" being the term of preference in the South and East portions of the United States.

Coconut Rice
SERVES 8

This rice is exotic, slightly sweet, and a space-saver. You can use all of your stovetop burners to prepare the rest of your meal while it bakes in the oven. It's especially good paired with fish or shellfish.

1 stick (4 ounces) unsalted butter
½ cup shallots, minced
¼ cup yellow bell peppers, minced
¼ cup carrots, finely diced
2 cups long-grain white rice, uncooked
1 can (13½ ounces) unsweetened coconut milk
1¼ cups hot water
½ teaspoon salt
⅛ teaspoon white pepper
½ cup coconut, shredded
½ cup toasted coconut, shredded

1. Preheat oven to 350°F.
2. Melt butter in a sauce pan and sauté the shallots, bell peppers, and carrots until tender. Add rice and sauté for 3 to 5 minutes with the vegetables.
3. Pour rice mixture into a glass casserole dish. Add coconut milk, water, salt, pepper, and shredded coconut. Stir to incorporate. Cover and bake for 1 hour.
4. Remove from oven and leave lid on until ready to serve. Before serving, sprinkle the toasted coconut on top.

ELSEWHERE ON THE WEB

▶ Coconut milk is actually a combination of equal parts shredded coconut and water, simmered and then strained through cheesecloth, squeezing out as much of the essence of the pulp as possible. You can find canned coconut milk and cream in most markets along with canned fruit juices, or try your hand at making your own. Do not confuse sweetened "cream of coconut" (used for desserts and mixed drinks) with unsweetened coconut milk or cream. For more information, visit www.thaifoodandtravel.com/ingredients/cocmilk.html.

Barley, Sun-Dried Tomatoes, and Scallions
SERVES 4

This method treats barley like rice, toasted in butter, then cooked with flavorful sun-dried tomatoes, garlic, and scallions. When rice gets boring, try this recipe.

3 tablespoons butter
1½ cups pearl barley
1 medium bunch scallions (white and green portions), sliced thin
2 cloves garlic, pressed
2 cups chicken broth
2½ cups hot water
10 oil-packed sun-dried tomato halves, chopped into large chunks
1½ teaspoons salt
½ teaspoon pepper, freshly ground
¼ cup pine nuts, toasted

1. Place a medium-sized saucepan over medium heat and melt butter. Add barley and stir-fry until it begins to turn white, about 2 minutes. Add scallions and garlic, stirring constantly for an additional minute.
2. Carefully add chicken broth and water while stirring with a long-handled spoon. Add sun-dried tomatoes, salt, and pepper.
3. Bring to a boil. Reduce heat to low. Cover and cook until barley is tender to the bite, about 40 to 45 minutes. Stir in pine nuts and serve warm.

▶ Grains are not only nutritious and delicious, but they're also wonderfully easy to prepare. Here is a list of some of the most common grains—along with a few that aren't so common: amaranth, pearl barley, bulgur, cornmeal, couscous, hominy, millet, rolled oats, steel-cut oats, quinoa, brown rice, rye berries, triticale, wheat berries, cracked wheat, and wild rice. For a resource on these alternative grains, refer to my Grains Recipes and Usage chart at http://about.com/homecooking/grains.

Ranch House Beans

SERVES 4

These are the perfect beans to serve with your barbecue. Throw every-thing in one pot and just let it simmer while you prepare the rest of the meal.

2 cups cooked canned pinto beans
¼ cup bacon, chopped
¼ cup onion, chopped
¾ cup tomato salsa
1 tablespoon cayenne pepper sauce
Salt, to taste
Pepper, to taste

1. Combine everything except salt and pepper in a saucepan and bring to a simmer.
2. Simmer for 45 minutes.
3. Season with salt and pepper to taste.

Savory Lemon Couscous
SERVES 4

Couscous makes a delicious alternative to rice or potatoes. This easy dish cooks up in less than 10 minutes with very little effort and goes well with meat, poultry, pork, and fish.

> ¼ cup sweet onion, minced
> 2 tablespoons butter
> 1½ cups chicken broth
> 1 teaspoon fresh lemon juice
> 1 teaspoon lemon zest, grated
> ½ teaspoon onion powder
> ½ teaspoon garlic powder
> 1½ teaspoons salt
> ½ cup frozen baby peas
> 1 cup plain quick-cooking couscous

1. Gently sauté sweet onion in the butter until the onion is translucent.
2. Add chicken broth, lemon juice, lemon zest, onion powder, garlic powder, salt, and baby peas.
3. Bring to a boil. Remove from heat, stir in couscous, cover, and let stand for 5 minutes to absorb the liquid.
4. Fluff couscous with a fork before serving.

ELSEWHERE ON THE WEB

▶ Today's couscous consists of small granules or pellets made from semolina flour (from the heart of durum wheat) which resembles farina, polenta, or grits, but slightly larger. However, the term "couscous" originally referred to the method of processing the flour, and couscous was often made from millet, barley, and other grains. Couscous is as old as pasta. In fact, many historians argue that couscous predates pasta, with references to couscous dating back as far as the tenth century. For more information, visit http://about.com/busycooks/couscous.

Refried Black Beans

SERVES 4

Refried beans are easy to make and you can't always find black beans prepared this way in a can. You can use canned beans or cook your own dried beans for this recipe.

½ cup onion, diced
1 clove garlic, minced
2 tablespoons olive oil
2 cups black beans, cooked, divided use
1 cup water, divided use
1 teaspoon ground cumin
1 teaspoon salt
¼ cup sour cream
1 tablespoon fresh cilantro, chopped
2 tablespoons fresh lime juice

1. Sauté onion and garlic in olive oil until translucent.
2. Mash beans and stir 1 cup of them into the onion mixture over medium heat.
3. Stir in ½ cup of water and then the remaining beans.
4. Stir in the rest of the water, cumin, and salt and cook over medium to medium-low heat for 10 minutes, stirring often. Turn off heat and stir in sour cream and cilantro.
5. Stir in the lime juice and serve hot.

WHAT'S HOT

▶ Black beans have long been a protein-rich staple food of many Latin cultures. Today, black beans are enjoyed around the world. Find out why some cook faster than others, what can toughen the beans, and how to ease any potential flatulence using herbs. Learn about the history of black beans, and get some cooking tips plus many black bean recipes at http://about.com/homecooking/blackbeans.

Get Linked

Here are some great links to my About.com site for more pasta, rice, grain, and bean recipes and related information.

PASTA RECIPES

Here is a resource for all kinds of pasta dishes to check out and refer to for dinner ideas.

 http://about.com/homecooking/pasta

RICE RECIPES

Brown rice, arborio rice, basmati rice, wild rice, and long-grain white rice are some of the different types of rice used in the recipes here for risotto, rice side dishes, rice stuffing, rice pudding, and more.

 http://about.com/homecooking/rice

BLACK BEAN RECIPES

This is a page dedicated entirely to recipes using black beans, such as black bean cakes, relish, and stew.

 http://about.com/homecooking/blackbeanrecipes

Chapter 5

Beef and Lamb

ASK YOUR GUIDE:

Can you give me some other pot roast ideas?
▶ **PAGE 72**

What is caponata and what if I can't find it?
▶ **PAGE 73**

What does a marinade do?
▶ **PAGE 78**

Can you advise me on lamb selection and storage?
▶ **PAGE 80**

What is ground beef?
▶ **PAGE 82**

Teriyaki Flank Steak
SERVES 6

Flank steak is best served medium-rare. It works well as an entrée, in fajitas, and in salads. Flank steak, like beef brisket, must be sliced against the grain or it can be tough and chewy. The marinade *not only adds flavor, but also acts as a tenderizer.*

3 tablespoons peanut oil
½ teaspoon kosher salt
2 cloves garlic, pressed
½ teaspoon black pepper, ground
1 flank steak (about 2½ pounds)
1 cup light soy sauce
2 tablespoons honey
1 tablespoon rice wine vinegar
1 tablespoon fresh gingerroot, grated
2 tablespoons sesame seeds
¼ cup scallions, sliced thinly on the bias

1. In a small bowl, mix the peanut oil, salt, garlic, and pepper. Spread on both sides of the steak. Cover and refrigerate overnight.
2. Combine soy sauce, honey, rice wine vinegar, gingerroot, sesame seeds, and scallions in a saucepan. Heat the mixture over low heat to melt the honey and meld the flavors.
3. Preheat the grill. Brush the steak with the warm sauce and grill it for 3 to 4 minutes on each side for medium-rare. Baste the steak with sauce while cooking.
4. Remove the steak from the heat and let it sit for a few minutes. Slice very thinly, diagonally across the grain. Serve warm or at room temperature.

WHAT'S HOT

▶ Ginger is native to Southern Asia and has long been a staple addition to Asian cuisines. It is quite popular in the Caribbean Islands, where it grows wild in lush tropical settings. Jamaican ginger is prized for its strong, perky flavor, and this island currently provides most of the world's supply, followed by India, Africa, and China. The gnarled, bumpy root of the ginger plant is the source of this wonderful spice.

Texas Brisket

SERVES 8 TO 10

Authentic Texas brisket is slow-roasted over a very low fire for many hours. This recipe makes it accessible to the home cook in a faster way without all the smoke.

1 tablespoon onion powder
1 tablespoon garlic powder
1 tablespoon paprika
1 teaspoon celery salt
1 tablespoon kosher salt
2 teaspoons sugar
2 teaspoons pepper
2 teaspoons dried oregano
1 teaspoon liquid smoke
1 beef brisket (5 to 6 pounds), rinsed and patted dry
½ cup beer

1. Mix the onion powder, garlic powder, paprika, celery salt, kosher salt, sugar, pepper, oregano, and liquid smoke together in a bowl.
2. Rub the spice mixture on the brisket, cover, and refrigerate overnight.
3. Put the brisket in an electric slow-roaster. Pour the beer around, but not on, the meat and put the lid on.
4. Turn the temperature to 325°F and roast for 1 hour. Reduce heat to 300°F and roast an additional 1½ to 2 hours, or until brisket is fork-tender.
5. Remove brisket to a platter, cover, and let rest for 15 minutes. Slice brisket diagonally across the grain and serve with warm barbecue sauce on the side.

TOOLS YOU NEED

▶ You might want to try perfecting your barbecued brisket recipe in a covered wood-burning grill or a smoker. A smoker will be easier to maintain the low temperature required for the long cooking time. A general rule for cooking time is 30 minutes per pound of meat at 275°F. Another way to go is an indoor smoker. No indoor smoker will work as well as an outdoor slow method, but it can be a convenient alternative. Check out my review at http://about .com/homecooking/smoker review.

ASK YOUR GUIDE

Can you give me some other pot roast ideas?

▶ You can use the same method in a large oval slow-cooker, cooking on low setting for six to eight hours. For a less sweet roast, make your pot roast Italian-style with red wine instead of cola. Omit the potatoes and add canned diced tomatoes and basil. Poke several holes in the meat with a paring knife and insert garlic cloves into them before cooking. Serve sliced pot roast and vegetables over creamy polenta.

Cola Seven-Bone Roast
SERVES 6 TO 8

You won't taste cola, but the gravy is to die for! Oven-baked pot roast and vegetables are enhanced by rich gravy. This can also be made in a slow cooker.

1 beef seven-bone roast (3 to 4 pounds)	1 cup cola, at room temperature
Kosher salt and pepper, to taste	1 cup tomato sauce
1 tablespoon olive oil	1 packet dry onion soup mix
1 pound baby red (creamer) potatoes, scrubbed, skins on	1 tablespoon sweet Hungarian paprika
1 cup celery, roughly chopped	2 teaspoons dried oregano, crushed
½ pound baby carrots, peeled	1 teaspoon garlic powder
1 red onion, very thinly sliced	

1. Prepare a 9" × 13" baking pan by lining it with foil. Preheat oven to 350°F.
2. Sprinkle roast with salt and pepper.
3. Heat a heavy-duty skillet until very hot, add the olive oil, and quickly sear the seven-bone roast on both sides. Place seared roast in baking pan. Surround with potatoes, celery, and carrots in an even layer. Spread sliced red onions evenly over the top of the meat and vegetables.
4. Mix cola, tomato sauce, onion soup mix, paprika, oregano, and garlic powder in a bowl until combined. Pour evenly over meat and vegetables. Cover tightly with foil.
5. Bake for 2 hours. Remove from oven and let rest at least 15 minutes. Carve meat. Serve with vegetables and pan gravy.

Sicilian Meatballs

SERVES 4

These meatballs can be served with spaghetti and other pastas, put into lasagna, or used to make scrumptious meatball sandwiches.

    4 cups tomato sauce
    1 can diced tomatoes
    ½ cup caponata, ready-made
    1 slice white bread, soaked in milk
    1 pound ground beef
    1 egg
    ¼ cup onion, minced
    2 tablespoons fresh parsley, chopped
    2 cloves garlic, pressed
    ¼ cup Parmesan cheese, grated

1. In a large pot combine the tomato sauce with the diced tomatoes and caponata and heat to a simmer while assembling the meatballs.
2. To make the meatballs, squeeze the milk out of the bread (discard the milk) and tear it into small pieces.
3. In a large bowl combine the bread with the ground beef, egg, onion, parsley, garlic, and Parmesan cheese.
4. With wet hands, shape the meat mixture into 2-inch balls and drop the meatballs into the simmering sauce.
5. Simmer for 1½ hours, stirring gently from time to time.

ASK YOUR GUIDE

What is caponata and what if I can't find it?

▶ Caponata is Sicily's zesty summer relish: A sweet-and-sour and salty dish made from eggplants, tomatoes, capers, olives, celery, onions, vinegar, and sugar. If you can't find it, you can add 1 tablespoon of capers, 1 tablespoon of chopped green or black olives, 1 tablespoon of balsamic vinegar, and 1 teaspoon of honey to the sauce in place of it in this recipe.

Brandy Peppercorn Filet Mignon
SERVES 4

Peppercorns enhance this tender filet mignon dish.

4 beef tenderloin steaks (filet mignon), 1½ inches thick (6 ounces each)
1 teaspoon olive oil
½ teaspoon kosher salt
1 tablespoon cracked black peppercorns

1 tablespoon butter
⅓ cup plus 1 teaspoon brandy, divided use
1 cup heavy cream
Chives, chopped, for garnish

1. Rub olive oil on both sides of filet mignon steaks evenly, then sprinkle with salt. Press the peppercorns into the meat.
2. Heat a large heavy skillet over high heat until very hot, but not smoking. Add 1 tablespoon butter and filets. Brown the steaks 7 minutes on one side, then turn and cook an additional 7 minutes on the other side to medium-rare doneness. (Turn only once.)
3. Remove filet mignon steaks and keep warm while preparing the sauce. Off the heat, add ⅓ cup of brandy to the same undrained skillet and carefully ignite the alcohol with a long match or firestick. Shake the pan gently until the flames die down, then stir, scraping up any browned bits from the bottom, over medium heat.
4. Add the cream and bring to a slow boil. Cook until the sauce begins to thicken, about 5 minutes.
5. Add the remaining brandy and adjust the seasoning with salt if necessary. Return the steaks to the pan, turning to coat both sides with sauce, and warm 1 minute. Serve pan sauce over warm filet mignon steaks and sprinkle with chopped chives.

1950s-Style Meatloaf

SERVES 6

This meatloaf version became a family favorite in many households in the 1950s. The key is in the onion soup mix and the mixture of ground beef and pork for added flavor and moisture. If you have any leftovers, make meatloaf sandwiches with ketchup, of course!

1½ pounds ground beef (chuck is best)
½ pound ground pork
2 eggs, lightly beaten
1 cup fine bread crumbs
1 large clove of garlic, pressed
½ cup sweet onion, minced
¼ cup pickle relish
1 teaspoon dried oregano, crushed

1 teaspoon kosher salt
Freshly ground pepper, to taste
1 tablespoon Worcestershire sauce
1 package dry onion soup mix
½ cup milk
¾ cup tomato ketchup, divided use
½ cup potato chips, crushed

1. Preheat oven to 350°F.
2. Combine ground beef, ground pork, eggs, bread crumbs, garlic, sweet onion, pickle relish, oregano, kosher salt, pepper, Worcestershire sauce, onion soup mix, milk, and half of the ketchup.
3. Gently mix only until combined. Do not overwork the meat or it will become tough. Form into a loaf. Cover with the remaining half of the ketchup. Sprinkle the potato chips over the top.
4. Bake 1 hour. Let meatloaf rest 15 minutes before cutting to serve.

WHAT'S HOT

▶ Meatloaf, the ultimate comfort food, has many possibilities; you can vary the ingredients, toppings, and sauces it is served with. Check out http://about.com/homecooking/meatloaf for different meatloaf recipes, such as Italian style in peppers, sweet-and-sour crockpot, country French chicken, bacon double cheeseburger, and Reuben loaf.

Individual Meatloaves

SERVES 4

This recipe is a twist on the camp-out method of making beef stew in a foil packet and cooking it over a fire. Here it is revised for the oven. As an added bonus, this method also reduces cooking time.

1 pound ground beef
½ cup carrots, shredded
¾ cup bread crumbs
1 egg, beaten
1 tablespoon heavy cream
1 tablespoon Worcestershire sauce

1 tablespoon tomato ketchup
1 tablespoon Dijon mustard
1 teaspoon onion powder
¼ cup Parmesan cheese
½ teaspoon pepper
½ teaspoon salt
½ cup onion slices

1. Preheat oven to 350°F. Tear off 4 large squares of heavy-duty aluminum foil. Set aside.
2. In a bowl, combine the ground beef, carrots, bread crumbs, egg, cream, Worcestershire sauce, ketchup, mustard, onion powder, Parmesan cheese, salt, and pepper with your hands, being careful not to overmix. Form the meat mixture into 4 oblong loaves.
3. Set one loaf on each foil square. Divide the onions into four servings and place each serving on top of each meat patty. Sprinkle with salt and pepper.
4. Wrap each foil square up around the meat and vegetables into a tightly sealed packet.
5. Place the packets on a baking sheet pan and bake the packets for 45 minutes. Remove packets from the oven and carefully open them, avoiding the steam that will be released.

TOOLS YOU NEED

▶ You don't need to cook these personal meatloaves in foil. For instance, you can bake them in little tea bread loaf pans, or you can braise them in an electric skillet. You can also bake them free-form on a baking sheet with sides. You could even use large muffin tins, if you don't mind meat "rounds" instead of loaves. The proportion of the loaves will make children happy at a family dinner party while adults enjoy meatloaf in its regular size.

Apple and Sausage–Stuffed Steak Roll
SERVES 4

This roulade is an elegant yet hearty entrée for a special occasion. It's easy to make and sure to please the most discriminating guest.

2 cups herb-seasoned stuffing mix
¼ pound bulk breakfast sausage
½ cup apple, chopped
1 egg, beaten
1 pound beef flank steak
1 tablespoon vegetable oil
½ cup apple juice

1. Prepare stuffing mix according to the directions on the container.
2. Brown sausage in a Dutch oven, drain on paper towels, and let cool.
3. Cover meat with plastic wrap and pound with a meat mallet to make a thin rectangle.
4. In a bowl, combine the sausage, apple, stuffing, and egg. Spread stuffing mixture over beef; roll up from long side and skewer to secure the roll.
5. Brown the roll in the Dutch oven with the sausage fat and vegetable oil. Add ½ cup apple juice. Cover and simmer for 1½ hours. Remove meat.
6. Slice into rounds and serve hot.

ELSEWHERE ON THE WEB

▶ Meat and fruit together? Oh my! I came across a news article telling of this newest concoction, which may soon be showing up in public-school cafeterias. Not only are blueberries being added to lean ground meat burgers, but so are cherries and prunes. Fruit is also being added to turkey and chicken burgers. The fruit lends moisture to the dry lean meats as well as added nutrition. To make blueberry burgers, visit www.american grassfedbeef.com/recipes/ blueberry-hamburgers.asp.

What does a marinade do?

▶ Marinades serve two different functions: as a tenderizer and a flavor enhancer. You probably already know that some tough cuts of meat benefit from the tenderizing effects of marinating, but how does it work? Take a look at how you can make marinades work for you at http://about.com/homecooking/marinades.

Easy Wine-Marinated Brisket
SERVES 8

Wine makes a flavorful marinade for slow-cooked brisket, and also helps to tenderize the meat.

I cup dry red or white wine
2 tablespoons soy sauce
I small onion, grated
I celery stalk, thinly sliced
3 garlic cloves, finely minced
3 to 4 pounds beef brisket
I medium-sized onion, thinly sliced
½ cup prunes, pitted

1. Preheat oven to 325°F.
2. Combine wine, soy sauce, grated onion, celery, and garlic in a heavy-duty, zip-top freezer bag large enough to accommodate the brisket.
3. Add the brisket to the bag, squeeze out the air, seal, and refrigerate 3 to 4 hours, turning occasionally.
4. Remove brisket and place fat-side up in a roasting pan or Dutch oven. Spread sliced onions and prunes around brisket and cover with half the marinade. Reserve remaining marinade. Cover tightly with heavy foil or a lid.
5. Bake 3 hours, until tender. Check midway during roasting time and add more marinade if needed to keep brisket from drying out. (Discard any remaining marinade when brisket is done.)
6. When done, remove brisket from oven and let rest 15 minutes. Carve slices against the grain and place on serving platter. Cover slices with pan juices and cooked onions to serve.

Chicken-Fried Steak

SERVES 6 TO 8

This take-off on chicken-fried steak starts with a quick browning in a skillet and is finished in the oven. The rich gravy makes itself.

2 pounds round steak, cut into
   serving sizes
1 teaspoon salt
½ teaspoon pepper
1 cup self-rising flour
½ teaspoon dry mustard
3 tablespoons canola oil
2 tablespoons butter

1 medium onion, chopped
1 cup mushrooms, chopped
1 clove garlic, chopped
¾ cup water
3 tablespoons cornstarch
3 tablespoons brown sugar
½ cup sour cream

1. Preheat oven to 300°F. Spray a baking dish with oil.
2. Pound steaks to tenderize, then season them with salt and pepper on both sides.
3. Combine flour and dry mustard. Coat steak pieces with flour mixture then brown them in the oil. Remove to baking dish.
4. Melt butter in the pan with the drippings and sauté the onion, mushrooms, and garlic in it. Arrange the sautéed mixture on top of the steak pieces.
5. Combine water, cornstarch, brown sugar, and sour cream in a small bowl until smooth. Pour this gravy mixture over the steaks. Bake 1 hour.
6. Serve hot with mashed potatoes and biscuits.

ELSEWHERE ON THE WEB

▶ Chicken fried steak is a favorite comfort food in the southern part of the United States. It is also called country fried steak, and I have seen boneless pork and chicken breasts cooked this way as well. White pan gravy is the usual accompaniment, with biscuits and honey on the side. For more recipes inspired by the South, visit http://southernfood.about.com.

Can you advise me on lamb selection and storage?

▶ Color is a good indicator of age. The lighter the color, the younger the meat. Baby lamb should be pale pink. Regular lamb is pinkish-red. Ground lamb and small lamb cuts should be wrapped and refrigerated up to three days. Ground lamb can be tightly wrapped and frozen up to three months, while larger roasts and solid pieces can be frozen up to six months. Frozen lamb should be thawed in the refrigerator, not at room temperature.

Mint Pesto–Crusted Lamb Chops
SERVES 4

Lamb is often served with icky mint jelly, and I created these lamb chops with that in mind. They can be prepared earlier in the day and refrigerated before the broiling step and then finished by broiling at serving time.

1½ cups fine dry bread crumbs
1 clove garlic, minced
2 tablespoons fresh mint, minced
2 tablespoons fresh basil, minced
2 tablespoons walnuts, ground
2 tablespoons olive oil

12 lamb chops
2 tablespoons Parmesan cheese, grated
Salt, to taste
Pepper, to taste
4 tablespoons unsalted butter

1. Combine bread crumbs, garlic, mint, basil, walnuts, Parmesan cheese, and olive oil. Set aside.
2. Season lamb chops with salt and pepper and sauté them in butter until medium-rare. Place browned chops on a broiler pan. Preheat the broiler.
3. Mound 2 tablespoons of breadcrumb mixture on each lamb chop.
4. Broil chops until crust is lightly browned.

Pomegranate Lamb
SERVES 8

Pomegranate juice, red wine, lemon, and spices make a tenderizing marinade for butterflied leg of lamb. Be sure to plan ahead for this recipe because the lamb needs to marinate overnight.

1 cup unsweetened pomegranate juice
½ cup dry red wine
2 large sweet onions
1 cup fennel, diced
1 whole lemon, unpeeled, chopped
3 cloves garlic, slightly crushed but whole
1 teaspoon black pepper
1 tablespoon fresh oregano, chopped
1 teaspoon salt
1 leg of lamb (5 to 6 pounds), boned and butterflied

1. Combine pomegranate juice, red wine, sweet onions, fennel, lemon, garlic, pepper, oregano, and salt in a large freezer zip-top bag.
2. Add lamb to the bag, squeeze out the air, and gently massage the marinade into the lamb. Refrigerate 12 hours or overnight.
3. To cook: Preheat coals in grill to medium or preheat oven to 325°F.
4. If grilling, wipe the lamb of excess marinade. Grill or roast until internal temperature of lamb reaches 145°F. Remove from oven or grill and cover lamb with foil and let rest 10 to 15 minutes before carving.

ELSEWHERE ON THE WEB

▶ To learn more about the wonderful qualities of pomegranate juice, visit www.pom wonderful.com. This company makes a full line of pomegranate juice and teas. Their Web site also features a pomegranate recipe for every type of meal so you'll never be left wondering what to do with the leftover juice.

What is ground beef?

▶ Well, it depends. Ground-beef labeling is extremely confusing. At least you can rest assured that it will be beef. By law, ground beef may not contain any added water, fillers, or binders. To find out the cut of beef and the fat content, you'll have to depend on the label or grind it yourself. Grinding effectively tenderizes other-wise tough cuts of meat into a form that won't give your teeth a workout. The ground fat adds flavor. Check out http://about.com/homecook ing/groundbeefinfo for more details.

Meat-Stuffed Peppers
SERVES 4

You don't have to use green peppers for this recipe. Try making these stuffed peppers with red, yellow, orange, or even purple bell peppers. Other vegetables, such as acorn squash, red onions, eggplants, zucchini, and cabbage leaves, can also be stuffed.

    4 large green peppers
    1 pound ground beef
    ¼ pound ground pork sausage
    ½ cup long-grain white rice, uncooked
    ½ cup onion, diced
    2 cups tomato sauce, divided use
    ½ teaspoon salt
    ¼ teaspoon black pepper

1. Preheat oven to 350°F.
2. Cut peppers in half lengthwise through the stem and discard seeds, stem, and membrane. Lay pepper cups in a casserole dish.
3. In a bowl, mix together the meat, rice, onion, ½ cup of tomato sauce, salt, and pepper.
4. Stuff each pepper half with meat mixture, mounding it on top.
5. Pour tomato sauce over the stuffed peppers, cover with foil, and bake 45 minutes to 1 hour. Serve hot.

Gyro Loaf
SERVES 4 TO 6

The Greek gyro is a sandwich made from spiced minced lamb that is heated on a vertical rotisserie and shaved off into strips with a knife. The meat is put in a pita with fresh tomatoes, onions, fresh parsley, and cucumber yogurt sauce. This Americanized version adds ground beef for a delicious homemade rendering.

½ pound ground beef
½ pound ground lamb
¼ cup onion, minced
2 cloves garlic, pressed
½ teaspoon celery salt
1 teaspoon Worcestershire sauce
1 tablespoon fresh parsley, chopped

1 egg
1 tablespoon dried oregano
1 teaspoon black pepper
½ teaspoon salt
¼ cup oatmeal
¼ cup breadcrumbs
1 tablespoon olive oil

1. Preheat oven to 350°F.
2. Combine all ingredients, except the olive oil, with your hands in a bowl.
3. Shape the mixture into a loaf and press it into a loaf pan. Brush the top with olive oil.
4. Bake, uncovered, until thermometer inserted in center reads 160°F, about 1 hour 15 minutes.
5. Let the loaf cool and refrigerate it until ready to use.
6. Slice thin and warm the slices in the oven wrapped in foil to make gyro sandwiches.

WHAT'S HOT

▶ Make your own cucumber yogurt sauce to go on your homemade gyros. Known as tzatziki sauce in Greek, this cool and refreshing sauce is easy to make. First, drain 6 cups of plain yogurt in a coffee filter or cheesecloth overnight in the refrigerator. This will thicken it up. Combine the thick yogurt with 3 peeled and grated pickle-sized cucumbers,

Get Linked

Here are some great links to my About.com site for more beef and lamb recipes and related information.

BEEF RECIPES

There are so many cuts of beef and even more ways to cook them that you just need to see this index of recipes.

 http://about.com/homecooking/beef

GROUND BEEF RECIPES

If you're tired of the same old ground beef recipes, you're sure to find something to spark your interest here.

 http://about.com/homecooking/groundbeefrecipes

LAMB RECIPES

Lamb chops, leg of lamb, lamb stews, and lamb roasts are all here for you to start cooking lamb.

http://about.com/homecooking/lamb

Chapter 6

Pork, Ham, and Sausage

ASK YOUR GUIDE:

Why is ham often the center of the Easter meal?
▶PAGE **87**

Can you recommend a good biscuit recipe to accompany gravy?
▶PAGE **91**

Pork Loin with Cherry Sauce
SERVES 8

Be sure to use pork loin here, not tenderloin! Pork loin has a sufficient amount of fat to keep moist while roasting.

1 boneless pork loin (4 pounds)	1 red onion, coarsely chopped
2 tablespoons fresh rosemary, finely chopped	½ teaspoon garlic powder
	¼ cup gold rum
1 tablespoon dried sage, crumbled	1 cup chicken broth
	¼ cup dried cherries
1 teaspoon herbs de Provence	1 tablespoon cornstarch
1 tablespoon kosher salt	¼ cup heavy cream
1 teaspoon ground black pepper	Additional salt and pepper, to taste
2 tablespoons olive oil	

1. Preheat oven to 450°F.
2. Coat the pork loin with rosemary, sage, herbs de Provence, kosher salt, and pepper. Rub olive oil over the meat.
3. Put the red onion in the bottom of a roasting pan to make a bed for the roast. Sprinkle the garlic powder over the onion and then lay the pork loin on top. Roast for 15 minutes.
4. Turn the oven down to 300°F and roast for 1 hour and 15 minutes.
5. Remove the meat from the roasting pan and keep warm on a platter with a tent of foil over the roast.
6. Add the rum to the roasting pan and scrape up any browned bits. Add the chicken broth and then pour the contents of the roasting pan into a saucepan. Skim grease off the top. Simmer until reduced by half.
7. Strain the sauce and return it to the saucepan. Add the cherries and any juices that have collected under the roast and

▶ In addition to cherries, a variety of other fruits pair nicely with pork. For example, apricots and prunes are excellent in a stuffed pork loin, and applesauce is a classic accompaniment to pork chops. Pineapple chutney is great with grilled pork tenderloin, and blackberries are wonderful warmed in Dijon mustard sauce and served over sautéed pork cutlets. Exotic and humble fruits alike make tasty pan sauces. Try lychees or sautéed cinnamon apples with pork chops.

simmer until the cherries plump, 5 to 10 minutes. Mix the cornstarch into the cream and then add it to the simmering sauce. Simmer until sauce thickens slightly.

8. Slice the pork roast. Arrange the slices overlapping on a platter and spoon the cherry sauce over them.

Peach-Glazed Ham

SERVES 15 TO 20

This recipe calls for a ham that has already been cooked and only needs reheating. If you use a partially cooked or uncooked ham, you will need to bake it longer before the glazing step.

1 boneless fully cooked ham (9 pounds)
1 can peaches in syrup, diced
1 cup peach jam
¼ cup balsamic vinegar
¼ cup orange juice

1. Preheat oven to 325°F. Cover ham with foil and bake for 45 minutes. Remove from oven. Score surface lightly in a uniform diamond pattern.
2. Strain peaches, reserving syrup. Set peaches aside. Stir together syrup from peaches, jam, balsamic vinegar, and orange juice. Pour glaze mixture on ham. Continue baking 30 minutes longer, basting frequently with glaze.
3. Garnish ham with reserved peaches.

ASK YOUR GUIDE

Why is ham often the center of the Easter meal?

▶ In the United States, ham is a traditional Easter food. In the early days, meat was slaughtered in the fall. There was no refrigeration, and the fresh pork that wasn't consumed during the winter months before Lent was cured for spring. The curing process took a long time, and the first hams were ready about the same time that Easter rolled around. Thus, ham was a natural choice for the celebratory Easter dinner.

Mango Mojo Pork Chops
SERVES 4

ELSEWHERE ON THE WEB

▶ The folks at Wild Oats market have prepared a helpful step-by-step guide, with pictures, to show you just the right way to cut a mango. Visit www.wildoats.com/u/department173. There is also a mango slicer on the market from the company OXO.

Quick and easy boneless pork chops are served with a tangy mango mojo sauce. Serve with rice, black beans, and plantains for a Caribbean meal with a tropical flair.

4 boneless pork chops, 1 inch thick
Salt and freshly ground pepper, to taste
1 tablespoon vegetable oil
¼ cup orange juice
¼ cup lemon juice
¼ cup lime juice
2 cups fresh mango, diced
½ cup sweet onion, sliced
4 cloves garlic, minced
1 jalapeño pepper, minced
½ teaspoon ground cumin
¼ cup fresh cilantro, chopped

1. Place pork chops between two pieces of plastic wrap and pound until they are ½-inch thick. Sprinkle both sides of pork chops with salt and pepper.
2. Heat a large skillet over medium heat. When hot, add the oil, swirling to coat the pan. Cook pork chops about 4 minutes on each side until browned and just slightly rosy in the center. Remove pork chops from skillet and keep warm.
3. To the juices in the pan add the orange, lemon, and lime juices, mango, onion, garlic, jalapeño, and cumin. Cook about 5 minutes until reduced and thickened, stirring occasionally to scrape up the browned bits. Return warm pork chops to the pan, turning to coat with sauce. Sprinkle the cilantro over the pork chops and serve hot.

Pineapple Ham Balls

YIELDS 20 TO 25

Sure to please your guests, this baked appetizer combines ham and fresh ground pork with vegetables, mustard, spices, pineapple juice, and a splash of whiskey.

1 pound ground cooked ham
½ pound ground fresh pork
1½ cups soft bread crumbs
    (about 3 slices)
2 tablespoons whiskey, divided
    use
2 tablespoons water
1 egg
¼ cup celery, minced
2 tablespoons onion, minced

½ teaspoon dry mustard
¼ teaspoon pepper
⅛ teaspoon cloves, ground
⅓ cup brown sugar, firmly
    packed
1 tablespoon prepared
    mustard
½ tablespoon vinegar
2 tablespoons pineapple juice

1. Preheat oven to 350°F. Line a baking sheet with nonstick foil.
2. In a large bowl, mix together ham, ground pork, bread crumbs, 1 tablespoon whiskey, water, egg, celery, onion, dry mustard, pepper, and cloves until evenly combined.
3. Using about 1 tablespoon of the mixture for each, form into balls, and place 1 inch apart on baking sheet. Bake for 15 minutes.
4. For the sauce, combine remaining 1 tablespoon whiskey, brown sugar, prepared mustard, vinegar, and pineapple juice in a saucepan over low heat. Whisk until combined and cook about 5 minutes.
5. Toss cooked ham balls in sauce. Serve warm in a chafing dish or low-heat crockpot.

TOOLS YOU NEED

▶ A very useful tool in the kitchen is an ice cream scoop. It can help you measure out muffin and cupcake batter, portion mashed potatoes and rice, and form meatballs, among other things. For appetizer-sized cocktail meatballs, get a smaller scoop, like the kind used for chocolate truffles.

Deviled Ham Wraps
SERVES 6 TO 12

Ham wraps are a favorite for those on low-carb diets. Ham slices are filled with a savory cheese mixture and then rolled into wraps. Wrap each ham roll in a leaf of lettuce for an easy sandwich.

> 8 ounces cream cheese, at room temperature
> 4 ounces sour cream
> 1 tablespoon Dijon mustard
> 1 tablespoon pickle relish
> ¼ cup sweet onion, minced
> 2 tablespoons chives, minced
> 1 teaspoon garlic powder
> ¼ teaspoon cayenne pepper sauce
> 1 pound deli sliced ham, sliced thin enough to easily roll into a tube

1. Blend cream cheese, sour cream, Dijon mustard, pickle relish, sweet onion, chives, garlic powder, and cayenne pepper sauce until smooth.
2. Spread cheese mixture on ham slices. Roll ham slices into logs. Refrigerate at least 1 hour. Cut ham wraps into thirds for serving as an entrée or into 1-inch-thick spirals to serve as an appetizer.

ELSEWHERE ON THE WEB

▶ Try making ham wraps with Italian ham. The meat is seasoned, salt cured, and air dried. It is not smoked. The meat is pressed into a dense, firm texture. Parma ham is true prosciutto. There are lots of other great recipes that use prosciutto, such as this one for a watermelon prosciutto salad that makes a great start to a summer meal: http://about.com/gourmetfood/salad.

Sausage Gravy and Biscuits
SERVES 6

You can serve this breakfast dish with eggs, potatoes, and fruit for a huge country breakfast, but it makes a hearty meal on its own.

1 pound bulk sausage
¼ cup flour
2 cups whole milk
1 teaspoon dried thyme
½ teaspoon black pepper, ground
¼ teaspoon cayenne pepper
Pinch nutmeg, ground
½ cup heavy cream
Salt, to taste
6 buttermilk biscuits (see sidebar)

1. Brown the sausage in a large skillet and separate it into crumbles.
2. Dust the sausage with the flour and stir over medium heat for a few minutes.
3. Add ½ cup of milk and whisk over medium heat until smooth and thick. Gradually add the rest of the milk, whisking between additions.
4. When the gravy is smooth, add the thyme, black pepper, cayenne pepper, and nutmeg. Simmer over medium-low heat until gravy thickens.
5. Stir in the cream and season with salt. Simmer, if necessary, to desired consistency.
6. Split biscuits horizontally and ladle sausage gravy over each half. Serve hot.

ASK YOUR GUIDE

Can you recommend a good biscuit recipe to accompany gravy?

▶ Of course! I've got a great recipe called Blitz Buttermilk Biscuits on my About.com site. Just visit http://about .com/homecooking/butter milkbiscuits. These flaky biscuits are the perfect ones to ladel gravy over, any time of day (or night!).

Ham Steak with Red-Eye Gravy
SERVES 4

Ham steaks are an economical way to feed your family. They are usually so large that one can serve two people.

2 ounces unsalted butter
2 ham steaks
¼ cup brewed coffee
½ cup boiling water
Cayenne pepper sauce, to taste
Black pepper, to taste

1. Heat the butter over medium high heat in a frying pan and fry the ham steaks in it, for 2 to 3 minutes on each side, or until they are browned. Only one ham steak will fit at a time so repeat in the same pan. Transfer them to a platter and set aside in a warm oven.
2. Pour the coffee and boiling water into the same pan and cook the mixture over high heat, scraping up the browned bits, for 2 minutes.
3. Season the gravy with the cayenne pepper sauce and pepper and pour it over the ham steaks. Serve hot.

ELSEWHERE ON THE WEB

▶ You may not have thought of doing anything with coffee besides using it as a way to wake up in the morning. However, there are lots of recipes out there that can use an extra caffeine kick. For more coffee recipes, visit www.vanhoutte.com/en/about_coffee and click on "recipes." You'll find gems such as coffee burgers and coffee spaghetti!

Spareribs, Apples, and Sauerkraut
SERVES 4

Oktoberfest would be a great time to serve this hearty meal with dark bread, hunks of sharp Cheddar cheese, and frosty steins of beer.

2 cans (16 ounces each) sauerkraut
3 pounds country-style spareribs
2 teaspoons paprika
6 beef bouillon cubes
½ teaspoon caraway seeds
½ teaspoon pepper
1 Granny Smith apple, cored, peeled, and diced
10 bacon slices, dipped in flour

1. Rinse and drain the sauerkraut. Place sauerkraut in large 4-quart Dutch oven. Add 2 quarts hot water.
2. Add uncooked spareribs, paprika, bouillon cubes, caraway seeds, and pepper. Cook covered, over low heat for 3 hours.
3. Add the apple and cook another hour.
4. Fry floured bacon slices. Break bacon into sauerkraut. Remove bones from the sauce before serving.

Pork Medallions with Apple-Rosemary Sauce
SERVES 4

If you were raised with applesauce as a condiment for pork dishes, this will evoke memories. This recipe incorporates fresh applesauce into the pan gravy with the delicious complementary flavors of rosemary and cinnamon.

2 pounds boneless pork loin
1 cup dry white wine
2 tablespoons vegetable oil
1 tablespoon fresh rosemary, chopped
1 teaspoon lemon zest, grated
1 teaspoon black pepper, freshly ground
⅔ cup sugar
⅔ cup water
2 sprigs fresh rosemary

16 whole black peppercorns
1 cinnamon stick
6 tablespoons cider vinegar
4 medium-sized firm, tart apples, peeled, cored, and quartered
2 tablespoons butter, divided use
1 tablespoon vegetable oil
⅓ cup dry calvados (apple brandy)

1. Trim any excess fat and gristle from pork loin. Cut into 4 medallions, each about 1 inch thick.
2. In a large, heavy-duty zip-top freezer bag, combine dry white wine, vegetable oil, chopped rosemary, lemon zest, and black pepper. Squish to combine. Add pork loin medallions to the marinade in the bag, squeeze out the air, and seal. Turn bag to distribute the marinade evenly around the pork. Refrigerate for at least 2 hours or up to 8 hours.
3. Remove pork from refrigerator and let rest at room temperature in the marinade for 1 hour before cooking.
4. Dissolve the sugar in the water over low heat in a medium saucepan. Add rosemary sprigs, peppercorns, cinnamon stick,

and vinegar. Stir and simmer uncovered over low heat for about 10 minutes. Add apples and simmer another 10 minutes until apples are soft, but not mushy. With slotted spoon, remove apples to a food processor. (Save the liquid.) Pulse apples until smooth. Boil reserved apple cooking liquid until reduced to 1 cup. Strain liquid, discarding solids, and add the liquid syrup to the apple purée. Set aside.

5. Remove pork medallions from marinade, discard marinade, and pat pork dry with paper towels. Heat a large, heavy skillet over medium-high heat. Add 1 tablespoon of butter and the oil to the hot pan, swirling to combine. Add pork medallions and cook about 4 minutes on each side. Do not overcrowd the pan (if necessary, cook in batches) and do not overcook. Remove pork medallions to a platter and cover with foil to keep warm.

6. Deglaze pan with the calvados, scraping up browned bits. Cook to reduce the liquid to about 2 tablespoons, lower heat, and add apple purée. Heat about 1 minute until warmed through. Return pork medallions to the pan along with any accumulated juices from the platter. Heat about 2 minutes. Remove pork medallions to serving dishes. Quickly swirl remaining tablespoon of butter into the apple pan gravy and season with salt if necessary.

7. To serve, spoon apple rosemary pan gravy over pork medallions and serve hot.

WHAT'S HOT

▶ Rosemary is an herb native to the Mediterranean area. A member of the mint family, it is an evergreen shrub also related to basil, marjoram, and oregano. Its Latin name equates to "dew of the sea." The small, gray-green leaves look similar to small pine needles and have a bittersweet, lemony, slightly piney flavor. Use of rosemary dates back to 500 B.C., when it was used as a culinary and medicinal herb. To learn more about rosemary, check out http://about.com/home cooking/rosemary.

Pork Shoulder Roast with Apple Walnut Stuffing
SERVES 8 TO 10

Savory apple stuffing is rolled up in the center of a deboned pork shoulder roast. Pork shoulder roast is a very inexpensive cut. Removing the bone—done either by yourself or by your butcher—yields a slab of meat that is easy to stuff and slow-roast.

1 cup celery, diced
1 cup sweet onion, diced
¼ cup butter (½ stick)
1 large Granny Smith apple, cut into ½-inch dice
½ cup walnuts, chopped
1 large clove garlic, pressed
3¼ cups chicken broth, divided use
¾ cup apple juice, divided use
1 tablespoon fresh sage, minced
4 cups corn bread stuffing mix
1 pork shoulder roast (about 7 pounds), deboned
Kosher salt and freshly ground black pepper, to taste
1 large clove garlic, cut into slivers

1. Line a large baking pan with heavy-duty foil. Preheat oven to 350°F.
2. In a large pot, gently sauté celery and sweet onion in butter until onion is translucent. Add apples, walnuts, and pressed garlic; cook about 1 minute longer, stirring often. Add 1½ cups chicken broth and ¼ cup apple juice. Bring to a boil. Remove from heat. Stir in sage. Then add stuffing mix, stirring to absorb liquid. Let rest to cool.

3. Place the deboned pork shoulder roast fat-side up on a cutting board. Sprinkle liberally with kosher salt and freshly ground black pepper. Turn roast over and again sprinkle liberally with salt and pepper. You may need to add a few cuts so that it lies open and flat. Poke holes in the meat with a sharp knife and insert garlic slivers into the pork.

4. Pack cooled stuffing on top of the pork roast. Roll both ends to the center to enclose the stuffing and tie with kitchen twine. Place roast skin-side up in baking pan. Pour in remaining chicken broth and apple juice. Cover with a layer of heavy-duty foil and seal edges to the rim of the pan.

5. Bake about 2 hours. Remove foil and bake an additional 30 minutes until skin is browned.

6. Serve roast hot, cut in slices.

TOOLS YOU NEED

▶ A good-quality, sharp, seven- or eight-inch boning knife will help you out with deboning the pork shoulder if your butcher won't. Some butchers will debone the pork shoulder roast for you at no extra cost, while others will charge a higher price. Don't worry—it's easy to debone the roast yourself in about fifteen minutes. Just follow my step-by-step instructions, complete with photos, at http://about.com/homecooking/debonepork.

▶ To scoop the choke out of the middle of an artichoke, a sharp melon ball scoop is preferred, but a serrated grapefruit spoon will do a good job. A cooked artichoke will give up its choke much easier, using just a teaspoon. Then you can fill the center with various things, such as crab salad or vinaigrette if served cold, or Béarnaise sauce if served hot.

Sausage-Stuffed Artichokes
SERVES 4

These artichokes make a nice entrée served with a side of pasta, a green salad, and crusty bread.

4 whole artichokes	¼ cup olive oil
1 lemon, cut in half	½ teaspoon crushed red
1¼ cups dry breadcrumbs	pepper
½ cup Parmesan cheese, grated	1 teaspoon salt
2 cloves garlic, minced	¼ teaspoon pepper
¼ cup parsley, chopped	1½ cups water
1 cup cooked bulk sausage, crumbled	½ cup dry white wine

1. Prepare the artichokes for stuffing by cutting the stems off the bottoms first. Rub the cut lemon on all the places of the artichokes that you will cut to prevent browning. Next, cut the top inch off of each artichoke with a serrated knife and rub the lemon on the cut. Discard the cut-off part. Snip the thorny tips off the remaining leaves and rub with the lemon.
2. Pull out the center leaves to expose the fuzzy choke in the center, and then scoop out the choke with a melon baller. Squeeze lemon juice into the center of each artichoke.
3. Mix the breadcrumbs, Parmesan cheese, garlic, parsley, sausage, olive oil, crushed red pepper, salt, and pepper. Spoon the stuffing into the center of each artichoke.
4. Pour the water and white wine into the bottom of a large pot. Place a steamer rack in the bottom of the pot and put the artichokes upright on the rack. Cover the pot with a tight-fitting lid and simmer for 50 minutes, or until a leaf can be pulled easily from an artichoke. Serve warm.

Sausage Cabbage Rolls
SERVES 4

These cabbage rolls can be frozen in a casserole dish and reheated to eat on another day if you're planning your meals ahead.

1 medium head cabbage, cored
1 large onion, chopped, divided use
1 tablespoon butter
2 14.5-ounce cans Italian-style stewed tomatoes
4 garlic cloves, finely minced
2 tablespoons brown sugar
1½ teaspoon salt, divided use

1 cup rice, cooked
½ cup currants or raisins
¼ cup ketchup
2 tablespoons Worcestershire sauce
Freshly ground pepper, to taste
½ pound ground pork
½ pound ground beef
¼ pound bulk Italian sausage

1. In a Dutch oven, cook cabbage in boiling water for 10 minutes or until outer leaves are tender; drain. Rinse in cold water; drain. Remove eight large outer leaves; set aside.
2. In a saucepan, cook ⅔ of the onion in butter until softened. Add tomatoes, garlic, brown sugar, and ½ teaspoon salt. Simmer for 15 minutes, stirring occasionally. Set aside.
3. In a bowl, combine rice, currants, ketchup, Worcestershire sauce, pepper, and remaining onion and salt. Add pork, beef, and sausage; mix well. Place ½ cup meat mixture on each cabbage leaf. Fold in sides and then roll up leaf to completely enclose filling. Place seam-side down in a large skillet.
4. Top cabbage rolls with the tomato sauce. Cover and cook over medium-low heat for 1 hour. Reduce heat to low and simmer for an additional 20 minutes, adding a little water if needed. Serve hot.

WHAT'S HOT

▶ The head variety of cabbage was developed during the Middle Ages by northern-European farmers. It was French navigator Jacques Cartier who brought cabbage to the Americas in 1536. Other related cabbage cousins include Brussels sprouts, broccoli, kale, kohlrabi, and cauliflower. Needing only three months of growing time, one acre of cabbage will yield more edible vegetables than any other plant. The world's largest cabbage is credited to William Collingwood of County Durham, England, whose prized cabbage weighed 123 pounds.

Mini Meatballs

SERVES 8

These meatballs are a mixture of pork sausage, ground chuck, onions, garlic, and herbs which are then simmered with mushrooms. The resulting incredibly rich gravy is to die for. Serve as an entrée or a party appetizer.

1 pound bulk pork breakfast sausage

1 pound ground beef

½ large sweet onion, finely chopped, divided use

6 medium cloves of garlic, pressed, divided use

¼ cup fresh parsley, chopped

1 teaspoon dried oregano, crumbled

½ teaspoon dried sage

½ teaspoon dried thyme

1 tablespoon plus 1 teaspoon kosher salt, divided use

10 grinds fresh black pepper, or to taste

1 cup seasoned bread crumbs

1 tablespoon Worcestershire sauce

2 eggs, lightly beaten with a fork

½ cup heavy cream, divided use

1 teaspoon olive oil

2 tablespoons butter

1 pound baby portobello or brown mushrooms, sliced into ½-inch slices

1 tablespoon all-purpose flour

2 cups beef stock, divided use

2 cups chicken stock

1 tablespoon port wine

2 tablespoons fresh chives, chopped

1. In a large bowl, combine sausage, ground beef, half of the chopped sweet onions, half of the pressed garlic, parsley, oregano, sage, thyme, 1 tablespoon kosher salt, black pepper, bread crumbs, Worcestershire sauce, eggs, and ¼ cup of the heavy cream. Fold together with a light touch using hands. Do not over-knead. Form into meatballs the size of a quarter.

2. Heat a large Dutch oven over medium heat and coat the bottom of the pan with the olive oil. Brown the meatballs in batches. Remove browned meatballs to a large bowl.
3. Melt butter in the pan drippings and add remaining sweet onions and garlic, plus the mushroom slices. Toss vegetables to coat with oil. Sprinkle with 1 teaspoon kosher salt and sauté about 5 minutes, until mushrooms release their water. Sprinkle with flour and cook another 2 minutes. Add ½ cup beef stock and cook, stirring, for another 2 minutes. Add chicken stock, port wine, and remaining beef stock, stirring constantly until flour is incorporated. Return meatballs to the pot and simmer on very low heat for another 30 minutes. Gravy should thicken.
4. Add remaining ¼ cup of heavy cream to the meatballs and gravy. Stir, bring back to a simmer, and then turn off the heat. Stir in chopped chives.
5. Serve over cooked white rice, pasta noodles, or couscous.

Oven-Barbecued Spareribs

SERVES 4 TO 6

You don't need a grill to make spareribs. These spareribs are oven-baked with a tangy, balsamic-orange barbecue sauce.

1 tablespoon paprika	4 pounds pork spareribs
2 teaspoons kosher salt	½ sweet onion, minced
2 teaspoons dried parsley	1 tablespoon olive oil
¾ teaspoon onion powder	¼ cup balsamic vinegar
1¾ teaspoon garlic powder, divided use	1 can (8 ounces) tomato sauce
	¼ cup ketchup
¼ teaspoon black pepper, ground	¼ cup orange juice
	1 tablespoon Worcestershire sauce
¼ teaspoon dried oregano	
¼ teaspoon dried basil	1 tablespoon mustard
¼ teaspoon dried thyme	¼ cup brown sugar
⅛ teaspoon celery salt	

1. Preheat oven to 350°F. Select a large baking pan to fit spareribs in one layer and line it with heavy-duty foil. Place baking rack (a cake rack works fine) inside lined pan to keep ribs from resting on the bottom of the pan.
2. Combine spice mix of paprika, kosher salt, dried parsley, onion powder, ¾ teaspoon garlic powder, ground black pepper, dried oregano, dried basil, dried thyme, and celery salt in a bowl. Season both sides of ribs with spice mix. Place ribs in pan with meaty side up and bake for 1 hour.
3. While spareribs are baking, make barbecue sauce. Sweat minced sweet onion in olive oil over low heat until translucent and cooked, but not browned. Add balsamic vinegar and

cook three minutes until slightly reduced. Add tomato sauce, ketchup, orange juice, Worcestershire sauce, and mustard. Stir to combine well. Stir in brown sugar and remaining garlic powder. Continue cooking over low heat for 10 minutes.

4. Remove spareribs from oven and pour off fat. Turn spareribs and brush the bony side lightly with barbecue sauce. Return spareribs to meaty side up and pour remaining barbecue sauce evenly over the ribs, making sure all spots are covered with sauce. Cover with heavy-duty foil.

5. Reduce oven heat to 325°F. Bake covered spareribs an additional 1 to 1½ hours, or until done. Meat should be shrinking back from the tips of the bones and the bones should wiggle fairly easily in the meat. Let rest 10 minutes before serving. Cut into 2- to 3-rib portions and serve.

WHAT'S HOT

▶ Balsamic vinegar's rich, slightly sweet flavor readily lends itself to vinaigrette dressings and gourmet sauces, and brings out the sweetness of fresh fruits such as raspberries, strawberries, and peaches. Although it is considered a wine vinegar, it's not a wine vinegar at all. It is not made from wine, but from grape pressings that have never been permitted to ferment into wine. Some balsamic vinegars have been aged for more than 100 years.

Get Linked

Here are some great links to my About.com site for more pork, ham, and sausage recipes and related information.

PORK RECIPES

Recipes using all cuts of pork are here, including bacon, ribs, chops, tenderloin, roasts, ham, and sausage.
 http://about.com/homecooking/pork

HAM RECIPES AND INFORMATION

There is information here about all the various types of hams, how to cook those hams, and recipes using ham as an ingredient. Historical information on ham is here as well.
 http://about.com/homecooking/ham

SAUSAGE RECIPES AND INFORMATION

Not only are there recipes using sausage here, but there are also recipes to make your own sausage, cooking information about sausages, and articles and information about the many different varieties of sausage.
 http://about.com/homecooking/sausage

Chapter 7

Poultry

Ab⬤ut

ASK YOUR GUIDE:

What is the best way to defrost frozen chicken?
▶ PAGE 108

What are Rock Cornish hens?
▶ PAGE 111

Did turkeys originate in Turkey?
▶ PAGE 114

Does buttermilk have butter in it?
▶ PAGE 119

Peach Amaretto Duck Breast

SERVES 4

Duck breast meat is best served on the rare side, sliced thin. A delicious sauce of fresh peaches and amaretto complement the rich duck flavor in this recipe.

2 boneless duck breasts
Salt and pepper, to taste
2 tablespoons butter
2 shallots, chopped
2 fresh peaches, chopped
¼ cup rice vinegar
2 tablespoons amaretto liqueur
1 cup chicken broth

1. Preheat oven to 375°F.
2. Score skin on duck breasts, season both sides with salt and pepper and sear them skin side down in a sauté pan over medium-high heat for 3 minutes. Remove duck breasts from sauté pan and place skin side up in a baking dish and put in the oven for 5 minutes to finish cooking.
3. While the duck is in the oven, make the sauce. In the same sauté pan, melt the butter and cook the shallots for 2 minutes. Add peaches, vinegar, and amaretto.
4. Cook to reduce liquid by half, add broth and cook for 5 to 10 minutes more. Adjust seasoning in the pan sauce with salt and pepper.
5. Serve the duck breasts with the peach sauce spooned over the meat.

Chicken-Fried Chicken Breasts

SERVES 4

Enjoy these crispy chicken breasts with mashed potatoes and pan gravy, or eat them on a biscuit with honey and a pickle slice as a sandwich.

> 4 boneless chicken breasts
> Salt and pepper, for seasoning chicken
> 2 eggs
> ¼ cup water
> 1½ cups self-rising flour
> ½ teaspoon black pepper
> 1 cup shortening with no trans-fats

1. Season chicken breasts with salt and pepper and refrigerate for 2 hours.
2. Beat the eggs and mix them with the water in a soup plate, or other shallow bowl.
3. Combine the self-rising flour with the black pepper in another shallow bowl.
4. Melt the shortening in a cast-iron skillet to 350°F.
5. Dip the chicken breasts in the egg mixture and then dredge them in the flour mixture. Be sure to coat the meat well.
6. Fry the chicken breasts, skin side down first, in the hot shortening. Cover with a lid and cook until crisp and golden, and then turn them over and fry the other side. A total of 8 to 10 minutes cooking time is necessary.
7. Drain chicken breasts on paper towels or brown paper.

ELSEWHERE ON THE WEB

▶ Hydrogenated fats are getting a bad rap (and rightly so!). Some polyunsaturated fats and all margarines undergo a process called hydrogenation, which not only makes them useful for baking, but also prolongs shelf life. This process creates trans-fatty acids, which act like saturated fats—increasing cholesterol production in the body and negating any potential positive benefits they had as polyunsaturated fats. Sources include vegetable oils, margarine, snack foods, fried fast foods, and cookies. Avoid these trans-fats whenever possible. Visit www.bantrans fats.com for more info.

What is the best way to defrost frozen chicken?

▶ The Food Safety and Inspection Service of the USDA recommends three ways to defrost chicken: in the refrigerator, in cold water, and in the microwave. Never defrost chicken on the counter or in other locations. It's best to plan ahead for slow, safe thawing in the refrigerator. Boneless chicken breasts will usually defrost overnight. Bone-in parts and whole chickens may take one or two days or longer.

Easy Chicken Piccata
SERVES 4

To save time, measure the ingredients before you start and you can have this delicious chicken piccata on the table in less than 15 minutes.

1 tablespoon all-purpose flour	1 tablespoon butter
½ teaspoon onion powder	¼ cup white wine
½ teaspoon garlic powder	1 tablespoon lemon juice
½ teaspoon kosher salt	(about ½ lemon)
¼ teaspoon black pepper, freshly ground	¼ cup green onions, sliced
4 chicken breast cutlets (about 1½ pounds total)	½ cup chicken stock
	2 tablespoons golden raisins
2 tablespoons olive oil	1 tablespoon small capers, drained

1. Combine flour, onion powder, garlic powder, kosher salt, and black pepper. Sprinkle evenly on both sides of chicken cutlets.
2. Heat a large heavy skillet over medium heat until hot. Add the olive oil and swirl to coat the bottom of the pan. Add the chicken in one layer and cook on the first side for 5 minutes, until golden brown.
3. Turn the chicken cutlets to the second side. Add butter, white wine, and lemon juice, swirling around chicken to combine. Add the green onions and cook about 1 minute.
4. Add chicken stock, golden raisins, and capers. Cook another 1 to 2 minutes until chicken is no longer pink in the center (internal temperature should be 180°F) and pan gravy has thickened. Serve with pan piccata sauce over the chicken cutlets.

Crab-Stuffed Chicken Breasts
SERVES 6

Sweet crab meat and butter enhance these crispy chicken breast rolls that are elegant enough for a formal dinner party.

1 cup butter, divided use
1 clove garlic, finely chopped
⅛ cup parsley
¼ cup green onion
¼ cup celery
8 ounces lump crabmeat or imitation crabmeat
½ teaspoon salt
Dash pepper
1 cup fine dry bread crumbs
⅓ cup half-and-half
6 boneless, skinless chicken breasts
1 cup seasoned breadcrumbs

1. Melt ½ cup butter in a large skillet. Add garlic, parsley, green onion, and celery; sauté vegetables until soft. Fold in crabmeat, salt, and pepper, being careful not to break up crabmeat. Bring to a simmer. Add bread crumbs and half-and-half a little at a time so mixture is not too dry. Let cool slightly.
2. Preheat oven to 350°F.
3. Flatten chicken breasts to ¼-inch thickness. Spread the cooled crab mixture on the chicken breasts and roll each one up jelly-roll style. Press edges to seal.
4. Melt the remaining ½ cup butter. Dip each chicken roll in melted butter and roll in seasoned breadcrumbs. Place them in a 9" × 13" baking dish.
5. Cover and bake for 45 minutes. Uncover and bake until golden brown, about 10 more minutes.

ELSEWHERE ON THE WEB

▸ There are lots of ways to get creative with the idea of "surf and turf." In this risotto recipe from the About.com Guide to Italian Food, the "turf" comes from mushrooms and the "surf" comes from shrimp: http://about.com/italianfood/surfandturf risotto.

▶ The word "garlic" comes from Old English *garleac*, meaning "spear leek." Dating back more than 6,000 years, it is native to Central Asia, and has long been a staple in the Mediterranean region and a frequent seasoning in Asia, Africa, and Europe. Egyptians worshipped garlic and placed clay models of garlic bulbs in the tomb of Tutankhamen. Garlic was so highly prized that it was even used as currency.

Chicken Scampi

SERVES 6

Scampi means "shrimp" in Italian, but it also refers to a preparation of shrimp with garlic, butter, and lemon. This recipe treats chicken in the same manner. It's great served with linguine.

1 cup seasoned bread crumbs
1 cup Parmesan cheese, grated
6 boneless, skinless chicken breasts
2 eggs, beaten
½ cup butter
1 garlic clove, minced
½ cup lemon juice

1. Preheat oven to 375°F.
2. Combine bread crumbs and Parmesan cheese.
3. Dip the chicken in the eggs, then coat with bread crumb mixture. Place the chicken in a 9" × 13" glass baking dish.
4. Melt butter, garlic, and lemon juice in a skillet. Gently pour half of this sauce over the chicken.
5. Bake, uncovered, for 45 minutes. Spoon the rest of the sauce over the chicken before serving.

Balsamic Cornish Hens
SERVES 4

Rock Cornish game hens are not only the perfect single serving size in one compact package, but they also make an impressive sight on the dinner plate.

> 4 Rock Cornish game hens
> 4 teaspoons olive oil
> Salt, to taste
> Pepper, to taste
> Garlic powder, to taste
> Paprika, to taste
> 1 cup chicken broth
> ½ cup dry sherry
> ¼ cup balsamic vinegar

1. Preheat oven to 350°F.
2. Rinse hens with cold water and pat dry with paper towels. Rub lightly with oil. Season inside and out with salt, pepper, garlic powder, and paprika. Place hens on a rack in a roasting pan.
3. Combine chicken broth, sherry, and balsamic vinegar and brush some on the hens.
4. Bake hens for 1 hour, basting every 15 minutes with the vinegar mixture. Insert an instant-read thermometer into the thickest part of the chicken after an hour. Internal temperature should read 180°F when done.

ASK YOUR GUIDE

What are Rock Cornish hens?

▶ One food historian says chicken mogul Donald John Tyson created the Rock Cornish game hen in 1965 by crossbreeding White Rock hens and Cornish hens. His intent was to create a specialty item at a higher price to appeal to foodies. However, other sources credit Alponsine and Jacques Makowsky of Connecticut for developing this small bird some ten years earlier.

Grape-Stuffed Cornish Hens
SERVES 4

These small birds make presentation easy since each person gets a hen. Alternatively, they may be stuffed with other fruits, such as blueberries.

> 4 Cornish hens (1½ pounds each)
> Salt and pepper, to taste
> ⅛ cup olive oil
> ⅛ cup lemon juice
> ⅛ cup Marsala wine
> 2 cups green seedless grapes
> 2 teaspoons sugar
> ¼ cup butter
> 4 small bay leaves

1. Preheat oven to 350°F.
2. Sprinkle game hens inside and out with salt and pepper.
3. Mix olive oil, lemon juice, and Marsala, and brush game hens with mixture inside and out.
4. Fill each bird with ½ cup grapes and ½ teaspoon sugar. Sew or skewer opening and place on a shallow pan. Spread soft butter over breasts of birds and place bay leaf on butter.
5. Roast in oven for 1 hour, or until leg is easily moved.

▶ Many markets carry fresh game hens ready to cook. Choose hens that look plump, with unbroken, unblemished skin, and cook them within twenty-four hours or get them into the freezer. To freeze fresh game hens, remove the giblets, wash, and pat dry before wrapping in an airtight package with all air removed. Properly frozen game hens may be stored in the freezer at 0°F for six to nine months. For more Cornish hen information, check out http://about.com/homecooking/cornishhens.

Cornish Hens à l'Orange

SERVES 4

You traditionally pair orange with duckling, but little Cornish hens are used here. The method couldn't be easier yet yields incredible flavor suitable for the most discriminating palate.

¼ cup orange marmalade
2 tablespoons butter
1 tablespoon Dijon mustard
1 tablespoon Worcestershire sauce
4 Cornish game hens, thawed in the refrigerator if previously frozen

1. Preheat oven to 375°F. Line a baking pan with foil, shiny side up.
2. Melt orange marmalade, butter, Dijon mustard, and Worcestershire sauce in a saucepan on the stove or a microwave-safe bowl in the microwave for about one minute. Stir until combined. You don't want it boiling hot, only melted.
3. Baste half the glaze onto the skins of the Cornish hens.
4. Bake uncovered about 1 hour. Halfway through baking time, baste with remaining glaze. Test with instant-read thermometer in center of thigh. It should be 165°F. Let rest 10 minutes before serving.

TOOLS YOU NEED

▶ A meat thermometer is a necessity for testing the internal temperature of meat instead of guessing. An instant read thermometer is your best bet because the chance of overcooking is lessened. Meat thermometers come in all sorts of varieties and prices from basic (where you open the oven and push the termometer in) to electric (where the temperature gauge stays in the oven while the electric portion stays outside and alerts you when the meat is done).

Did turkeys originate in Turkey?

▶ The wild turkey (*Meleagris gallopa*) is native to North America and was a staple in the Native American diet. It was imported to Europe in the early part of the sixteenth century by the Spaniards via Turkey (the country). It was confused in those early times with the Guinea fowl which also arrived via Turkey, and both birds were called "turkeys" in those days. When it was assigned its Latin name in the eighteenth century, the name "turkey" still stuck.

Roasted Herbed Turkey Breast
SERVES 12

If you're having a small Thanksgiving gathering, cooking a turkey breast is the right size as opposed to a whole bird. Your only leftovers will be white meat to slice for sandwiches.

1 5- to 7-pound fresh (or frozen and thawed) turkey breast
1 tablespoon olive oil
Kosher salt and ground pepper, to taste
1 teaspoon dried thyme
1 teaspoon dried sage
¼ teaspoon onion powder
½ teaspoon Hungarian sweet paprika

1. Preheat the oven to 325°F.
2. Brush the turkey breast with olive oil.
3. Sprinkle turkey breast with salt, pepper, and herbs. Pat the herbs into the skin with your palms.
4. Place turkey breast on a wire rack in a shallow roasting pan. Cover tightly with foil and roast 2 hours.
5. Remove the foil and roast another 30 to 45 minutes, basting 2 times with the drippings. Breast is done when a meat thermometer inserted into the thickest part reaches 180°F.

Apricot Bacon Chicken Breasts
SERVES 6

The bacon keeps the chicken white meat moist while the apricot jam makes a delightful contrast to the smoky flavor of the bacon. Fast and easy to put together, this chicken dish bakes in less than 30 minutes.

6 boneless, skinless chicken breasts
½ teaspoon poultry seasoning
Salt and freshly ground pepper, to taste
6 slices bacon
¼ cup (½ stick) butter, melted
1 tablespoon Worcestershire sauce
½ cup apricot jam

1. Preheat oven to 375°F. Line a shallow baking pan with nonstick foil. (Omit foil and reduce temperature by 25°F if using a glass baking dish.)
2. Sprinkle each chicken breast evenly with poultry seasoning, then season generously with salt and pepper.
3. Wrap each chicken breast with one slice of bacon and place in baking pan with bacon ends tucked under.
4. Melt together butter, Worcestershire sauce, and apricot jam in the microwave for about 45 seconds on high. Stir until combined. Pour evenly over bacon-wrapped chicken breasts.
5. Bake until bacon is crisp and chicken tests done in the center (180°F), about 25 to 30 minutes. (If the chicken breasts are thick, bake an additional 5 to 10 minutes.)

TOOLS YOU NEED

▶ If packaged sliced bacon is cold from the refrigerator, slowly slide the dull edge of a butterknife along the length between the strips, gently rocking to separate slices. Plan ahead and take the bacon out of the refrigerator thirty minutes before cooking. The slices should separate easily. If you must watch your fat intake, lean smoked ham or prosciutto can be substituted in many recipes where the rendered bacon fat is not needed. Turkey, chicken, and vegetarian bacon products are also available.

Boneless Stuffed Turkey with Pistachios

SERVES 8 TO 10

You can fit more stuffing in a boneless turkey and have an easier time carving it to boot. Your guests will never know by looking at it that the turkey has been deboned. Visually, it looks just like a standard stuffed turkey. This recipe was designed for use in a counter-top roaster oven but may be prepared in a standard oven as well.

STUFFING:

1 medium sweet onion, diced

1½ cups (about 3 large stalks) celery, diced

½ cup (1 stick) butter

3½ cups (about two 14-ounce cans) chicken broth

1 teaspoon ground sage

1 teaspoon dried thyme

¼ teaspoon pepper, freshly ground

2 cups dry bread cubes

2 cups dry corn bread cubes

Kosher salt, to taste

1 cup whole berry cranberry sauce

1 cup pistachios, shelled

POULTRY SEASONING BLEND:

1 teaspoon ground sage

1 teaspoon dried thyme

1 tablespoon kosher salt

½ teaspoon black pepper, freshly ground

1 teaspoon garlic powder

1 teaspoon onion powder

1 tablespoon paprika

TURKEY:

1 (12 to 14 pounds) turkey, deboned

1 teaspoon browning sauce (such as Gravy Master or Kitchen Bouquet)

1 tablespoon butter, melted

Boneless Stuffed Turkey with Pistachios (continued)

1. Prepare Stuffing: Sweat onions and celery in ½ cup of butter until limp. Add chicken broth, sage, thyme, and pepper. Stir to combine. Remove from heat. Fold in bread and corn bread. Taste and add salt if necessary. Fold in whole berry cranberry sauce and pistachios. Let stuffing cool to room temperature.
2. Poultry Seasoning Blend: Combine sage, thyme, kosher salt, pepper, garlic powder, onion powder, and paprika.
3. Preheat countertop roaster oven to 400°F.
4. Turkey: Open deboned turkey and place meat-side down, skin-side up on the work surface. Combine browning sauce with melted butter and brush over the entire exterior skin of the turkey. Sprinkle ⅔ of poultry seasoning spice mix on the skin of the turkey. Turn turkey over and sprinkle remaining spice mix on meat side.
5. Mound cooled stuffing on meat side of turkey. Pull skin together over stuffing. Sew closed using cooking string or secure with a metal skewer.
6. Place stuffed turkey on rack in countertop roaster oven, making sure the lifter handles are in the upright position. Turn down temperature to 350°F. Bake for about 2 hours, or until meat thermometer in the thickest part of the meat registers 180°F. If necessary, turn up temperature to 400°F. during the last half hour of cooking to promote browning.

WHAT'S HOT

▶ Frozen turkeys are available year-round. They are quite good roasted with the bones in, but the bones can make carving difficult. Some butchers will debone the turkey for you, usually at a higher price. It's easy to do it yourself in about fifteen minutes and your guests will never guess it is deboned until you cut it. Easy instructions and photos on how to debone a turkey yourself are included in on my About.com site at http://about.com/homecook ing/deboneturkey.

Parmesan Chicken Tenders
SERVES 4

These nuggets are not deep fried but baked in the oven instead. They are still crunchy and less greasy than fried. Additionally, they are made with olive oil—a good fat.

½ cup olive oil
3 cups breadcrumbs
1 cup Parmesan cheese
1 tablespoon onion powder
2 teaspoons paprika
2 teaspoons salt
1 teaspoon pepper
3 boneless, skinless chicken breasts, cut into strips

1. Preheat oven to 350°F. Line a baking sheet with foil and set aside.
2. Put olive oil in a bowl and set aside.
3. Combine breadcrumbs, Parmesan cheese, onion powder, paprika, salt, and pepper in a bowl. Set aside.
4. Toss chicken strips in the olive oil, and then dredge them in the crumb mixture.
5. Arrange the coated chicken chunks on the foil and bake for 1 hour. Serve warm or at room temperature.

▶ Believe it or not, fat is actually necessary to our diets—it's a tool your body needs. Some vitamins are strictly fat-soluble, meaning they cannot be delivered to the body via any other method. Vitamins A, D, E, and K provide energy reserves and are fat-soluble vitamins. Of course, fat is the insulator for the body and protects body organs. However, not only do we need to follow the old adage of "all things in moderation," but we also need to choose the right fats for the needs of our bodies.

Oven-Fried Chicken
SERVES 4

This chicken tastes like fried chicken but it is only fried briefly to seal the coating, then it is baked to finish cooking.

>2 cups buttermilk
>½ teaspoon cayenne pepper sauce
>1 chicken (3 pounds), cut into eight pieces
>1 cup self-rising flour
>1½ teaspoons salt
>1½ teaspoons black pepper
>1 cup peanut oil

1. Mix the buttermilk and the cayenne pepper sauce. Soak the chicken pieces in the buttermilk mixture overnight.
2. Preheat the oven to 350°F.
3. Combine the flour, salt, and pepper in a large bowl. Remove the chicken from the buttermilk and coat each piece with the flour mixture. Pour the oil into a large skillet and heat to 360°F on a thermometer.
4. Place several pieces of chicken in the oil and fry for about 3 minutes on each side until the coating is a light golden brown. Remove the chicken from the oil and place the pieces on a metal baking rack nestled inside a jellyroll pan.
5. Bring the oil back to 360°F before frying the next batch. When all the chicken is fried, bake for 30 to 40 minutes. Serve hot.

ASK YOUR GUIDE

Does buttermilk have butter in it?

▶ In days gone by, nothing went to waste in the standard homestead, and this included the liquid left over after churning butter. When combined with natural airborne bacteria, this liquid thickened and soured, taking on a pleasingly tangy flavor. Nowadays, most commercial buttermilk is made by adding a lactic-acid bacteria culture to pasteurized sweet whole milk or, more commonly, skim milk or nonfat milk. Most commercial varieties are salted, so check the label if you are on a sodium-restricted diet.

Garlic Buffalo Wings
SERVES 6

Serve these spicy wings with celery sticks and blue cheese dressing for the classic presentation.

I cup all-purpose flour
I teaspoon salt
3 pounds chicken wings
I cup butter, melted
I tablespoon garlic, minced
I teaspoon garlic powder
I tablespoon Worcestershire sauce
½ cup cayenne pepper sauce

1. Preheat oven to 375°F.
2. Combine the flour and salt in a large bowl and toss the chicken wings in it. Shake off the excess flour and put the wings on a foil-lined baking sheet pan. Repeat in batches if necessary to get all the wings on baking sheets.
3. Bake wings for 30 minutes. Remove from oven, turn the wings over, and bake another 15 minutes.
4. Combine butter, garlic, garlic powder, Worcestershire Sauce, and cayenne pepper sauce in a large bowl.
5. Remove the chicken wings from the oven, toss them in the sauce, and return them to the baking sheets. Bake for 15 minutes more.

ELSEWHERE ON THE WEB

▶ There is some dispute about who came up with the original hot wing appetizer, but most credit the Anchor Bar in where else but Buffalo, New York. The historic creation date for Buffalo Wings was October 30, 1964, when owner Teressa Bellissimo was faced with feeding her son and his friends a late snack. For wing facts and recipes, visit www.buffalo wings.com.

Get Linked

Here are some great links to my About.com site for more poultry recipes and related information.

CHICKEN RECIPES

From cutlets to bratwurst, hot wings to Cornish hens, you'll find a variety of recipes at this link.

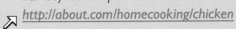
http://about.com/homecooking/chicken

TURKEY RECIPES AND INFORMATION

Before and after Thanksgiving, be sure to check out my recipes and information on this page.

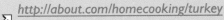
http://about.com/homecooking/turkey

POULTRY

For a complete list of poultry recipes and information check out this link.

http://about.com/homecooking/poultry

Chapter 8

Seafood

About

ASK YOUR GUIDE:

How did the catfish get its name?
▶PAGE 131

What's the difference between a bay scallop and a sea scallop?
▶PAGE 136

Should shrimp be deveined?
▶PAGE 138

Where did shrimp get its name?
▶PAGE 140

Crab Puffs

YIELDS 40

Crab Puffs, like all Choux pastry, are best made under low humidity conditions. If you cannot use beer, you may substitute chicken or clam broth. As a last resort, use water, but they will not be as flavorful. Crab-puff appetizers may be served warm or at room temperature.

1 cup lump crabmeat, picked clean (pasteurized canned is fine)

½ cup Swiss cheese, shredded (Gruyère suggested)

2 tablespoons chives, chopped

1 teaspoon Worcestershire sauce

1 teaspoon dry mustard

1 teaspoon lemon juice

½ cup (1 stick) butter

1 cup lager beer (not light beer)

½ teaspoon salt

¼ teaspoon lemon pepper

1 cup all-purpose flour

4 large eggs

2 tablespoons fresh dill weed, chopped

1 cup cream cheese, whipped

1. Preheat oven to 400°F. Line baking sheets with parchment paper or Silpats.
2. Combine crabmeat, Swiss cheese, chives, Worcestershire sauce, dry mustard, and lemon juice in a bowl. Set aside.
3. In a large saucepan, melt butter, beer, salt, and lemon pepper. Bring to a boil. Add flour, remove from heat, and stir vigorously with a wooden spoon. Return to heat. Continue to beat until a dough ball forms. Remove from heat.
4. Add eggs to dough, one at a time, beating vigorously after each addition until well combined. Fold crab mixture into dough.

Crab Puffs (continued)

5. Pour Choux puff dough into a large zip-top bag, squeeze out the air, and seal. Cut about ⅓-inch from one corner of the bag. Pipe the dough onto prepared baking sheets into mounds about 1½ inches in diameter.
6. Bake crab puffs 25 to 30 minutes until crispy and golden brown.
7. While puffs are baking mix the fresh dill with the whipped cream cheese.
8. Split and fill puffs with a little of the cream-cheese mixture to serve.

WHAT'S HOT

▶ There are many different types of crab, and you can check out a handy chart at http://about.com/homecook ing/typesofcrab to learn more about them. One popular variety is the King Crab, Latin name *Paralithodes camtschaticus*. This giant crab is also often called "Alaskan King crab," "Japanese crab," and "Russian crab" due to its size, which can reach up to twenty-five pounds and measure up to ten feet. It may be large, but only about ¼ is edible—primarily the legs and claws.

Miniature Crab Cakes
SERVES 4 TO 6

Tiny crab cakes are delicious served as finger food with lemon aioli for dipping. Serve on a salad with baby greens and rémoulade, in a sandwich with tartar sauce, or in a bowl of corn chowder.

1 pound crabmeat, picked over and shell pieces discarded (canned is fine)
¼ cup shredded Monterey jack cheese
½ cup mayonnaise
¼ cup green bell pepper, minced
¼ cup sweet onion, minced
1 tablespoon lemon juice
1 slice white bread, soaked in milk and squeezed dry
½ teaspoon salt
¼ teaspoon pepper
1 egg, beaten
2 cups bread crumbs

1. Pick any shells or cartilage that may be left in crabmeat and discard.
2. Combine crabmeat with Monterey jack cheese, mayonnaise, green bell pepper, sweet onion, lemon juice, bread, salt, and pepper in a bowl until well mixed. Chill for one hour up to overnight.
3. Put egg in one bowl and breadcrumbs in another. Shape crab mixture into cakes that are 2 inches around and 1 inch thick. Dip the cakes first in beaten egg, then in breadcrumbs.
4. Fry the crab cakes in butter until browned on both sides.
5. Serve warm.

ELSEWHERE ON THE WEB

▶ Most of the Stone crab harvest comes from Florida, where it is a prized delicacy harvested from October 15 to May 15. Only the claws are eaten, so fishermen twist off one claw from crabs and toss them back to grow a new one, leaving them with one claw to defend themselves. Crabs will regenerate their claws within eighteen months. The law requires these claws to be boiled for seven minutes and then either put on ice or frozen. For ordering information, visit www.crabs.com.

Baked Citrus Salmon

SERVES 4

This preparation makes the salmon meat flaky and tender with a sweet-tart punch of flavor. The cooked meat is delicate, so have the plates close by when serving.

2 tablespoons orange juice, freshly squeezed
2 tablespoons blood orange juice, freshly squeezed
2 tablespoons lemon juice, freshly squeezed
1 tablespoon olive oil
1 teaspoon shallot, minced
⅛ teaspoon salt
Pepper, to taste
1¼ pound salmon fillet
4 orange slices

1. Preheat oven to 450°F.
2. Mix the orange juice, blood orange juice, lemon juice, olive oil, shallot, salt, and pepper in a small bowl.
3. Place salmon in a baking dish skin-side down. Spoon the juice mixture over the fish. Place the slices of orange on top of the fish.
4. Bake 12 to 15 minutes, or until cooked through.
5. Serve by dividing the salmon in four and carefully lifting the meat off the skin with a metal spatula.

WHAT'S HOT

▶ Salmon are anadromous, which means they migrate from saltwater to freshwater to lay their eggs. Freshwater salmon are salmon that became landlocked, and have less flavor than saltwater varieties. Likewise, although farm-raised salmon live in a saltwater habitat, they just don't have the same degree of rich flavor as their wild counterparts. Salmon get that beautiful pink color from astaxanthin, a pigment in the insects and crustaceans that the fish feed upon.

Crab-Stuffed Mushrooms

SERVES 8

Served as an appetizer or entrée, these crab-stuffed portobello mush-rooms are rich and elegant. Other large mushroom caps will also work, but reduce cooking time accordingly. Plan ahead for chilling the stuffing mixture.

16 ounces canned pasteurized crab claw meat, picked over for shells
½ cup sweet onion, minced
2 tablespoons fresh parsley, minced
1 tablespoon garlic powder
½ tablespoon dry mustard powder
½ tablespoon kosher salt
Freshly ground pepper, to taste
Juice of 1 fresh lemon
1 tablespoon Worcestershire sauce
½ cup mayonnaise

¼ cup heavy cream
1 cup seasoned dry stuffing mix, pounded into coarse crumbs
1 tablespoon dried porcini mushrooms, crumbled
1½ cups mozzarella cheese, shredded, divided use
½ cup fresh Parmesan cheese, grated, divided use
8 portobello mushroom caps
3 tablespoons olive oil
Hungarian sweet paprika, to taste
¼ cup dry sherry

1. In a large bowl, combine crab, sweet onion, parsley, garlic powder, mustard powder, salt, pepper, lemon juice, Worcestershire sauce, mayonnaise, heavy cream, stuffing crumbs, dried porcini mushrooms, 1 cup of mozzarella cheese, and ¼ cup of Parmesan cheese until well combined. Cover and refrigerate 4 hours or overnight.

2. Preheat oven to 400°F. Select a shallow baking pan large enough to hold portobellos and line it with nonstick foil.
3. Brush portobello mushrooms clean. Remove the stem. Scrape out the dark gills with a large spoon. Rub olive oil over the tops of the portobello mushroom caps and place bottom-side up in baking pan. Mound crab mixture into caps. Top the stuffing with the remaining ½ cup mozzarella cheese and ¼ cup Parmesan cheese. Sprinkle lightly with paprika. Carefully pour sherry down the side of the baking pan.
4. Bake 25 to 30 minutes, until golden on top and mushrooms are cooked through.

TOOLS YOU NEED

▶ Of course if you are using lump crabmeat you don't need any special tools to sort through the meat to pick out any cartilage. However, if you are cooking whole crabs or crab legs, a special pick can be used to help extract the crabmeat from the shells.

Nutty Parmesan Sole
SERVES 4

This fish is baked instead of fried, but it is still crisp crunchy. Feel free to experiment with other nuts, such as pecans or hazelnuts.

2 large eggs
¾ cup Parmesan cheese, freshly grated
2 tablespoons all-purpose flour
4 sole fillets (4 to 6 ounces each)
3 tablespoons vegetable oil
3 tablespoons butter, melted
½ cup walnuts, finely chopped

1. Place a 10" × 15" baking pan (with sides) in the oven and pre-heat to 425°F.
2. Beat eggs in a shallow pie plate with a fork. Mix the Parmesan cheese and flour together on a large dinner plate.
3. Rinse the sole and pat dry. Dip into the egg, drain off excess, and coat with the cheese mixture. Set the coated fish filets on a cookie sheet.
4. Remove heated pan from oven. Add the oil and place the pieces of fish in the hot pan. Drizzle the top of the fish with the melted butter. Sprinkle the walnuts over the fish.
5. Bake uncovered 7 to 10 minutes.

▶ Sole is a flatfish that feeds on the bottom of bodies of water. Its flesh is white, mild tasting, and flakey when cooked. This baking method is a healthy alternative to frying fish while keeping the crunchy texture. Try it for your next fish "fry"!

Pecan Cornmeal Catfish

SERVES 4

These crispy critters are a filling entrée accompanied by hush puppies, coleslaw, biscuits or corn bread with honey butter and, of course, tartar sauce and lemon wedges.

> 1¼ to 1½ pounds catfish fillets
> ¾ cup yellow cornmeal
> ¼ cup pecans, finely chopped
> ½ teaspoon salt
> ¼ teaspoon cayenne pepper
> 4 lemon wedges
> Tartar sauce, to taste

1. Rinse the catfish fillets and then pat them dry, but not completely.
2. Mix together the cornmeal, pecans, salt, and cayenne pepper.
3. Heat about 1 inch of oil in a large skillet over medium-high heat. Dip each catfish fillet into the cornmeal mixture, then place in hot oil.
4. Turn fillets over when browned and fry the other side. Catfish is done when the meat just begins to flake when pierced with a fork. Serve hot with lemon wedges and tartar sauce.

ASK YOUR GUIDE

How did the catfish get its name?

▶ Catfish are named as a result of the whisker-like feelers the fish have on their heads that make them resemble cats.

Champagne Salmon with Asparagus
SERVES 8

This is a favorite for a springtime afternoon get-together. It's elegant, yet easy to prepare.

1 whole salmon (6 to 8 pounds), dressed
6 shallots, minced
1 pound fresh mushrooms, chopped
1 bottle (25.4 ounces) champagne or sparkling wine
1¾ cups heavy cream
4 tablespoons (½ stick) unsalted butter, cut into pats

Salt and freshly ground black pepper, to taste
2 tablespoons fresh lemon juice
2 tablespoons butter, melted
1 tablespoon fresh dill, chopped
3 cups asparagus tips
Fresh dill sprigs, for garnish

1. Preheat the oven to 450°F.
2. Butter a large baking dish and place the salmon in it. Add the shallots and mushrooms and pour in the champagne. Bake the salmon, uncovered, for 45 minutes, basting several times during cooking.
3. Remove the salmon from the pan and set it aside. Strain the cooking liquid into a saucepan and save the shallots and mushrooms. Boil the liquid over high heat until it is reduced to about ½ cup. Add the heavy cream and boil until the sauce is reduced and thickened. Whisk the unsalted butter into the sauce, one pat at a time, until emulsified. Season with salt and pepper, to taste.
4. Meanwhile, mix the lemon juice, melted butter, and chopped dill. Steam the asparagus tips. Toss with the lemon dill butter and the reserved shallots and mushrooms.

5. Make a bed for the salmon with the asparagus on a platter. Skin the salmon and place it on the platter. Pour the sauce over and garnish with fresh dill sprigs.

Hazelnut Trout Filets
SERVES 4

Try this dish with almonds and amaretto instead of hazelnuts and Frangelico for a slightly different flavor that goes equally well with trout.

> 4 whole (small) rainbow trout, deboned
> Salt and pepper, to taste
> 1 cup hazelnuts, chopped
> 1 cup bread crumbs
> ½ cup butter, melted
> 2 tablespoons Frangelico (hazelnut liqueur)

1. Preheat oven to 400°F. Place fish opened, skin side down, on 2 baking sheets and season the flesh with salt and pepper.
2. Combine hazelnuts with breadcrumbs and pat the mixture onto the trout flesh, coating thoroughly. Melt the butter with the hazelnut liqueur and then pour it over the coated fish.
3. Bake for 10 to 13 minutes, and then broil to brown the crust for about 1 minute, if necessary. Serve hot.

TOOLS YOU NEED

▶ A boning knife with a small, flexible blade is the perfect tool for deboning fish. Try to find a knife that fits comfortably in your hand to make the process go more smoothly. When buying knives, never be afraid to ask the salesperson if you can hold the knife before purchasing. It's the only way to ensure a perfect fit in your hand.

ELSEWHERE ON THE WEB

▶ For correct zester use and information about different kinds of zesters you might find in a kitchen gadget store, visit the About.com Guide to Entertaining at http://about .com/entertaining/zesters, where there is information on other favorite gadgets such as garlic gadgets, immersion blenders, and pizza stones.

Orange Roughy with Leeks and Sun-Dried Tomatoes
SERVES 4

You can make this dish with frozen fish filets too. It is actually easier to spread the butter on them. Just bake the dish 10 to 15 minutes longer.

4 tablespoons (½ stick) unsalted butter, softened
1 tablespoon lemon zest, grated
¼ cup sun-dried tomatoes, diced
1 cup leeks, diced
4 orange roughy filets (about 1 pound), thawed if frozen
Salt and pepper, to taste
1 cup panko breadcrumbs
¼ cup dry white wine

1. Preheat oven to 350°F.
2. Mix the soft butter with the lemon zest and sun-dried tomatoes.
3. Spread the leeks out on the bottom of a baking dish large enough to accommodate the fish in one layer. Season the fish filets with salt and pepper and place them on top of the leeks.
4. Divide the butter mixture into 4 parts and spread evenly on each fish filet. Sprinkle the breadcrumbs on top of the butter.
5. Pour the wine around the fish into the baking dish. Bake uncovered for 15 minutes. Serve hot with leeks and baking juices.

Baked Halibut in Napa Cabbage
SERVES 4

Serve with jasmine rice or cooked rice sticks (noodles).

4 large leaves Napa cabbage
4 tablespoons unsalted butter, softened
1 tablespoon fresh gingerroot, grated
1 shallot, minced
4 halibut filets (1-inch thick)

Salt and pepper, to taste
½ cup coconut milk
¼ cup fresh lime juice
1 piece of lemongrass (3 inches), thinly chopped
½ cup heavy cream

1. Preheat oven to 375°F.
2. Blanch the Napa cabbage leaves in boiling water to soften and make them flexible, then plunge them into ice water to cool. Lay them out on paper towels to drain.
3. Combine the soft butter, grated gingerroot, and shallot to make a compound butter.
4. Divide the compound butter among the blanched cabbage leaves and place in the middle. Season the halibut filets with salt and pepper and place one on each cabbage leaf. Wrap the cabbage leaves around the fish filets to make packages.
5. Place cabbage-wrapped packages seam-side down in a baking dish. Pour the coconut milk and lime juice over the packages and sprinkle with the chopped lemongrass.
6. Bake uncovered for 15 minutes. Remove the packages from the baking dish and place on a serving platter. Strain the baking liquid into a saucepan and bring to a boil. Add the heavy cream and simmer to reduce into a slightly thickened sauce. Season with salt and pepper if necessary, then pour sauce over the packages on the platter. Serve hot.

WHAT'S HOT

▶ If you're having trouble finding lemongrass in the produce section of your local supermarket, try looking in an Asian market or grocery store. Many cities and even smaller towns have Asian markets that specialize in ingredients that are found often in Asian cuisine, such as lemongrass, and you can often buy hard-to-find ingredients that are not available in American grocery stores.

What's the difference between a bay scallop and a sea scallop?

▶ The bay scallop is tiny and tender and the deep-sea scallop is larger and less tender. The entire scallop within the shell is edible, but it is the adductor muscle, which hinges the two shells, that is most commonly sold and consumed by the general public in the United States. Be forewarned that some unscrupulous markets may try to pass imposter seafood (usually shark meat) as scallops. Learn how to spot a true scallop at http://about .com/homecooking/ truescallop.

Broiled Bay Scallops with Garlic and White Wine
SERVES 4

Once you've tried this, you'll crave the sweet simplicity of this dish. The tender bay scallops shine through without getting lost in cream sauces or deep-fried breading.

2 tablespoons butter
2 pounds bay scallops
¼ cup dry white wine
Salt and pepper, to taste
½ cup breadcrumbs
1 garlic clove, pressed
2 tablespoons parsley, chopped
4 to 8 lemon wedges

1. Preheat oven to 400°F.
2. Butter 4 individual gratin dishes with ½ tablespoon butter each.
3. Arrange ½ pound of scallops in each gratin dish and sprinkle with dry white wine. Season scallops with salt and pepper.
4. Combine bread crumbs with garlic and parsley and sprinkle scallops with breadcrumb mixture.
5. Bake gratin dishes in the oven for 12 minutes. Serve hot with lemon wedges.

Lobster Purses
YIELDS 2 DOZEN

You can try mixing and matching seafood in this recipe if lobster is out of your budget. Crabmeat, shrimp, and, of course, imitation crabmeat are all good options.

8 ounces cooked lobster meat
¼ cup Monterey jack cheese, shredded
2 tablespoons chives, chopped
1 tablespoon fresh gingerroot, grated
4 ounces cream cheese, softened
Salt and pepper, to taste
1 tablespoon lemon zest, grated
1 tablespoon rice wine
24 wonton wrappers
Vegetable oil cooking spray

1. Preheat oven to 375°F.
2. Toss the lobster meat with the jack cheese, chives, and ginger in a medium-sized bowl. Mix the cream cheese, salt, pepper, lemon zest, and rice wine into the lobster mixture.
3. Spray mini-muffin tins with vegetable cooking spray. Place one wonton wrapper in each cup and gently press down. Place a heaping teaspoon of lobster mixture in each cup. Twist tops of wonton wrappers to enclose the filling. Spray each bundle with the cooking spray.
4. Bake for 12 to 15 minutes or until lightly brown. Serve immediately.

TOOLS YOU NEED

▶ Wonton wrappers are thin square noodles that are used to contain dumpling fillings for pot stickers and wontons. You can usually find them in the refrigerated section of the produce area in most supermarkets or at your local Asian grocery store.

Should shrimp be deveined?

▶ This is pretty much a question of aesthetics. With large shrimp, it's fairly easy to devein them by slitting along the back and lifting out the vein with a knife. Most cooks won't bother deveining medium-sized or smaller shrimp, unless they look particularly dirty. You can see the vein through the shell and meat, so use your own judgment.

By the way, it's easier to peel and devein raw shrimp than cooked shrimp. However, shrimp cooked in the shell has more flavor than shrimp peeled before cooking.

Easy Baked Shrimp
SERVES 4

Slightly spicy with a hint of sweetness, this shrimp recipe bakes quickly in the oven. Be careful not to overcook the shrimp or they will become rubbery.

¼ cup olive oil
½ cup orange juice
2 tablespoons tomato paste
1 tablespoon soy sauce
2 tablespoons honey
2 garlic cloves, pressed

1 pound peeled fresh or frozen thawed shrimp, tails optional
½ teaspoon ground cayenne pepper (red pepper), or to taste
1 cup panko bread crumbs
½ teaspoon kosher salt
¼ cup Parmesan cheese, grated

1. Preheat oven to 450°F (425°F for glass). Line a shallow baking dish with nonstick foil or spray a glass baking dish with vegetable oil.
2. Combine olive oil, orange juice, tomato paste, soy sauce, honey, and garlic in a zip-top plastic bag. Add the shrimp and squeeze out the air. Seal, and toss to coat shrimp. Refrigerate 15 minutes.
3. Combine cayenne pepper, panko, and kosher salt until well blended.
4. Remove shrimp from marinade with a slotted spoon and place in baking dish along with ½ cup of the marinade. Spread shrimp into a single layer. Sprinkle evenly with the seasoned panko mix, then top with grated Parmesan cheese. Refrigerate for 15 minutes.
5. Bake shrimp 12 to 15 minutes until lightly browned.

Honey-Cider-Glazed Shrimp Kebabs
SERVES 4

These tangy, sweet shrimp are perfect for adding to a salad or serving over a bed of rice with sautéed vegetables. They also make an impressive appetizer on their own.

8 bamboo skewers
¼ cup apple cider
¼ cup cider vinegar
¼ cup olive oil
1 tablespoon honey
Salt and pepper, to taste
24 raw shrimp, peeled

1. Soak the skewers in water.
2. Combine apple cider, vinegar, olive oil, honey, salt, and pepper in a zip-top plastic bag and squish to combine. Place shrimp in the bag, press out all the air, and seal. Toss to coat shrimp.
2. Marinate the shrimp in the bag while heating the grill.
3. Thread 6 shrimp onto two parallel skewers to keep them stable. Repeat 3 more times with the remaining shrimp and skewers.
4. Grill skewered shrimp for about 3 minutes per side.
5. Serve hot off the grill.

TOOLS YOU NEED

▶ I love steamers! There are various types of steamers available for steaming vegetables, fish, and dim sum. Choices include plastic, bamboo, and metal steamers in a variety of shapes for use in the microwave or over a pot of boiling water on the stove. There are even specialized steamers for asparagus, whole fish, and corn on the cob. Some foods, such as whole artichokes, benefit from steaming because they get cooked through without becoming waterlogged from boiling or dried out from baking.

Where did shrimp get its name?

▶ The word "shrimp" comes from the Middle English *shrimpe*, meaning "pygmy" or the crustacean itself. In the seventh century, shrimp and other seafood composed most of the Chinese diet, and they still do today. Harvesting of shrimp dates back to the seventeenth century, when Louisiana bayou residents used seines up to 2,000 feet in circumference to scoop up the delicacy. Mechanized shrimping didn't come about until after 1917.

Sautéed Fennel Shrimp
SERVES 4

The sun-splashed flavors of the famous fish soup from southern France, bouillabaisse, are in this dish made of shrimp, orange peel, and anise.

¼ cup olive oil
½ cup fresh orange juice
1 tablespoon Pernod (anise liqueur)
1 tablespoon orange zest, grated
1 tablespoon Dijon mustard
2 cloves garlic, pressed
1 tablespoon fresh tarragon, minced
½ teaspoon fennel seed
1 teaspoon kosher salt

¼ teaspoon ground black pepper
1 to 1½ pounds fresh shrimp, peeled and deveined, tails left on for presentation, if you wish
1 tablespoon vegetable oil
1 cup fresh fennel bulb, thinly sliced
½ cup tomatoes (canned or peeled), diced
¼ cup heavy cream

1. Put olive oil, orange juice, anise liqueur, orange zest, Dijon mustard, garlic, tarragon, fennel seed, salt, and pepper into a large zip-top bag. Seal and squish contents to mix. Add shrimp to marinade, squeeze out all the air, and seal. Turn bag to coat shrimp. Refrigerate for 1 hour.

2. Heat a large, heavy skillet over medium-high heat. Add vegetable oil to hot pan and swirl to coat. Remove shrimp from marinade, reserving marinade, and place in a single layer in the hot pan. Cook for 1 minute, then flip the shrimp to the other side. Do not overcook the shrimp or it will become rubbery. Add the reserved marinade to the pan. Cook 1 minute, then remove shrimp and keep warm.

3. Add the sliced fennel bulb and the tomatoes and cook until the fennel is tender.
4. Add the cream and continue cooking until the liquid reduces and thickens into a sauce. Turn off heat, return the shrimp to the pan, and toss in the sauce. Serve hot.

WHAT'S HOT

▶ You can make a wonderful broth by boiling the shells from shrimp with spices, onion, garlic, and perhaps some celery and carrot. Cool and sift through cheesecloth when the desired strength is achieved, and freeze it for later use in soups or chowders.

Get Linked

Here are some great links to my About.com site for more seafood recipes and related information.

SHRIMP RECIPES AND INFORMATION

To find recipes and cooking tips for the most popular shellfish in the United States, check my Web page.

 http://about.com/homecooking/shrimp

CRAB RECIPES AND INFORMATION

Dungeness, peekytoe, blue crab, soft shell crab. Find out more about different types of crab and how to cook them here.

 http://about.com/homecooking/crab

LOBSTER AND INFORMATION

You'll find a wealth of information on this page concerning lobsters, including recipes, history, and terminology.

 http://about.com/homecooking/lobster

Chapter 9

Soups and Stews

ASK YOUR GUIDE:

What are some other types of stew?
▶**PAGE 144**

Can soup be served cold?
▶**PAGE 151**

What is rouille?
▶**PAGE 152**

What is the best way to thicken soup?
▶**PAGE 156**

What are some other types of stew?

▶ Brunswick stew is a hearty squirrel meat and onion stew originating in Brunswick County, Virginia. Modern versions substitute chicken or rabbit for the squirrel and may also add other vegetables such as okra, lima beans, tomatoes, and corn. Mulligan stew is made from whatever happens to be on hand, including meat, potatoes, and vegetables in any combination.

Chuck Wagon Stew
SERVES 8

Imagine yourself eating this around the campfire.

3 pounds beef chuck, cut into 1½-inch chunks
¾ teaspoon salt
½ teaspoon pepper
2 tablespoons bacon drippings
1 large onion, chopped
2 cloves garlic, minced
2 cans (4 ounces each) chopped mild green chilies, drained
2 pounds red-skinned potatoes, scrubbed and cut into 1-inch pieces
4 cups beef broth
1 cup tomatoes, diced
2 cups fresh or thawed frozen corn kernels
¼ cup fresh parsley, chopped
1 cup flour

1. Season the beef with salt and pepper. Melt the bacon drippings in a Dutch oven and cook the beef chunks in it, turning occasionally, until browned on all sides, about 8 minutes. Remove the beef and reserve.
2. Add the onion and garlic to the pot and cook until the onion is softened, about 4 minutes. Stir in the beef broth. Return the beef to the pot and add the chilies. Bring to a simmer over high heat, skimming off any foam that forms on the surface. Reduce the heat to low, cover, and simmer until the beef is tender, about 2½ hours.
3. During the last 30 minutes, stir in the potatoes, tomatoes, corn, and parsley. Remove from the heat and let stand 5 minutes. Skim the fat from the top of the stew.
4. In a jar, shake 1 cup of the cooking liquid with the flour until smooth. Stir into the stew and simmer until the sauce is thickened, about 3 minutes. Adjust seasoning with salt and pepper.

Artichoke Hazelnut Soup

SERVES 6

Creamy, pale green, and nutty describes this refined soup. Canned artichoke hearts are used here for convenience. If you can find frozen artichoke hearts, do use them. They will give the soup a fresher flavor.

1 small onion, diced
2 stalks celery, diced
1 shallot, minced
2 tablespoons butter
¼ cup flour
1 can artichoke hearts, packed in water
1 potato, peeled and cubed
6 cups chicken broth
½ cup heavy cream
1 tablespoon cognac
Salt and freshly ground black pepper, to taste
¼ cup roast hazelnuts, chopped

1. Sauté onion, celery, and shallot in butter until tender. Dust vegetables with flour, stir, and cook for 2 minutes.
2. Add drained artichoke hearts, potatoes, and chicken broth and bring to a boil over medium heat. Reduce the heat and simmer, covered, for 1 hour.
3. Remove from the heat and purée the solids with a small amount of the liquid in a food processor or blender in batches.
4. Return purée to the pan. Add the cream and cognac while stirring over low heat. Season the soup with salt and pepper to taste and then serve hot with hazelnuts scattered on top.

WHAT'S HOT

▶ Here are unusual and exotic soups: Authentic Bird's Nest Soup is a Chinese soup actually made from the white or black nests of a small Asian bird. The nests are difficult to harvest, thus making the soup very expensive. *Billy-bi* (or *billi-bi*) is a French soup made with mussels, onions, wine, cream, and seasonings. The classic recipe strains the mussels to leave a smooth soup, but the mussels are often left in as an added bonus these days.

Tortilla Soup
SERVES 6

This soup is a staple of Southwestern cuisine. It has many variations, but the constant ingredient is corn tortillas.

1 small onion, diced
2 tablespoons vegetable oil
1 cup corn kernels (frozen)
1 can tomatoes, diced, with chilies (Ro*Tel)
4 cups chicken broth
2 cups cooked chicken, diced
3 corn tortillas, cut in ¼-inch strips

1 teaspoon ground cumin
2 limes
Salt and pepper, to taste
Cayenne pepper sauce, to taste
¼ cup cilantro, chopped
2 avocados, peeled and diced
1 cup tortilla chips, crushed
1 cup Cheddar cheese, shredded

1. In a soup pot, sauté the onion in the oil until translucent. Add corn, tomatoes with chilies, and chicken broth. Bring to a boil.
2. Add chicken meat, tortilla strips, and cumin. Simmer for 15 minutes. Remove from heat.
3. Cut one lime in half and add the juice to the soup pot. Cut the other lime in wedges to serve with each bowl.
4. Season the soup with salt and pepper. Stir in the cayenne pepper sauce and cilantro.
5. Put diced avocado in soup bowls and ladle hot soup on top. Garnish with tortilla chips and cheese. Serve with lime wedges.

ELSEWHERE ON THE WEB

▶ Feeling ambitious? To make this meal truly homemade, try making the corn tortillas yourself. It's easier than you might think. Try this recipe, from the About.com Guide to Southern Cooking: http://about.com/southernfood/tortillas. Tortilla presses are sold in most kitchenware stores.

Chili con Carne
SERVES 6

Chili con Carne is literally "chili with meat." Period. No beans. No vegetables. And a purist would say no tomatoes; just chilies, spices, and meat.

2 pounds beef chuck roast, cut
   into small cubes
2 tablespoons olive oil
½ teaspoon salt
1 can (8 ounces) tomato sauce
1 cup beef broth
½ cup chicken broth
6 tablespoons chili powder
1 tablespoon ground cumin

½ teaspoon paprika
1 teaspoon cayenne pepper
1 teaspoon dried oregano
2 tablespoons garlic powder
1 tablespoon onion powder
½ teaspoon black pepper,
   ground
1 teaspoon brown sugar
¼ cup toasted cornmeal

1. Brown beef in olive oil, drain off grease, and return to pot.
2. Season the beef with salt, then add tomato sauce, beef broth, and chicken broth. Simmer for 1 hour.
3. Add chili powder, cumin, paprika, cayenne pepper, oregano, garlic powder, onion powder, black pepper, and brown sugar. Simmer for 1 additional hour.
4. Toast the cornmeal in a dry skillet for about 5 minutes (do not burn!), then add it to the chili and simmer another 10 minutes.
5. Serve hot, with tortilla chips.

TOOLS YOU NEED

▶ There are special kitchen gadgets on the market that can help you drain the fat out of a pan; they look like very long, flat, slotted spoons. These can be burdensome to use while holding the pan, though, so I suggest using a piece of stale bread to soak up any extra grease left in the pan after browning ground meat.

Cincinnati-Style Chili
SERVES 6

This Cincinnati chili was once served in "chili parlors" all over "Porkopolis" but is now made with beef.

2 large onions, diced
1 garlic clove, pressed
2 tablespoons vegetable oil
2½ pounds ground beef
2 tablespoons chili powder
1 tablespoon paprika
1 teaspoon cumin
1 teaspoon oregano
2 teaspoons ground cinnamon
2 teaspoons ground cayenne pepper
1 teaspoon ground allspice
1½ tablespoons unsweetened cocoa powder
1 bay leaf
4 cups water
1 can (6 ounces) tomato paste
1½ tablespoons cider vinegar
1 teaspoon Worcestershire sauce
Salt and pepper, to taste
3 cups cooked spaghetti

1. In a large, heavy-bottom pot, cook the onions and garlic in the oil over moderate heat, stirring, until the onions are softened. Add the beef and cook the mixture, stirring and breaking up the lumps, until the beef is no longer pink.
2. Add the chili powder, paprika, cumin, oregano, cinnamon, allspice, cayenne, and cocoa powder and cook the mixture, stirring, for 1 minute.
3. Add the bay leaf, water, tomato paste, vinegar, and Worcestershire sauce. Simmer the mixture, uncovered, stirring occasionally and adding more water if necessary to keep the beef barely covered, for 2 hours, or until it is thickened but soupy

enough to be ladled. Discard the bay leaf and season the chili with salt and pepper.

4. Serve the chili as is or in the traditional Cincinnati "five-way" style: Ladle the chili over the spaghetti and top it with the Cheddar cheese, chopped onions, and beans.

Fresh Tomato Bisque
SERVES 4

Bisque is a creamy soup traditionally made with puréed seafood and cream. In this recipe, fresh tomatoes take the place of the seafood, while rice is added for thickening and texture.

¾ cup onion, chopped
2 tablespoons butter
2 cups tomatoes, peeled and chopped
3 cups chicken broth
¼ cup long-grain rice, uncooked
½ cup cream
Salt and pepper, to taste

1. Sauté onions in butter until tender.
2. Add tomatoes and sauté 2 minutes.
3. Add chicken broth and rice. Simmer for 25 minutes, until rice is tender.
4. Purée soup in a blender and return to the pan. Over low heat add cream and season with salt and pepper.

WHAT'S HOT

▶ Fresh tomatoes are the best thing on earth when they are vine-ripened, and they really shine in an uncooked soup from Spain known as gazpacho. It is made of a puréed mixture of fresh tomatoes, sweet bell peppers, onions, celery, cucumber, bread crumbs, garlic, olive oil, vinegar, and sometimes lemon juice, and is served cold. It is also served chunky-style, much like a salsa that you eat with a spoon. You may also see this spelled "gaspacho."

Rich Corn Chowder

SERVES 6

I prefer frozen or fresh corn in this recipe, but you may substitute canned corn in a pinch.

6 slices bacon, diced
1 small onion, diced
1 stalk celery, diced
4 cups frozen corn kernels, thawed
1 large potato, peeled and diced
4 cups chicken broth, preferably low-salt
1 tablespoon cornstarch
¼ cup water
2 cups heavy cream
Salt and pepper, to taste

1. Sauté the bacon in a soup pot until crispy. Add onions and celery and sweat until vegetables are tender and translucent.
2. Add the corn kernels and sauté 5 minutes. Add potatoes and chicken broth and bring to a boil.
3. Simmer 45 minutes, until potatoes are cooked.
4. Dissolve cornstarch in ¼ cup cold water. Add heavy cream to soup pot and bring to a boil. Stir in the cornstarch mixture and cook, stirring constantly, until thickened. Remove from heat.
5. Season with salt and pepper, to taste.

▶ Chowder is a thick, rich soup containing chunks of food, such as clams, and there are usually potatoes in it. Other types of chowder include fish, lobster, shrimp, crab, vegetable, pumpkin, sweet potato, mushroom, and chicken. Almost anything that can be chunked can be chowdered.

Cheesy Onion Potato Soup
SERVES 6

This soup may be dressed up by garnishing with bacon bits, green onions, or salsa. Try different cheeses as well, such as jack or Swiss.

1 large onion, diced
2 tablespoons butter
4 cups chicken broth
5 large potatoes, peeled and diced
1 can evaporated milk (not sweetened condensed milk)
¼ cup cream cheese
Salt, to taste
½ teaspoon pepper
1 cup Cheddar cheese, shredded

1. Sauté the onion in butter until translucent, 5 to 10 minutes.
2. Add the chicken broth to the onion, and then add the potatoes.
3. Bring to a boil and simmer until potatoes are cooked, about 15 minutes.
4. Add the evaporated milk and bring soup back to a simmer.
5. Add the cream cheese, salt, and pepper. Stir and remove from heat.
6. Add the Cheddar cheese and stir to combine as it melts from the residual heat.

ASK YOUR GUIDE

Can this soup be served cold?

▶ Yes. For this recipe I would purée and strain it and add fresh cream to refine it. Vichyssoise is a rich, creamy, potato and leek soup garnished with chives that is served cold. Borscht is another soup that can be served cold. Borscht comes from Russia and Poland and is made with fresh beets, assorted vegetables, and sometimes with meat and/or meat stock. It is traditionally garnished with a dollop of sour cream. Borscht may also be served hot.

What is rouille?

▶ Rouille is the garlicky, red peppery condiment traditionally served with the French seafood stew, bouillabaisse. It is similar to the garlic mayonnaise, aioli, but with red peppers. To prepare rouille, combine ½ cup olive oil, 6 garlic cloves, 1 fresh seeded red chili pepper, 1 pinch saffron, and 1 peeled, cooked potato in a food processor. Process rouille until smooth and then season with salt and pepper to taste.

Seafood Stew
SERVES 6 TO 8

This is a version of the seafood stew native to the south of France called bouillabaisse. The ingredient list looks daunting, but this is very easy to make. Be sure to begin with a large, deep pot to accommodate all the seafood. If you cannot find pastis liqueur, you may substitute the more commonly found Pernod.

½ medium onion, diced
2 celery stalks, diced
1 carrot, diced
½ fennel bulb, diced
5 garlic cloves
2 tablespoons olive oil
1 tablespoon tomato paste
2 large tomatoes, diced
3 tablespoons pastis (licorice-flavored alcohol)
1 cup white wine
2 cups clam juice
2 cups chicken broth
2 cups water
1 teaspoon black peppercorns, freshly ground
1 teaspoon dried red chili pepper
1 teaspoon orange peel, grated
1 bay leaf
2 sprigs of thyme
1 pinch saffron
5 parsley stems
Salt, to taste
2 pounds rock fish filets
1 pound John Dory filets (or other white flatfish, such as porgy or sole)
2 pounds red snapper filets
1 pound striped bass filets
2 pounds grouper filets
2 lobster tails (½ pound each)
16 small squid
1 cup mussels
1½ cups rouille (see sidebar)
8 to 10 small potatoes, cooked
1 baguette

Seafood Stew (continued)

1. In a large pot sweat the onion, celery, carrot, fennel, and garlic in olive oil for 3 minutes. Stir in the tomato paste and coat all of the vegetables. Add the tomatoes and cook until soft. Add the pastis, and cook until dry. Add the white wine and reduce by half.
2. Add the clam juice, chicken broth, water, peppercorns, chili pepper, orange peel, bay leaf, thyme sprigs, saffron, and parsley stems. Cook until the liquid has reduced by a third. Remove bay leaf, thyme sprigs, and parsley stems from the bouillon and season it with salt to taste.
3. Bring the bouillon to a simmer and add each filet of fish individually based on its thickness (thickest filets first). Cut the lobster tails through the shell into large pieces. Add the lobster, squid, and mussels to the bouillon. Cook until the mussels open.
4. Ladle soup directly out of the pot and serve with rouille, cooked potatoes, and toasted baguette slices on the side.

Hearty Beef Stew
SERVES 6

Beef stew is a basic comfort food that warms the heart on a cold autumn or winter night. As with many hearty stews, this tastes even better the next day, so consider doubling this recipe.

1 pound beef chuck roast, cut into 1½-inch cubes
¾ cup onions, diced
2 tablespoons vegetable oil
¼ cup flour
1 tablespoon tomato paste
4 cups beef broth
½ cup carrots, peeled and sliced
1 potato, peeled and diced
1 teaspoon dried thyme
1 tablespoon Worcestershire sauce
½ cup frozen peas
Salt, to taste
Pepper, to taste

1. Brown the beef cubes and onions in oil. Dust browned meat with flour and stir to coat.
2. Add tomato paste and stir again. Add beef broth, carrots, potatoes, thyme, and Worcestershire sauce.
3. Bring to a boil then simmer for 1½ to 2 hours, until beef is tender.
4. Add peas, and season with salt and pepper. Cook 10 minutes longer.

Veggie Potpie
SERVES 4 TO 6

Potpie is often made with both a bottom and top pie crust. This recipe is made with just the top crust and uses rich, flakey puff pastry.

½ medium onion, diced
2 carrots, peeled and diced
1 celery stalk, diced
½ cup mushrooms, sliced
2 tablespoons butter
¼ cup flour
3 cups vegetable broth
1 potato, peeled and cubed

½ cup green beans, cut
1 bay leaf
½ cup frozen peas
½ cup cream
Salt and pepper, to taste
¼ cup parsley, chopped
1 sheet puff pastry, thawed
1 egg, beaten

1. Sauté onion, carrots, celery, and mushrooms in butter until tender. Dust with flour, stir, and cook a few minutes. Add vegetable broth, potato, and green beans. Bring to a boil, add bay leaf, and simmer for 40 minutes, until vegetables are cooked and liquid is thickened.
2. Stir in peas and cream and remove from heat. Remove bay leaf, season with salt and pepper, and stir in chopped parsley. Pour filling into a deep-dish pie pan and place on a baking sheet with sides.
3. Preheat oven to 400°F. Unfold puff pastry and cut the corners off to make a rough circle. Cut a 1-inch circle out of the center. Brush the pastry with beaten egg and place it on top of the filling, egg-brushed side up. Bake potpie for 20 minutes, until puffed and golden. Scoop out individual portions and serve hot.

TOOLS YOU NEED

▶ The best soups are made with a base of homemade stock and fresh ingredients. Obviously, this can be a time-consuming endeavor. You can reduce your time in the kitchen by using canned or frozen broths or bouillon bases. Even so, plan on taking your time with a good soup or stew.

What is the best way to thicken soup?

▶ The best method for thickening soups and stews is to remove some of the cooked vegetables, purée them, and return the puréed mixture to the pot. If you are short on veggies or there are none in your soup, make a paste of flour mixed with twice as much cold stock, milk, or water. Add the paste and stir slowly at a simmer for 5 to 10 minutes. The ratio is 1½ teaspoons of flour to 1 cup of soup.

Sweet Potato and Sausage Stew
SERVES 4

You can substitute lamb shanks for the beef if you prefer.

6 Italian sausages
3 tablespoons vegetable oil
2 pounds beef, cut in 1½- to 2-inch pieces
1 carrot, diced
1 celery stalk, diced
2 medium onions, diced
1 teaspoon salt
½ teaspoon pepper
1½ teaspoons curry powder
2 cans peeled diced tomatoes, drained
¼ cup water
1½ pounds sweet potatoes, cut in ½-inch slices and soaked in water

1. Place sausages in a deep skillet with 1 inch of water and bring to a boil. Lower heat and simmer for 10 minutes. Remove sausages to a platter.
2. Heat oil in a large, oven-proof casserole, brown beef on all sides, and remove to a platter. In the same oil, lightly brown sausages on all sides. Remove sausages and drain fat from casserole, leaving just a film of oil.
3. Add carrot and celery to the casserole and sauté for 4 minutes. Add onions and cook for 3 minutes, until wilted. Return beef and sausages to casserole and sprinkle with salt. Cover, turn heat to low, and cook for 15 minutes. Uncover casserole and stir in pepper and curry powder. Add tomatoes and water. Cover and cook over low heat for 1 hour, adding additional water as needed.
4. Drain the sweet potatoes and add them to the casserole. Continue cooking for 30 minutes or until the meat and potatoes are tender.

Vegetable Soup with Pesto
SERVES 8

This soup is similar to minestrone, but without the pasta or beans. The pesto adds a bright kick to it.

½ cup onion, chopped
½ cup carrots, peeled and sliced
½ cup celery stalks, sliced
1 clove garlic, crushed
2 tablespoons olive oil
½ cup cabbage, shredded
½ cup potatoes, peeled and cubed
1 can tomatoes, peeled and chopped
½ cup green beans, cut in 1-inch pieces
1 cup zucchini, diced
6 cups chicken broth
Salt and pepper, to taste
½ cup pesto

1. Sauté onion, carrots, celery, and garlic in olive oil for 15 minutes.
2. Add cabbage and cook another 10 minutes.
3. Add potatoes, tomatoes with their liquid, green beans, zucchini, and chicken broth. Bring to a boil and then reduce heat to simmer 45 minutes.
4. Season with salt and pepper and stir in pesto.

TOOLS YOU NEED

▶ A mini food processor is great to use for small amounts of fresh pesto. Just add 1 clove of chopped garlic, 1 cup of fresh basil leaves, 1 tablespoon of pine nuts, ¼ cup olive oil and 1 tablespoon of Parmesan cheese to the bowl. Process until smooth.

Clam Chowder
SERVES 6

Creamy New England—style clam chowder is traditionally eaten with oyster crackers floating in it. The milk and cream are essential parts of this recipe, so don't skimp!

½ cup celery, diced
½ cup onions, diced
2 tablespoons butter
1 clove garlic, minced
2 tablespoons flour
1 cup (8 ounces) clam juice
4 cups milk
3 large potatoes, peeled and diced
½ teaspoon thyme
1 cup cream
1 cup clams, drained and chopped
Salt and pepper, to taste
2 tablespoons fresh parsley, chopped

1. Sauté the celery and onions in butter in a large pot until translucent. Add the garlic and cook another minute.
2. Sprinkle the flour over the vegetables and cook for 1 minute. Add the clam juice, milk, potatoes, and thyme and bring to a boil. Simmer until the potatoes are tender, about 15 minutes.
3. Add the cream and clams and simmer for 10 minutes. Season the chowder with salt and pepper and stir in the parsley.

ELSEWHERE ON THE WEB

▶ If making this clam chowder recipe has piqued your curiousity about the region in which it originated, take a visit to http://gonewengland.about.com. Here the guide gives helpful tips on where to stay and what to do in New England. You'll also find places from which to mail order clam chowder, along with more clam chowder recipes.

Cream of Mushroom Soup
SERVES 2 TO 4

The canned version comes in handy for casseroles, but for a stand-alone cream of mushroom soup, go for the real thing with lots of mushrooms.

8 ounces mushrooms
4 tablespoons butter, divided use
1 tablespoon sherry
1 medium sweet onion, chopped
1 teaspoon salt
¼ cup flour

2 cans (10¾ ounces each)
    chicken broth
⅛ teaspoon ground nutmeg
¼ teaspoon white pepper, or
    to taste
1 cup heavy cream
Chives, chopped, for garnish

1. Clean mushrooms with a mushroom brush or damp paper towel. Cut half of the mushrooms into slices. Chop the remainder.
2. Melt half of the butter in a large saucepan and sauté sliced mushrooms until golden. Add sherry and reduce liquid until almost dry. Remove and reserve sliced mushrooms.
3. Add remaining butter to the same pan, along with the chopped mushrooms and sweet onions. Sprinkle with salt. Cook, stirring often, until onion is soft.
4. Return sliced mushrooms to the pan. Add flour and cook, stirring constantly, about 2 minutes, until smooth. Slowly add chicken broth while stirring. Simmer until thickened, stirring often. Add nutmeg and pepper. Taste and adjust seasoning, if need be.
5. Add heavy cream and bring to a simmer. (Do not boil.) Ladle into soup bowls and garnish with chopped chives.

Get Linked

Here are some great links to my About.com site for more soup and stew recipes and related information.

SOUP AND STEW INFORMATION

Not a glossary, but a thorough explanation on what makes a soup a soup and a stew a stew, with links to recipes.

 http://about.com/homecooking/soupandstewrecipes

SOUP, STEW, AND CHOWDER RESOURCES

Here you'll find resources focusing on hot and cold soup, stew, and chowder recipes.

 http://about.com/homecooking/soupresources

SOUP GLOSSARY

Bisque, chowder, consommé—whatever you call it, you can find the definitions here for all types of soups and stews.

 http://about.com/homecooking/soupglossary

Chapter 10

Casseroles and One-Dish Meals

About.

ASK YOUR GUIDE:

Are almonds seeds?
▶PAGE 164

What exactly are chives?
▶PAGE 166

Where is broccoli from?
▶PAGE 170

Where can I buy frozen pierogies and which brands do you recommend?
▶PAGE 173

Is ricotta the same as cottage cheese?
▶PAGE 176

▶ The combination of onion, celery, and green bell pepper is called "the trinity" in Bayou and Caribbean cuisine. It is used in the same manner as mirepoix is in classic French cooking. (Mirepoix, the combination of onion, celery, and carrot, is the flavor base for sauces, soups, and more.) To make an authentic jambalaya, use ingredients that are indigenous to Louisiana. For example, the sausage should be andouille, the shellfish should be crawfish, and if you use ham, it should be tasso.

Jambalaya
SERVES 6

There are two variations of Louisiana's famous spicy rice concoction jambalaya: Creole and Cajun. This recipe is a combination of the two, made with shellfish, chicken, and sausage

3 boneless, skinless chicken breasts, cubed
½ cup olive oil
1 cup onion, diced
1 cup celery, diced
1 cup green bell pepper, diced
5 cloves garlic, minced
½ teaspoon dried thyme
½ teaspoon ground black pepper
¼ teaspoon cayenne pepper

3 cups long-grain white rice, uncooked
4 cups chicken broth
2 bay leaves
¼ teaspoon salt
1 fully cooked smoked sausage, sliced
½ cup tomatoes, diced
½ pound shrimp, peeled and deveined

1. Brown the chicken in the olive oil in a large pot; remove chicken and set aside.
2. Add the onion, celery, green pepper, and garlic to the pot and sauté until tender.
3. Add the thyme, black pepper, cayenne pepper, and rice and cook for 5 minutes, stirring occasionally.
4. Add chicken broth, browned chicken, bay leaves, salt, smoked sausage, and tomatoes. Stir to combine, bring mixture to a simmer over medium heat, and cover the pot with a lid.
5. Simmer 20 minutes, add the shrimp on top, return the lid, and continue to cook 5 to 7 more minutes. Make sure the shrimp are pink, which means they're cooked. Remove the bay leaves and serve hot.

Scalloped Potato and Ham Casserole
SERVES 4

Hearty and satisfying, this dish is good served with any green vegetable, such as asparagus or green beans.

1 tablespoon olive oil
1 tablespoon butter
¼ cup all-purpose flour
2½ cups milk
¼ teaspoon salt
⅛ teaspoon ground black pepper
½ cup Parmesan cheese, grated
4 cups potatoes, peeled and sliced, divided use
1 cup onion, chopped
3 cups zucchini, shredded
1 pound boiled ham, cut into 1-inch chunks

1. Preheat oven to 400°F. Coat shallow 2-quart casserole with olive oil and set aside.
2. Melt butter, add flour, and cook over medium heat for about 5 minutes to form a roux.
3. Add the milk, salt, and pepper, and cook until thickened, whisking out lumps to make a white sauce. Stir in the Parmesan cheese.
4. Layer half the potatoes into prepared casserole and top with the onions, zucchini, and half the sauce. Arrange ham on top and cover with remaining potatoes and sauce.
5. Cover and bake 40 to 45 minutes. Remove cover and bake 15 minutes longer.

▶ You may have noticed a glistening, sometimes greenish, rainbow iridescent effect on cut ham. This is not necessarily an indication of spoilage. Hams using nitrates and/or nitrites as curing agents undergo pigment changes when exposed to light and air due to a chemical reaction. These same chemicals are the cause of the meat color remaining rosy red, even when fully cooked.

Are almonds seeds?

▶ Botanically speaking, almonds are a fruit. On the tree, the fruit or drupe looks like a small, elongated peach with a hard, greenish-gray husk. When mature, the husk splits open to reveal the shell, which in turn contains the nutmeat. Spanish missionaries are credited with bringing the almond to California, now the world's largest producer of more than 100 varieties of almonds. Part of the plum family, the almond tree (*Prunus dulcis*; *Prunus amygdalus*) is native to North Africa, West Asia, and the Mediterranean.

Green Bean and Roasted Pepper Casserole
SERVES 4 TO 6

Baby boomers fondly remember the simple classic green bean casserole as a Thanksgiving favorite. It is considered almost decadent these days with cream of mushroom soup and crispy fried onions on top. I've updated it by adding roasted red bell peppers and toasted almonds.

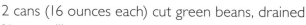

 2 cans (16 ounces each) cut green beans, drained
 ¾ cup milk
 1 can (10¾ ounces) condensed cream of mushroom soup
 ⅛ teaspoon black pepper
 1 can (2.8 ounces) French-fried onions, divided use
 1 cup roasted red bell peppers, cut into strips
 ½ cup almonds, sliced

1. Preheat oven to 350°F.
2. Dump green beans, milk, cream of mushroom soup, pepper, and half of the fried onions into a large bowl and mix until combined.
3. Pour green bean mixture into a 1½-quart casserole dish. Lay the red bell pepper slices out on top of the bean mixture, sprinkle the almonds on the peppers, and bake uncovered for 30 minutes.
4. Remove from oven and top with the remaining fried onions. Bake an additional 5 to 10 minutes until onion topping is browned and crispy.

Hash Brown Potato Casserole
SERVES 10 TO 12

Easy and quick to put together, this potato casserole is great for parties, potluck dinners, buffets, or family dinners. Serve it as a side dish, or add meat to make it a meal in one dish. You can prepare this ahead of time and refrigerate until ready to bake. The baked dish may be frozen. Let thaw before reheating.

½ cup (1 stick) butter, softened
1 can cream of celery soup, undiluted
1½ cups sour cream
1 teaspoon dried thyme
12 ounces Cheddar cheese, shredded, divided use
1 package (24 ounces) frozen hash brown potatoes (break up any frozen clumps)
1 cup sweet onion, chopped
1 cup mushrooms, chopped
½ cup sweet red bell pepper, diced
Paprika, to taste

1. Preheat oven to 350°F. Grease an 8" × 11" shallow glass oven-proof casserole dish.
2. In a large bowl, combine softened butter, celery soup, sour cream, and thyme. Mix well.
3. To the soup mixture, add 8 ounces of the Cheddar cheese, frozen hash brown potatoes, onion, mushrooms, and bell pepper. Mix well. Pour into greased casserole dish. Top with remaining 4 ounces of shredded Cheddar cheese. Sprinkle top with paprika.
4. Bake for 1 hour, 30 minutes, uncovered. Let rest for 15 minutes before serving.

ELSEWHERE ON THE WEB

▶ For more hashbrown meal ideas, visit http://about.com/southernfood/hashbrowns. Here the About.com Guide to Southern Food provides both breakfast and main dish meal ideas all featuring the star ingredient: hash browns.

What exactly are chives?

▶ Chives (*Allium schoenoprasum*), a member of the onion family and native to Asia and Europe, have been around for more than 5,000 years. Yet, they were not actively cultivated until the Middle Ages. The botanical name is derived from the Greek, meaning "reed-like leek." The English name "chive" comes from the Latin *cepa*, meaning "onion," which became *cive* in French. Prized for their flavor, this smallest member of the onion family has many wild cousins growing throughout the northern hemisphere.

Lobster Puff Casserole
SERVES 4

This delicious seafood dish is somewhere in between a soufflé and a mousse. It is elegant enough for any occasion, yet easy to make. You may make individual lobster puff servings by using single-serving ramekins. Reduce the cooking time accordingly. Try substituting crab or shrimp for the lobster for a less expensive dish.

> 3 tablespoons granulated tapioca
> 1 cup milk
> 1½ cups cooked lobster meat, chopped
> 1 cup Gruyère cheese, shredded
> ¼ teaspoon salt
> ¼ teaspoon paprika
> 2 teaspoons lemon juice
> ⅛ cup chives, chopped
> 2 egg yolks, beaten
> 2 egg whites, beaten until stiff

1. Preheat oven to 350°F. Butter an 8" × 8" glass baking dish or equivalent round baking dish.
2. In the top of a double boiler, stir tapioca and milk until tapioca is clear and transparent. Remove from heat.
3. Add lobster, Gruyère cheese, salt, paprika, lemon juice, chives, and beaten egg yolks, stirring to combine. Fold in stiff egg whites. Pour into prepared baking dish and bake 40 minutes or until firm. Serve hot.

Tuna Casserole

SERVES 6

I didn't mess with the classic, but this recipe is from scratch and not from canned soup.

8 ounces (when dry) egg noodles, cooked
1 cup mushrooms, sliced
2 tablespoons butter
2 tablespoons flour
2 cups milk
2 cans tuna packed in water, undrained
¾ cup frozen peas
Salt and pepper, to taste
1 cup bread crumbs
½ cup Cheddar cheese, shredded

1. Preheat oven to 375°F. Butter a 9" × 13" casserole dish. Lay the cooked noodles in the dish.
2. Sauté mushrooms in butter until they release their water and begin to brown.
3. Sprinkle flour over the mushrooms, stir, and cook for two minutes.
4. Add milk and cook until thickened, stirring occasionally. Fold in tuna (with its water) and peas. Season with salt and pepper.
5. Pour mushroom sauce mixture over noodles and gently toss to distribute sauce evenly.
6. Mix the bread crumbs with the Cheddar cheese and then sprinkle over the top of the casserole. Bake for 20 minutes.

ELSEWHERE ON THE WEB

▶ For information on different packaged tuna brands including the history and lots of recipe ideas, visit www .starkist.com, www.bumble bee.com, or www.chickenof thesea.com.

Three-Cheese Potatoes
SERVES 6 TO 8

Not for the faint of heart, thyme and three cheeses make this potato dish very rich. To make this a one-dish meal (as if it couldn't already be considered such), you can add diced ham, sausage, and so on, when layering the potatoes.

1 sweet onion, finely diced
1 clove garlic, pressed
4 tablespoons butter
3 tablespoons flour
1 cup chicken broth
1 cup whole milk
1 cup heavy cream
1½ cups Monterey jack cheese, divided use
4 ounces cream cheese, cut into small cubes
⅛ teaspoon nutmeg
1 teaspoon parsley
Salt and pepper, to taste
2 pounds red potatoes, boiled, cooled, peeled, and sliced ¼- to ½-inch thick
1 sweet potato, peeled and sliced ¼-inch thick
¼ cup Parmesan cheese, grated
Hungarian sweet paprika, to taste

1. Preheat oven to 375°F.
2. Gently sauté sweet onions and garlic in butter until translucent, being careful not to brown. Add flour to make a roux.

3. Cook roux, stirring constantly for about 3 minutes to get rid of the raw taste. Add chicken broth, while stirring constantly, then milk and cream. Let this mixture get hot, then add ½ cup of jack cheese and all the cream cheese.

4. Cook over low heat, stirring constantly, until all the cheese has melted and is incorporated. Add nutmeg, parsley, salt, and pepper to taste. (Remember that the potatoes will absorb most of the salt, so don't be afraid to use a healthy dose of salt if you are so inclined!)

5. Layer red and sweet potatoes in an oven-proof casserole dish sprayed with vegetable oil. Pour cheese sauce evenly over potatoes, but don't stir. Sprinkle remaining jack cheese over top, then sprinkle with Parmesan and paprika.

6. Bake uncovered for 45 to 60 minutes, until top becomes brown and bubbly.

WHAT'S HOT

▶ Sweet onion varieties have been traced back to a packet of seeds from the Canary Islands that were shipped to South Texas in 1898. Those Bermuda onion seeds were planted near the city of Cotulla. The sweet onion crop was an instant success. In 1933, the Texas Agricultural Experiment Station began a cooperative breeding program with the U.S. Department of Agriculture to develop new hybrids and varieties. For more information and history, visit http://about.com/homecooking/sweetonion.

Where is broccoli from?

▶ Broccoli is native to the Mediterranean. It was engineered from a cabbage relative by the ancient Etruscans, who were considered to be horticultural geniuses. Its English name, "broccoli," is derived from the Italian *brocco* and the Latin *bracchium* meaning arm, branch, or shoot. When first introduced in England, broccoli was referred to as "Italian asparagus." Although commercial cultivation of broccoli dates back to the 1500s, it did not become a popular foodstuff in the United States until the early 1920s.

Broccoli Cheese Rice
SERVES 4

Feel free to substitute other vegetables for the broccoli in this recipe. It is a colorful and yummy dish. Best of all, you can mix it up in advance and bake at will.

¼ cup (½ stick) unsalted butter
½ cup onion, diced
1 cup uncooked long-grain white rice
2 cups fresh broccoli, chopped
1¾ cups chicken broth
½ teaspoon salt
¼ teaspoon ground pepper
1 cup American cheese, grated

1. Preheat oven to 350°F.
2. Melt butter in a sauce pan and sauté the onion until tender.
3. Add rice and sauté for 3 to 5 minutes with the onion. Stir the broccoli into the rice mixture.
4. Pour mixture into a 9" × 13" glass baking dish, add chicken broth, salt, pepper, and cheese. Stir to incorporate.
5. Cover with foil and bake for 45 minutes.

Savory Turkey Bread Pudding

SERVES 8 TO 10

This easy-to-make meal is Thanksgiving dinner all in one dish. Serve with a side salad and you have a satisfying meal for any time of the year.

10 cups stale bread cubes
½ cup celery, diced
½ cup sweet onion, diced
1½ cups turkey, cooked and diced
1 cup yams, peeled and diced
5 egg yolks
7 eggs
2½ cups chicken broth

3½ cups cream
½ cup Parmesan cheese, grated
½ teaspoon thyme
¼ teaspoon ground black pepper
1 teaspoon kosher salt
4 ounces butter, melted

1. Preheat oven to 350°F. Generously butter a 9" × 13" baking dish.
2. Put the bread cubes in the buttered dish. Sprinkle the celery, onion, turkey, and yams over the bread cubes and toss them together lightly with your hands. Set aside.
3. In a bowl, mix together the egg yolks, eggs, chicken broth, cream, Parmesan cheese, thyme, pepper, and salt. Pour this custard mixture evenly over the bread cubes. Press down the bread cubes to submerge them in the custard to soak it up.
4. Drizzle the melted butter over the top of the bread/custard mixture.
5. Bake for about one hour, or until the custard is set. Serve warm with cranberry sauce.

WHAT'S HOT

▶ Here are some fun onion facts: The onion is a member of the pungent *Allium* genus of the lily family, which also includes garlic, leeks, shallots, scallions, and chives. The bustling city of Chicago was named for a variety of onion the Native American Indians called "chicago" (*A. canadense*). The onion was considered as valuable as gold in the Middle Ages. It has long been a symbol of eternity due to its structural composition of layers within layers that form a sphere.

Hamburger Macaroni
SERVES 6

It's basic and very good. Kids love it with cheese stirred into it so it melts like a gooey cheeseburger.

1 pound ground beef
½ cup onion, diced
¼ cup celery, diced
1 teaspoon garlic, minced
1 tablespoon olive oil
1 teaspoon dried basil
1 teaspoon salt
½ teaspoon pepper
1 pound (dry weight) elbow macaroni, cooked
1 tablespoon fresh parsley, chopped

1. Brown the ground beef. Drain and discard the fat. Set aside the cooked meat.
2. In the same pot, sauté the onions, celery, and garlic in the olive oil until translucent. Add the dried basil and sauté another minute.
3. Return the ground beef to the pot and season with salt and pepper.
4. Add the cooked macaroni and stir over low heat to evenly heat the mixture.
5. Stir in the parsley, adjust seasoning with salt and pepper, and remove from heat.

ELSEWHERE ON THE WEB

▶ For another variation on the classic cheeseburger, check out this recipe for cheeseburger pie on the About.com Southern Food Web site: http://about.com/ southernfood/cheeseburger pie. There is some added flavor with the pizza sauce that goes on top of the pie, so any burger or pizza lover is sure to enjoy.

Pierogi Bake

SERVES 4

Pierogies are Polish dumplings that are most often filled with mashed potatoes and cheese or onions, but there are a variety of other fillings including sweet cheese, cabbage, or prunes. They are typically boiled, then pan-fried in butter. This recipe steams and crisps them as they bake in butter.

    1 package frozen potato pierogies
    ½ cup sweet onions, diced
    ¼ cup (½ stick) butter, melted
    ½ cup Cheddar cheese, shredded
    ¼ cup sour cream

1. Preheat oven to 350°F.
2. Butter a casserole dish and place the frozen pierogies in it in one layer.
3. Scatter the onions over the pierogies and drizzle them with melted butter.
4. Cover and bake for 45 minutes to one hour, until onions are a bit **caramelized** and pierogies are steamed and partially crisped in the butter.
5. Serve with Cheddar cheese and sour cream.

ASK YOUR GUIDE

Where can I buy frozen pierogies and which brands do you recommend?

▶ Pierogies are available in the frozen prepared food section of most supermarkets in a variety of flavors. Any brand is fine, but be sure you are getting the right filling for your taste, whether it's potato, potato and cheese, potato and onion, or cabbage, for instance.

Eggplant Lasagna
SERVES 12

This is a delicious, meatless meal that can serve a large family or group easily.

2 cups eggplant cubes
1 teaspoon kosher salt
2 tablespoons olive oil
5 cups tomato sauce, divided use
1 pound box lasagna noodles, cooked
3 eggs

16 ounces ricotta cheese
2 cups mozzarella cheese, shredded, divided use
¼ cup fresh basil, chopped
½ teaspoon salt
¼ teaspoon pepper
½ cup Parmesan cheese, grated

1. Put the eggplant in a colander in the sink and sprinkle it with salt. Toss the eggplant and let it drain for 15 minutes.
2. Heat the olive oil in a sauté pan and cook the eggplant until tender. Set aside. Preheat oven to 350°F.
4. Oil a lasagna (baking) pan and spread 1 cup tomato sauce on the bottom. Mix the remaining tomato sauce with the cooked eggplant. Set aside.
5. In a bowl combine the eggs, ricotta, and 1 cup mozzarella cheese until well blended. Stir in the basil, salt, and pepper.
6. Lay a layer of noodles over the sauce in the pan. Spread half of the ricotta over the noodles, then top with a layer of noodles. Ladle 2 cups of the eggplant sauce over the noodles then top with another layer of noodles.
7. Spread the remaining ricotta mixture over the noodles then top with noodles. Ladle the remaining eggplant sauce over the noodles.
8. Scatter the remaining mozzarella cheese, then sprinkle with the Parmesan cheese. Bake for 1 hour 15 minutes.

ELSEWHERE ON THE WEB

▶ **For more vegetarian recipes, visit** http://vegetarian.about.com**. There you will find not only recipes, but information about vegetarianism, the different types of vegetarians, and raw food diets. Try the recipe for jicama "fries."**

American Shepherd's Pie
SERVES 4 TO 6

This is an American variation of traditional shepherd's pie.

1 pound ground chuck beef
8 ounces mushrooms, chopped
½ cup onion, chopped
2 large cloves garlic, pressed or finely minced
1 teaspoon kosher salt
Freshly ground pepper, to taste
1 tablespoon Worcestershire sauce
1 tablespoon flour
½ cup beef broth

½ cup heavy cream
½ cup frozen peas, unthawed
2 cups mashed potatoes
2 tablespoons fresh parsley, chopped
2 cups Cheddar cheese, shredded
¼ cup mayonnaise
Sweet Hungarian paprika, to taste

TOOLS YOU NEED

▶ A good pepper grinder, or peppermill, is the best way to make freshly ground pepper. However, for cooking with larger quantities of freshly ground pepper, you may want to invest in a coffee grinder to be used just for grinding spices.

1. Preheat oven to 375°F.
2. Make stew by cooking the ground beef, mushrooms, onion, garlic, salt, and pepper together in a large pot. Sauté, breaking up the ground beef until most of the liquid has evaporated.
3. Stir in Worcestershire sauce, then flour. Cook 1 minute, stirring often. Add beef broth, stirring to combine, then heavy cream. Simmer until gravy thickens.
4. Pour meat mixture into a glass baking dish. Let cool slightly, then sprinkle green peas evenly on top of beef.
5. In a bowl, combine mashed potatoes with parsley, cheese, and mayonnaise. Spread the potato mixture over the stew, then sprinkle with paprika.
6. Bake for 30 to 40 minutes. Let cool 10 minutes before serving.

Is ricotta the same as cottage cheese?

▶ No—ricotta is a fresh, soft, snowy white cheese with a rich but mild, slightly sweet flavor. The texture is much like a grainy, thick sour cream. Ricotta is naturally low in fat, with a fat content ranging from 4 to 10 percent. It is also low in salt, even lower than cottage cheese. Technically, ricotta is not a cheese at all, but a cheese byproduct. Its name, "ricotta," means "cooked again"—an obvious reference to the production method used to make it.

Lasagna Roll-Ups
SERVES 4 TO 6

These roll-ups are an easy way to serve lasagna on a buffet. They are portioned ahead of time and they are less messy than the usual squares cut in a big pan. Try adding seafood or spinach to the filling for a treat.

2 cups ricotta cheese
1 cup Parmesan cheese, grated
1 large egg, beaten
¾ teaspoon salt
½ teaspoon black pepper, freshly ground
12 lasagna noodles, cooked and reserved in cold water
1 tablespoon olive oil
2 cups tomato sauce, divided use
1 cup mozzarella, shredded

1. Preheat the oven to 450°F.
2. Whisk the ricotta, Parmesan cheese, egg, salt, and pepper in a medium bowl to blend.
3. Drain the lasagna noodles, toss them with olive oil and then lay them out in a single layer on a baking sheet.
4. Butter a 9" × 13" glass baking dish. Pour 1 cup tomato sauce over the bottom of the baking dish.
5. Spread 3 tablespoons of ricotta mixture evenly over each noodle. Starting at one end, roll each noodle like a jelly roll. Lay the lasagna rolls seam-side down, not touching, in the dish. Repeat with the remaining noodles and ricotta mixture.
6. Spoon remaining tomato sauce and sprinkle the mozzarella over the lasagna roll-ups. Cover with foil.
7. Bake 20 minutes. Uncover and bake 15 minutes longer. Let stand for 10 minutes.

Chicken Divan

SERVES 6

This is a rich, velvety one-dish meal that is perfect for a potluck dinner. You can fiddle around with it by adding different flavorings, such as curry powder or sherry.

4 boneless, skinless chicken breasts
Salt and pepper, to taste
1 large bunch broccoli, cut into florets
1 can cream of chicken soup
1 cup mayonnaise
¼ cup chicken broth
1 tablespoon lemon juice
1½ cups sharp Cheddar cheese, grated
¼ cup Parmesan cheese, grated
½ cup bread crumbs

1. Preheat oven to 350°F.
2. Season chicken with salt and pepper and put in a glass baking dish with a small amount of water in the bottom. Bake for 20 minutes, then let cool and cut into bite-sized pieces.
3. In a large saucepan of boiling, salted water, cook the broccoli for 6 to 8 minutes, or until it is just tender, and then drain it well on paper towels.
4. Put the chicken in a 2-quart gratin dish and put the broccoli on top of the chicken.
5. Mix together the soup, mayonnaise, broth, and lemon juice in a bowl until smooth. Fold the Cheddar cheese into the mixture and pour it over broccoli and chicken. Toss gently to distribute the sauce.
6. Mix together the Parmesan cheese and bread crumbs and sprinkle over the casserole. Bake uncovered 40 minutes, until the sauce is golden and bubbling.

Get Linked

Here are some great links to my About.com site for more casserole and one-dish meal recipes and related information.

CASEROLE RECIPES

Here you will find a great resource for casserole recipes using noodles, rice, potatoes, vegetables, meat, and more.

 http://about.com/homecooking/casserole

CHILI RECIPES

Chili is the ultimate one-dish meal and there are many different variations in addition to traditional beef or bean chili. Check out these recipes.

http://about.com/homecooking/chili

OMELET AND FRITTATA RECIPES

Omelets and frittatas are not just for breakfast! Consider omelets and frittatas for a hearty meal-in-one that goes together fast and helps use up your leftovers. The variations are endless.

http://about.com/homecooking/omeletandfrittata

Chapter 11

Condiments and Sauces

What is extra-virgin olive oil?

▶ Cold-pressing, a chemical-free process using only pressure, produces a higher quality of olive oil that is naturally lower in acidity. When purchasing olive oil, it's important to check labels for the percentage of acidity, grade of oil, volume, and country of origin. The level of acidity is a key factor in choosing fine olive oil, along with color, flavor, and aroma. Extra-virgin olive oil is the cold-pressed result of the first pressing of the olives, with only 1 percent acid.

Champagne Vinaigrette
YIELDS 1¼ CUPS

This is an excellent neutral dressing for salads and vegetables. You may substitute less expensive white wine vinegar for the champagne vinegar, if you wish.

½ teaspoon Dijon mustard
1 tablespoon shallot, minced
¼ cup champagne vinegar
1 cup olive oil
Salt and pepper, to taste

1. Put mustard, shallot, and vinegar in a food processor and combine briefly.
2. Add the olive oil slowly through the top while the food processor is running.
3. Season with salt and pepper, to taste.

Fresh Herb Ranch Dressing
YIELDS 2 CUPS

The basic buttermilk ranch dressing is made with fresh herbs in this recipe. It is the buttermilk that gives ranch dressing that signature tang. There really is a difference when you make it fresh, so give it a try.

1 cup buttermilk
1 cup mayonnaise
1 teaspoon lemon juice
¼ teaspoon onion powder
¼ teaspoon garlic powder
½ teaspoon fresh basil, chopped
½ teaspoon fresh dill, chopped
½ teaspoon fresh chives, chopped
½ teaspoon fresh thyme, chopped
1 teaspoon flat-leaf parsley, chopped
Salt and pepper, to taste

1. Put the buttermilk and mayonnaise in a blender and process until smooth.
2. Add the lemon juice, onion powder, and garlic powder, and combine well.
3. Add the fresh herbs and combine.
4. Adjust seasoning with salt and pepper.

WHAT'S HOT

▶ Commercial mayonnaise has an undeserved bad reputation as a cause of food spoilage. In fact, commercial mayonnaise is loaded with acid and preservatives that can actually extend the life of salads by killing bacteria. The eggs used in prepared mayonnaise are pasteurized to kill harmful bacteria. Truth be told, it is usually cross-contamination of uncooked foods that causes foodborne illness, not the prepared mayo.

Caesar Salad Dressing
YIELDS 1½ CUPS

To make the classic Caesar salad, lightly combine romaine lettuce with this dressing, then toss it with garlic croutons and Parmesan cheese.

1 tablespoon anchovy paste
1 garlic clove, pressed
1 teaspoon Dijon mustard
3 tablespoons lemon juice
2 egg yolks
1 cup olive oil
2 tablespoons Parmesan cheese, grated
Salt and pepper, to taste

1. Put the anchovy paste, garlic, and mustard in a food processor and pulse briefly.
2. Add the lemon juice and egg yolks, then process to combine until smooth.
3. Add the olive oil slowly through the feed tube while the food processor is running and process until thickened.
4. Add the Parmesan cheese, and season with salt and pepper to taste.

Blue Cheese Balsamic Dressing

YIELDS 1¼ CUPS

This is a different take on blue cheese dressing. Rather than being served in a creamy base, this one has a balsamic vinaigrette background.

1 teaspoon Dijon mustard
1 garlic clove, pressed
2 tablespoons balsamic vinegar
1 tablespoon red wine vinegar
1 cup olive oil
¼ cup blue cheese, crumbled
Salt and pepper, to taste

1. Place mustard, garlic, balsamic vinegar, and red wine vinegar in a blender and process to combine.
2. Add the olive oil slowly through the top while blender is running.
3. Add the blue cheese and combine.
4. Season with salt and pepper.

TOOLS YOU NEED

▶ At a minimum, the aging process can take up to twelve years for true balsamic vinegar, which is legally labeled *aceto balsamico tradizionale*. The longer it is permitted to age, the higher the quality and price. Indeed, some balsamic vinegars, depending on age, can cost hundreds of dollars for a mere half cup! Half a teaspoon of this expensive aged vinegar is enough flavor for a vinaigrette that serves four. Luckily, there are less expensive balsamic vinegars available.

Honey Barbecue Sauce
YIELDS 3 CUPS

Use this ketchup-based barbecue sauce as a glaze or mop sauce while grilling meat, or as a condiment on burgers.

2 cups ketchup
⅓ cup honey
⅓ cup brown sugar
2 garlic cloves, pressed
¼ cup onion, finely minced

2 tablespoons cayenne pepper sauce
3 tablespoons cider vinegar
1 teaspoon paprika
1 teaspoon salt
1 teaspoon pepper

1. Combine ingredients in a saucepan and simmer for 15 minutes.
2. Cool and refrigerate until ready to use.

Mustard Barbecue Sauce
YIELDS 3 CUPS

This barbecue sauce is excellent for marinating chicken, fish, shrimp, or vegetables that are to be grilled. It also makes a nice mop sauce for chicken, ribs, and steak, or a dipping sauce for grilled sausages.

1 cup Dijon mustard
½ cup yellow mustard
½ cup whole grain mustard
⅔ cup honey
2 tablespoons butter

2 garlic cloves, pressed
3 tablespoons distilled white vinegar
1 teaspoon salt
1 teaspoon pepper

1. Combine all ingredients in a saucepan and simmer for 15 minutes.
2. Cool and refrigerate until ready to use.

Caramelized Onions

YIELDS 1½ CUPS

Use caramelized onions as a relish with sausages, cold meats, or crackers and pâté. They can also be used as a base for French onion soup or a casserole, or as a topping for pizza.

> 4 tablespoons butter
> 2 large sweet onions
> 1 teaspoon sugar
> 1 tablespoon Worcestershire sauce
> 2 tablespoons red wine
> Salt and pepper, to taste

1. Melt the butter in a large sauté pan.
2. Slice the onions and sweat them in the butter over medium-low heat until they are limp.
3. Sprinkle the sugar over the onions, add the Worcestershire sauce, and cook the onions to a rich mahogany color over medium heat. This may take 20 minutes or more.
4. Deglaze the pan with the onions still in it by adding the wine, scraping up all the browned bits, and cooking over medium-low heat to make a reduction of caramelized onions.
5. Season with salt and pepper and cool the onions.

ASK YOUR GUIDE

What is in Worcestershire sauce?

▶ The original recipe is closely guarded, but basically consists of anchovies layered in brine, tamarinds in molasses, garlic in vinegar, chilies, cloves, shallots, and sugar. After sitting for two years with periodic stirrings, the mixture is sifted of the solids and bottled. Now a generic term, Worcestershire sauce is manufactured by many different commercial retailers, as well as under the original Lea and Perrins label. Learn more about Worcestershire sauce, including how to make your own at home, at http://about.com/homecooking/worcestershiresauce.

Berry Vinegar
YIELDS 2 CUPS

You can make this one when the berries are at their peak and enjoy their essence all year long. Other berries, such as blueberries or cranberries, may also be used.

> 2 cups red wine vinegar
> 1 pint raspberries, crushed
> 2 tablespoons sugar

1. In a bowl stir together the vinegar, berries, and sugar.
2. Cover the bowl with cheesecloth or plastic and let the mixture steep at room temperature for 2 days.
3. Take the berries out with a slotted spoon, discard them and then strain the vinegar through a cheesecloth-lined sieve. (Use a triple layer of cheesecloth that has been rinsed and squeezed damp-dry.)
4. Transfer the flavored vinegar to a bottle or jar and store in a dark, cool cabinet.

Steak Seasoning Spread

YIELDS ¾ CUP

Try using this wet spread instead of a dry seasoning blend the next time you grill steaks. It's faster than a marinade, but adds lots of rich flavor.

> 1 teaspoon garlic powder
> ½ teaspoon kosher salt
> ¼ teaspoon pepper
> 3 tablespoons Dijon mustard
> 2 tablespoons balsamic vinegar
> ½ cup canola oil

1. Place the garlic powder, salt, pepper, mustard, and balsamic vinegar in a food processor and pulse to combine.
2. Add the oil slowly through the feed tube while the food processor is running and process until smooth.
3. Spoon the marinade onto steaks and spread it around to coat both sides just before grilling.

TOOLS YOU NEED

▸ When using an acid-based marinade, be sure to use only containers made of glass, ceramic, or stainless-steel—*never* aluminum. The chemical reaction produced between alkaline and aluminum not only imparts an unattractive discoloration to the food but can also darken and pit the aluminum container.

Banana Ketchup
YIELDS 3½ CUPS

Although there is little tomato in this ketchup, it's the flavor of the bananas that shines through. Banana ketchup is especially good with pork and chicken.

½ cup mangoes, peeled and chopped
¼ cup golden raisins
⅓ cup sweet onions, chopped
2 large garlic cloves, quartered
⅓ cup tomato paste
4 large very ripe bananas, peeled and sliced
1⅓ cup cider vinegar, divided use
½ cup pineapple juice
3 cups water

½ cup dark brown sugar, packed
1½ teaspoons salt
½ teaspoon fresh habanero pepper, diced
¼ cup honey
2 teaspoons ground allspice
1 teaspoon ground cinnamon
½ teaspoon nutmeg, freshly grated
¼ teaspoon ground cloves
2 tablespoons dark rum

1. Place the mangoes, raisins, onions, garlic, tomato paste, bananas, and ⅔ cup vinegar in the bowl of a food processor fitted with the metal blade. Process until smooth and pour into a large, heavy saucepan.
2. To the banana mixture in the saucepan, add remaining ⅔ cup vinegar, pineapple juice, water, brown sugar, salt, and habanero pepper. Stir to combine.
3. Bring mixture to a boil over medium-high heat, stirring often. Reduce heat to low and cook uncovered, stirring the ketchup occasionally, for 1 hour and 15 minutes. If the ketchup gets too thick and begins to stick, add water.

Banana Ketchup (continued)

4. Add honey, allspice, cinnamon, nutmeg, and cloves. Cook over medium-low heat, stirring often, for another 15 minutes or until it is thick enough to coat a metal spoon. Stir in the rum and remove from heat. Let cool for 10 minutes.
5. Purée ketchup through a food mill fitted with the finest disk. Let cool to room temperature, pour into glass bottles, cover, and refrigerate. Use within 1 month.

Cuban Mojo Sauce
YIELDS 1 CUP

This sauce and marinade is usually made with bitter orange juice, but I've adapted it here using three different citrus juices.

10 cloves garlic, pressed
1 teaspoon kosher salt
4 tablespoons orange juice
4 tablespoons lime juice
2 tablespoons lemon juice
¼ cup olive oil
¼ teaspoon ground cumin

1. Put the garlic and salt in a bowl and mix it to form a paste.
2. Add the orange, lime, and lemon juices and mix well.
3. Whisk in the olive oil and add the cumin.
4. Use as a condiment or marinade for pork chops, fish, shrimp, or chicken.

ASK YOUR GUIDE

What can I do with leftover marinade?

▶ It seems a shame to discard that flavorful mixture, but do *not* be tempted to reuse leftover marinade without first cooking it. During the contact with raw foods, the marinade most likely has picked up harmful bacteria that could make you very ill. For that reason, it's wise to boil leftover marinade for at least five minutes before using it as a sauce.

Cranberry Chutney
YIELDS 3 CUPS

Try this tangy condiment on turkey sandwiches or as an accompaniment to charcuterie and smoked meats.

16 ounces fresh cranberries
¾ cup brown sugar, packed
½ cup golden raisins
½ cup apples, chopped
½ cup pears, chopped
½ cup sweet onion. chopped
½ cup water
2 tablespoons candied ginger, minced
2 tablespoons cider vinegar
¼ teaspoon ground cloves

1. In a nonreactive 3-quart saucepan, combine cranberries, brown sugar, raisins, apples, pears, onion, water, ginger, vinegar, and cloves.
2. Heat to boiling over high heat. Reduce heat and simmer for 15 minutes. Stir occasionally to prevent sticking.
3. Cool and store covered in the refrigerator for up to one week.

Pico de Gallo
YIELDS 3 CUPS

The fresh cilantro gives this fresh and delicious chunky salsa its flavor.

I cup fresh tomatoes, seeded
  and diced
I cup red onion. diced
I cup cucumber, seeded,
  peeled, and diced

I teaspoon cayenne pepper
  sauce
I tablespoon lime juice
I tablespoon fresh cilantro,
  chopped
Kosher salt, to taste

1. Combine all of the ingredients in a bowl.
2. Serve with tacos, tortilla chips, or as a garnish in black bean soup.

Olive Tapénade
YIELDS I CUP

Tapénade is a rich olive spread popular in the Mediterranean. It's quite easy to make at home.

20 pitted Kalamata olives,
  coarsely chopped
¼ cup green olives, chopped
I teaspoon fresh lemon juice

2 teaspoons olive oil
½ teaspoon anchovy paste
  (optional)
Fresh cracked black pepper

1. Combine Kalamata olives, green olives, lemon juice, olive oil, anchovy paste, and pepper.
2. Mix well. Refrigerate and use within two weeks.
3. Use as a spread for sandwiches, such as panini and muffulletta, or as a condiment.

ELSEWHERE ON THE WEB

▶ For more Spanish recipes, visit the About.com Guide to Spanish Food at http://spanish food.about.com. You'll find classic cusine from Spain, like gazpacho and potato tortilla (omelet).

Get Linked

Here are some great links to my About.com site for more condiment and sauce recipes and related information.

CONDIMENT RECIPES

You'll find recipes for various types of ketchup, relish, salad dressing, and more in this index.

http://about.com/homecooking/condiment

SAUCE RECIPES

This is where you'll find a multitude of recipes for sauces both familiar and unique, such as Béarnaise Sauce and Cranberry Jezebel Sauce.

http://about.com/homecooking/sauce

MARINADE RECIPES

Marinades are used not only to flavor, but also to tenderize, and they can also be boiled down for sauces. Be sure to plan ahead for potential marinating time with these recipes.

http://about.com/homecooking/marinaderecipes

ASK YOUR GUIDE:

What is paprika?
▶PAGE 197

What if I want to make
my own mayonnaise?
▶PAGE 198

What is allspice?
▶PAGE 203

Chapter 12

Herbs and Spices

Cajun Spice Blend
YIELDS 2 CUPS

Use this mixture for blackened chicken, fish, or steak. It's also great in sauces, pastas, and Cajun soups. Keep in mind that this mixture is supposed to be spicy, but you can cut back on the chili powder and peppers to suit your tastes.

2 tablespoons lemon pepper
½ cup paprika
1 tablespoon brown sugar
½ cup kosher salt
½ cup chili powder
2 tablespoons onion powder
1 teaspoon garlic powder
1 teaspoon celery salt
½ teaspoon white pepper
¾ teaspoon cayenne pepper
1½ tablespoons dried thyme
2 tablespoons dried basil

1. Whisk together all ingredients. Place in a sealed container.
2. Store in a cool, dark place for up to four months.

▶ If you are just setting up house, you'll need to keep some basic herbs and spices on hand to be prepared for any recipe. Although those spice racks and turntables may be attractive and handy on your countertop, it is best to store all herbs and spices in a cool, dark place away from heat and light sources. You can purchase inexpensive turntables to fit inside your cabinet for easier accessibility.

Classic Pesto

YIELDS ¾ CUP

This classic Italian sauce is so easy and versatile, you'll want to keep some always on hand in the refrigerator. Pesto is traditionally made with pine nuts, garlic, olive oil, basil, and Parmesan cheese. Its most popular use is tossed with pasta. Walnuts may be substituted for pine nuts in a pinch.

2 tablespoons pine nuts, coarsely chopped
2 garlic cloves, peeled
3 tablespoons extra-virgin olive oil
3 cups basil leaves (about 4 ounces)
1 cup flat parsley leaves
½ cup (2 ounces) fresh Parmesan cheese, grated
¼ teaspoon salt

1. You will need a food processor or heavy-duty blender for this recipe. With the motor running, drop the pine nuts and garlic through the feed chute.
2. Process until finely minced. Add the olive oil and pulse three times. Add basil, parsley, Parmesan cheese, and salt to the processor bowl. Process until finely minced, scraping down sides.
3. Refrigerate leftovers and use within 1 week.

WHAT'S HOT

▶ To the ancient Romans, it was a symbol of hatred, but basil eventually became a token of love in Italy. Young maidens would wear a sprig of basil in their hair to profess their availability. In some regions of Italy, basil is known as "kiss-me-Nicholas." One can only wonder if the conflicting symbolism of basil in Rome is the origin of a love-hate relationship. In Romania, if a boy accepts basil from a girl, it means they are engaged to be married.

Tomato Pesto

YIELDS 1 CUP

This pesto is delicious in vegetable soups, pastas, and pasta salads.

2 tablespoons walnuts, coarse-chopped
2 garlic cloves, peeled
¼ cup chopped sun dried tomatoes (packed in oil)
3 tablespoons extra-virgin olive oil

4 cups basil leaves (about 4 ounces)
½ cup (2 ounces) fresh Parmesan cheese, grated
¼ teaspoon salt

1. Drop the walnuts and garlic through the feed chute of a food processor with the motor running. Process until finely minced.
2. Add the sun-dried tomatoes and process until minced.
3. Add the olive oil and pulse three times. Add basil, Parmesan cheese, and salt. Process until finely minced, scraping down sides.

Roasted Garlic

YIELDS ABOUT 20 CLOVES

This simple preparation is so easy to prepare at home. Try spreading it directly onto crostini and crackers.

2 whole garlic bulbs
1 teaspoon olive oil

¼ teaspoon salt

1. Preheat oven to 350°F.
2. Slice off and discard the tops of the garlic heads and toss the remaining bulb with the olive oil. Place on a large piece of aluminum foil, and sprinkle with salt.
3. Fold up the foil to seal in a packet and bake for 1 hour.

Grilled Vegetable Seasoning
YIELDS 1 TABLESPOON

Before grilling, sprinkle this herb and spice mixture onto vegetables such as zucchini. This recipe is easily multiplied.

¼ teaspoon oregano
½ teaspoon garlic powder
¼ teaspoon thyme
¼ teaspoon onion powder
¼ teaspoon paprika
¼ teaspoon parsley

¼ teaspoon celery salt
¼ teaspoon dried lemon peel, grated
¼ teaspoon ground black pepper
½ teaspoon kosher salt

Mix all the ingredients together in a bowl. If making in larger quantities, store in a jar in a cool, dark place.

Herbs de Provence
YIELDS ¾ CUP

Add a bit of flair from southern France to your dishes by using this classic herb combination to season chicken, vegetables, or meat.

3 tablespoons dried marjoram
3 tablespoons dried thyme
3 tablespoons dried savory
1 teaspoon dried basil

1 teaspoon dried rosemary
½ teaspoon dried sage
½ teaspoon fennel seeds

1. Combine all ingredients. Mix well and spoon into a tightly sealed jar.
2. Store in a cool, dark place for up to four months.

ASK YOUR GUIDE

What is paprika?

▶ Paprika comes from dried and ground chili peppers (*Capsicum annuum*), which originate in southern Mexico. By the 1560s, these peppers had reached the Balkans where they were called *peperke* or *paparka*. The peppers soon migrated to Hungary, now renowned for its paprika. It wasn't until the mid-1900s that paprika stepped into the limelight of Western kitchens. Learn more about paprika and how to use it by visiting http://about.com/homecooking/paprika.

What if I want to make my own mayonnaise?

▶ Traditional homemade mayonnaise contains raw egg yolks. The perfect solution is to purchase irradiated eggs, which are now available in most markets. Irradiated eggs carry no risk of salmonella contamination and are perfectly safe to use in raw preparations. However, if you are unable to find irradiated eggs and don't want risk using raw eggs, visit http://about.com/home cooking/mayonnaise.

Pickling Spice
YIELDS ¼ CUP

This spice mixture can be used to flavor pickling brines or poaching liquids. It is also an ingredient in crab boil seasoning.

2 teaspoons black peppercorns
1 tablespoon yellow mustard seeds
2 teaspoons celery seeds
1 teaspoon allspice berries

1 tablespoon dill seed
1 cinnamon stick
½ teaspoon ground cloves
1 teaspoon ground ginger

1. Combine all ingredients.
2. Store in a sealed jar in a dark, cool place

Garlic Mayonnaise
YIELDS 1 CUP

This is an easier version of aioli, which is usually made with raw egg yolks. Use as a condiment with fish instead of tartar sauces.

4 cloves garlic, pressed
¼ teaspoon salt
1 cup mayonnaise

1 teaspoon lemon juice
1 tablespoon olive oil

1. In a bowl, mash the garlic and salt into a paste with a fork.
2. Whisk the mayonnaise into the garlic paste. Add lemon juice and whisk again.
3. Pour oil in a slow stream while whisking it into the mayonnaise mixture. Refrigerate any leftovers.

Crab-Boil Spice Mix
YIELDS 1 CUP

Use this mix for poaching shrimp, lobster, and crab.

¼ cup pickling spices
¼ cup sea salt
1 teaspoon white pepper
2 tablespoons cracked black
   peppercorns
2 teaspoons cayenne pepper

½ teaspoon nutmeg
⅛ teaspoon ground cloves
2 teaspoons ground ginger
2 teaspoons dried basil
2 tablespoons dried chives
5 bay leaves

1. Add all of the ingredients to the bowl of a food processor fitted with the metal blade.
2. Process, pulsing, until the mixture forms a coarse powder.
3. Store in a sealed jar in a cool, dark place.

Dry Marinade Spice Rub
YIELDS 1 CUP

Rub this spice mixture on ribs, brisket, or chicken and let marinate from one hour up to overnight before grilling.

2 tablespoons kosher salt
1 teaspoon black pepper,
   freshly ground
1 tablespoon onion powder

1 teaspoon dried basil
1 teaspoon chili powder
2 tablespoons paprika
¼ cup brown sugar, packed

1. In a small bowl, combine salt, pepper, onion powder, basil, chili powder, paprika, and brown sugar until evenly mixed.
2. Store in a sealed jar in a dark, cool place.

TOOLS YOU NEED

▶ Unless you use a particular spice blend often or intend to split up a batch to give as gifts, don't plan on making a huge batch at once. It's best to make smaller batches that can be used within a month's time. Spices lose potency and flavor over time. Light, moisture, and heat are the worst enemies of spices, so keep them in a tightly sealed container in a cool, dark place. Although it may be more convenient, you should not store your spices near your stove or in open racks on the counter.

► Dill weed contains the carminative agent *carvone*, which has a calming effect and aids with digestion by relieving intestinal gas. Romans considered dill good luck and also used it as a tonic. A couple of centuries ago, parents would give dill seeds to children to chew during church services to keep them quiet and alert during long sermons. This usage caused them to be called "meetin' seeds."

Dill Dip Mix
YIELDS ¼ CUP

Mix this seasoning with 1 cup mayonnaise and 2 cups sour cream and chill for 1 to 2 hours. Serve with chips and raw vegetables.

1 teaspoon kosher salt
¼ teaspoon ground bay leaf
2 teaspoons white pepper
1 teaspoon black pepper

¼ teaspoon nutmeg
2 teaspoons onion powder
2 tablespoons dried dill weed
½ teaspoon celery salt

Mix thoroughly and store in a sealed jar in a cool, dry place.

Fajita Seasoning
YIELDS 1 CUP

Sprinkle this seasoning on sliced beef or chicken before grilling.

½ cup chili powder
¼ cup paprika
1 tablespoon ground cumin
1 teaspoon garlic powder

1 teaspoon ground cayenne
  pepper
2 teaspoons dried oregano
1 teaspoon onion salt

1. Combine all and mix well.
2. Store in an airtight container in a cool, dark place up to four months.

Five-Spice Powder

YIELDS ¼ CUP

Five-spice seasoning mix is used to flavor meat and poultry dishes in Chinese cooking. It's easy to make your own.

2 tablespoons Szechwan
    peppercorns
2 teaspoons white
    peppercorns

3 star anise
2 cinnamon sticks (3 inches each),
    broken into small pieces
6 whole cloves

1. In a small, heavy, dry skillet, toast peppercorns over medium heat until they become fragrant, about 1 to 2 minutes. Shake pan often to prevent burning.
2. Remove to a bowl. Repeat toasting process separately with star anise, cinnamon, and cloves.
3. Pour all of the toasted spices into a spice grinder (or clean coffee grinder) and grind to a fine powder. Let rest in the grinder for 1 minute, then transfer to a glass container and tighten lid. Store in a cool, dark place up to one month.

WHAT'S HOT

▶ Humans have been using spices for almost as long as they've been eating. Just as classic recipes evolved, so did spice blends. By making your own mixes, you can adjust flavors to suit your personal needs. Probably the most widely recognized spice blend is curry powder. Curries can contain as little as two or three different spices or up to fifty or more. They have evolved based on personal tastes and should always be adjusted to suit your own needs.

All-Purpose No-Salt Seasoning
YIELDS ⅓ CUP

Similar to the commercial Mrs. Dash mixture, use this salt-substitute herb mix on all types of savory foods and you won't miss the salt at all.

1 tablespoon ground white pepper
1 tablespoon garlic powder
1 tablespoon onion powder
1 teaspoon dried basil
1 teaspoon dried oregano

1 teaspoon dried thyme
1 teaspoon dried parsley flakes
1 teaspoon ground nutmeg
1 teaspoon dried marjoram
1 tablespoon lemon pepper

1. Combine white pepper, garlic powder, onion powder, basil, oregano, thyme, parsley flakes, nutmeg, marjoram, and lemon pepper.
2. Mix well. Place in a glass airtight container and store in a cool, dark place for up to four months. Use on all types of savory foods.
3. Recipe may be easily multiplied.

TOOLS YOU NEED

▶ If you plan on making your own spice blends at home, you will want to invest in an electric spice grinder. Luckily, they are inexpensive. If you should have difficulty finding a spice grinder, for some odd reason, you can also use an electric coffee grinder with equal success. You should be able to find either for around $15. Of course, you can always resort to grinding by hand with a mortar and pestle.

Pumpkin Pie Spice Mix

YIELDS 1 TEASPOON

This shortcut spice mix is often called for in quick pumpkin pie recipes, but it is also good in savory baked pumpkin or squash recipes, cookies, sweet potato pie, custard, cheesecake, and more.

½ teaspoon ground cinnamon
¼ teaspoon ground ginger
⅛ teaspoon ground allspice berries
⅛ teaspoon ground nutmeg
⅛ teaspoon coriander

1. Blend cinnamon, ginger, allspice, nutmeg, and coriander together until evenly mixed.
2. If making in larger quantities, store in an airtight container in a cool, dark place for up to 6 months.

ASK YOUR GUIDE

What is allspice?

▸ Although it sounds like a mix, allspice is one spice. Allspice is a popular spice in Caribbean and Latin savory dishes as well as in desserts. Today, allspice is enjoyed by most cultures around the world.

Get Linked

Here are some great links to my About.com site for more herb and spice recipes and related information.

SPICE-MIX RECIPES

This page has an index of spice mix recipes and a link to a full article on spices that includes information, tips, and hints on making your own spice mixes.

http://about.com/homecooking/spicemix

HERB AND SPICE CHART

Here's a quick reference chart to help you choose herbs and spices for specific dishes.

http://about.com/homecooking/herbandspicechart

SPICE AND HERB SUBSTITUTION CHART

You may find yourself in a situation where you are out of a specified spice in a recipe or perhaps you just don't care for that specific spice. This chart will help you choose substitutions or alternatives that should work with your recipe.

http://about.com/homecooking/spiceandherbsub

Chapter 13

Cookies, Brownies, and Candy

ASK YOUR GUIDE:

What is cream cheese?
▶**PAGE 208**

Why are hazelnuts called filberts?
▶**PAGE 219**

What are graham crackers?
▶**PAGE 223**

Berry Cheesecake Bars
SERVES 24

Feel free to use other berries or fruit, such as blackberries.

I can raspberries in light syrup
2 tablespoons cornstarch
2 cups flour
2 cups quick-cooking oats
1½ cups brown sugar, packed
I teaspoon baking soda
½ teaspoon salt
1½ cups butter or margarine

2 packages (8 ounces each)
   cream cheese, at room
   temperature
2 eggs, at room temperature
1½ cups powdered sugar
2 teaspoons vanilla
I teaspoon lemon juice

1. Preheat oven to 350°F. Line a 13" × 9" × 2" baking pan with nonstick foil.
2. Strain and process raspberries, with their syrup, over a saucepan with a food mill to remove the seeds. Add cornstarch to the liquid and mix until smooth. In the saucepan, bring berry mixture slowly to simmer, stirring constantly, until it begins to thicken. Remove from heat and let cool.
3. Combine flour, oats, sugar, soda, and salt. Cut in butter until crumbly. Press half of the mixture into the baking pan. Bake for 15 minutes. Let cool slightly.
4. Blend cream cheese, eggs, powdered sugar, vanilla, and lemon juice until smooth.
5. Spread berry mixture evenly over bottom crust. Place dollops of cream cheese mixture evenly over blackberry mix and swirl gently. Top with other half of crumb mixture. Bake 45 minutes.
6. Cool to room temperature. Lift out the entire pastry by the foil insert and cut into 24 bars. Chill before serving.

▶ If you don't have a food mill you may purée the berries in a food processor or blender and then strain the seeds out with a sieve. If you don't have a food processor or a blender, you may strain the berries over a bowl to catch the syrup and then force the berry pulp through a sieve with a rubber spatula or wooden spoon to remove the seeds. Or, try seedless jam and eliminate the cornstarch and the saucepan cooking step.

Chocolate Raspberry Meringue Cookies

YIELDS 5 DOZEN

These little meringue bites are lighter than air but packed with rasp-berry flavor and kicked up with chocolate chips for extra decadence.

3 large egg whites, at room temperature
¼ teaspoon cream of tartar
1 cup superfine granulated sugar
½ teaspoon raspberry flavoring
1 tablespoon lemon zest, grated
½ cup miniature semisweet chocolate chips

1. Chill mixing bowl and beaters for 15 minutes.
2. Preheat oven to 250°F. Line cookie sheets with Silpats or parchment paper.
3. Beat egg whites and cream of tartar on high speed until soft peaks form. Add sugar 1 tablespoon at a time until all sugar is incorporated and melted into the meringue. The meringue should be shiny and form stiff peaks.
4. Fold in raspberry flavoring, grated lemon zest, and miniature chocolate chips.
5. Drop by scant teaspoonfuls (or use a pastry bag) onto pre-pared cookie sheets, placing cookies about 1 inch apart. (You want these bite-sized, to pop the whole cookie into your mouth. Larger ones are fine but make a crumbly mess when you bite into them.)
6. Bake about 1 hour until stiff and dry. Turn off oven, but leave cookies in the oven until cool to further dry out, another 2 hours. Store in an airtight container.

ELSEWHERE ON THE WEB

▶ For other low-fat baked goods, try the About.com Guide to Low-Fat Cooking at http://about.com/lowfatcooking/bakedgoods. Here you'll find low-fat versions of some classics like chocolate chip cookies, banana bread, and cherry turnovers.

Chocolate Cherry Buttermilk Bars
SERVES 24

The cherries give a hint of sweet-and-sour flavor to these bars.

1 can (14.5 ounces) pie cherries packed in water (not syrup), drained
1 package (18.25 ounces) chocolate cake mix, divided use
3 eggs, divded use
8 ounces cream cheese, divided use
½ cup butter (1 stick), melted
1 cup white chocolate chips
1 cup buttermilk
1 cup powdered confectioners' sugar
3 tablespoons unsweetened cocoa powder
Powdered confectioners' sugar, for topping

1. Put cherries in a strainer to drain. Preheat oven to 350°F. Reserve 1 heaping cup dry cake mix and set aside.
2. In large bowl, combine remaining cake mix, 1 egg, 4 ounces cream cheese, and butter; blend well. Spread batter into bottom of foil-lined 9" × 13" baking pan. Press chocolate chips and batter. Bake for 15 minutes and set aside.
3. In medium bowl, cream 2 eggs, buttermilk, remaining cream cheese, 1 cup powdered sugar, and cocoa until well blended. Slowly add reserved cake mix and beat on medium speed until mixture is smooth and thickened (about 3 minutes).
4. Place drained cherries on paper towels and gently blot dry. Spread cherries evenly over baked crust. Top with batter, and bake for 45 to 50 minutes, until lightly browned on top. Cool completely and cut into bars.
5. Dust bar tops generously with sifted powdered sugar just before serving as the moisture in the bars will cause the sugar to melt within a matter of hours.

Two-Chip Cookies
YIELDS 3 TO 4 DOZEN

Potato chips, chocolate chips, and cookies—all your favorite junk foods in one tasty package! These cookies are quick, easy, and indescribably delicious. Have fun asking your guests to guess the secret (potato chip) ingredient.

1 cup flour
¾ cup cornstarch
1 cup butter (two sticks), softened
¾ cup sugar
1 teaspoon vanilla
1 cup (about 4 ounces) salted plain potato chips, finely crushed and packed
1 cup swirled white and dark chocolate chips, chilled
½ cup powdered sugar

1. Whisk together flour and cornstarch. Set aside.
2. Cream together butter and sugar. Gradually add flour mixture and mix well. Add vanilla and potato chips and mix well. Fold in cold chocolate chips. Chill 15 to 30 minutes.
3. Scoop out walnut-sized balls of dough with a small ice cream scoop or spoon and drop onto ungreased parchment-covered cookie sheets about 2 inches apart. Take a flat-bottomed drinking glass, dip it in powdered sugar, and gently flatten the cookies slightly with it. (Don't flatten too much or make them too large as they will be too thin and will crumble easily.)
4. Bake at 350°F for 12 to 14 minutes until edges are faintly golden. Let cool 5 minutes before removing with a spatula to racks. Let cookies cool before serving and storing.

TOOLS YOU NEED

▶ To crush the potato chips, place them in a plastic bag and use a rolling pin, shifting frequently to be sure they are uniformly crushed. The crushed chips should be just slightly larger than large grains of kosher salt. Use the thin-style plain potato chips, not the thicker wavy, ruffled, or kettle chips. Do not use the composite chips like Pringles.

Dalmatian Zebra Bars
SERVES 24 TO 36

These are a chocolate-lover's nirvana. They are called Dalmatian Zebra Bars because of the black and white polka dot chocolate chips and the black and white layers of chocolate and vanilla. They are quite decadent, so cut them into smaller portions than you normally would for brownies.

2¼ cups all-purpose flour
2½ teaspoons baking powder
½ teaspoon salt
¾ cup butter (1½ sticks), softened
1 cup granulated sugar
1 cup light brown sugar, firmly packed
1 teaspoon vanilla extract
3 large eggs
½ cup sour cream
⅓ cup unsweetened cocoa powder
2 tablespoons butter or margarine, melted
½ cup white chocolate chips
1 cup semisweet chocolate chips

TOPPING:
6 ounces semisweet chocolate
1 tablespoon shortening (not butter or margarine)
2 cups swirled white and dark chocolate chips

1. Preheat oven to 375°F. Line a 13" × 9" × 2" baking pan with nonstick foil.

2. In a medium bowl, whisk together flour, baking powder, and salt. Set aside.

3. In a large bowl, cream butter and sugars until light and fluffy. Beat in vanilla and eggs. Add half of the flour to creamed butter mixture, mixing until thoroughly combined. Repeat with the other half of the flour mixture. Beat in sour cream. Mixture will be very thick. Divide mixture in half.

4. Blend together cocoa powder and melted butter or margarine. Stir into one half the flour mixture. Spread evenly in foil-lined baking pan. Press white chocolate chips into chocolate layer.

5. Carefully spoon remaining vanilla batter on top of chocolate layer and gently spread to cover with a spatula, taking care not to disrupt chocolate layer. Sprinkle with semisweet chocolate chips on top and press gently into dough.

6. Bake 20 to 25 minutes in center of the oven. Cool on a rack to room temperature.

7. For the topping, melt 6 ounces chocolate with 1 tablespoon shortening over a double boiler until smooth. Remove from heat and cool slightly. Gently spread melted chocolate over the cooled bars. Sprinkle the swirled chocolate chips over the melted chocolate topping. Refrigerate for about 1 hour to set the chocolate.

8. Cut into bars. Store leftovers in a tightly covered container.

WHAT'S HOT

▶ Vanilla was discovered in Mexico by the Spanish conquistadors, who dubbed it *vainilla* meaning "little sheath." They brought it to Europe, where it was quickly adopted. The first written mention of vanilla was in 1662, in reference to an ingredient used with chocolate by the Native Americans. By the nineteenth century, the great innovation of ice cream had created a love affair with vanilla.

Mint-Chocolate Mousse Bars
SERVES 16 TO 24

Light but rich, these bars pack a big flavor punch so you can get away with cutting them into smaller bars than normal bar cookies. A little goes a long way.

> 1½ cups vanilla wafer crumbs (about 40 wafers)
> ¼ cup butter (½ stick), melted
> ¾ cup heavy whipping cream
> 1 cup semisweet chocolate chips
> 3 eggs
> ⅓ cup sugar
> ⅛ teaspoon salt

TOPPING:
> ½ cup mint chocolate chips
> 1 tablespoon shortening

1. Preheat oven to 350°F. Line an 8" × 8" × 2" baking pan with nonstick foil.
2. Combine vanilla wafer crumbs with melted butter until well mixed. Press into the bottom of the baking pan. Bake for 10 minutes.
3. In a double boiler, warm whipping cream and chocolate chips. Stir until melted and smooth. Remove top of double boiler to a trivet or pad and let chocolate cool at least 5 minutes. It needs to remain lukewarm and liquid.
4. In a large bowl, beat eggs, sugar, and salt until light and foamy. While constantly stirring, gradually add melted chocolate to the egg mixture. Pour mousse mixture into baking pan on top of the baked crust.

5. Bake 25 to 35 minutes. Center should be slightly puffed up and should spring back when lightly touched. Set on a rack to cool at least 15 minutes while making the chocolate topping.
6. To make topping, melt mint chocolate chips and shortening in the top of a double-boiler, stirring until smooth. Spread on top of cooled mousse bars. Refrigerate at least two hours to firm up before cutting into bars and serving.

ELSEWHERE ON THE WEB

▶ For another mint-chocolate recipe, try these mint-chocolate cups from the About.com Guide to Candy at http://about.com/candy/chocolatemintcups. Consult this site for basic candymaking information and more candy recipes as well.

YIELDS 4 DOZEN

As if brownie bites aren't decadent enough, these are stuffed with butterscotch chips. Semisweet chocolate chips perform a dual purpose as a filling and frosting.

¾ cup unsweetened cocoa
⅔ cup vegetable oil
2 cups sugar
4 eggs
2 teaspoons vanilla extract
1¼ cups all-purpose flour
1 teaspoon baking powder
½ teaspoon salt
1⅓ cups butterscotch chips, divided use
⅔ cup (about) semisweet chocolate chips

1. Preheat oven to 350°F. Line mini-muffin tins with papers.
2. Combine cocoa and oil in large bowl until smooth. Mix in sugar. Add eggs and vanilla, mixing until combined.
3. In a separate bowl, whisk together flour, baking powder, and salt. Add to cocoa mixture, stirring to combine. Fold in 1 cup butterscotch chips, reserving remaining ⅓ cup for decoration. Fill each muffin paper with about 1 rounded tablespoon of batter.
4. Bake 12 to 14 minutes or just until set and small cracks appear on surface. Remove from oven. Immediately place about 6 semisweet chocolate chips on center of each hot brownie bite. Let rest 2 to 3 minutes to soften, then swirl melted chips with the back of a spoon to frost brownie bites.
5. Garnish each with 1 butterscotch chip placed in the center.

WHAT'S HOT

▶ Imitation vanilla is made from artificial flavorings, most of which come from wood byproducts that often contain chemicals. Discerning palates find the imitation vanilla products to have a harsh quality with a bitter aftertaste. Twice as much imitation vanilla flavoring is required to match the strength of pure vanilla extract. Vanilla flavoring is usually a combination of imitation vanilla and pure vanilla extract.

Nickel Bars

SERVES 36

These bars have a combination of five different flavors in each bite—chocolate, peanut butter, marshmallows, cashews, and toasted coconut.

½ cup butter (1 stick or ¼ pound)
1 cup sugar
2 eggs, at room temperature
1 teaspoon vanilla
¾ cup all-purpose flour
½ cup cashews, chopped
3 tablespoons unsweetened cocoa powder

½ teaspoon baking powder
¼ teaspoon salt
2 cups miniature marshmallows
1 cup smooth peanut butter
1 cup (6 ounces) semisweet chocolate chips
1½ cups coconut, toasted and shredded

1. Preheat oven to 350°F. Line a 9" × 13" baking pan with non-stick foil.
2. In a large mixing bowl, cream butter and sugar until smooth. Add eggs and vanilla, mixing until combined.
3. In a separate medium bowl, whisk together flour, cashews, unsweetened cocoa powder, baking powder, and salt.
4. Add dry ingredients to egg mixture, stirring to combine. Pour into baking pan and smooth.
5. Bake 15 to 20 minutes, or until a toothpick inserted in center comes out clean. Evenly distribute marshmallows on top. Bake an additional 2 minutes until marshmallows puff up, but do not brown. Cool to room temperature.
6. Melt peanut butter and chocolate chips in the top of a double boiler over simmering water, stirring until smooth. Fold in toasted coconut. Spread topping over cooled bars. Chill until firm. Keep chilled until time to serve. Refrigerate leftovers.

TOOLS YOU NEED

▶ Silicone hot mitts are wonderful. They protect your hands and wrists from being burned better than cloth mitts because they won't get holes in them, and they also clean up easier with a rinse of soap and water.

Chocolate Cashew-Butter Pretzel Candy
YIELDS 8 DOZEN

These delicious candies have a cashew butter filling sitting on top of a pretzel and covered with chocolate. Let the kids help.

1 cup of cashew butter
½ cup butter (1 stick), at room temperature
½ cup graham-cracker crumbs
½ cup club-cracker crumbs
2 cups of confectioners' sugar
8 dozen small pretzel twists or square butter snaps pretzels
(about 4 cups, approximately 5 ounces)
10 ounces special dark chocolate (two 5-ounce bars)
1 ounce paraffin, shaved

1. In a large bowl, combine cashew butter, butter, graham-cracker crumbs, club-cracker crumbs, and confectioners' sugar on low to medium-low speed until well mixed. Scrape sides often. Mixture will be very thick.
2. Using your hands, roll mixture into small balls about the diameter of a dime and place each on a pretzel. Press down gently to cover the pretzel and place on a jelly roll pan. Repeat until all of the cashew-butter mixture is used. Refrigerate at least one hour to firm up.
3. Melt chocolate and paraffin in the top of a double-boiler until smooth. Remove from heat. Swirl the tops of each of the pretzel candies in the melted chocolate, shaking gently to remove excess and return to the jelly roll pan with pretzel-side down. Refrigerate again to set chocolate.
4. Store leftovers between sheets of wax paper or plastic wrap. Cover and refrigerate.

Orange Chocolate Cream Cheese Bars
YIELDS 24

Try experimenting with other flavors of chocolate chips.

1½ package (12 ounces) cream cheese, at room temperature, divided use

3 egg, at room temperature, divided use

½ cup butter, melted, but at room temperature (1 stick)

1 tablespoon orange zest, grated

1 box (18.25 ounces) chocolate devil's food cake mix

1 cup semisweet chocolate chips, divided use

2 cups powdered sugar

1 tablespoon cocoa powder

1 teaspoon orange extract

1. Preheat oven to 350°F. Line a 9" × 13" baking pan with foil.
2. Cream together 4 ounces of cream cheese, 1 egg, and butter on low speed until combined, about 1 minute. Blend in orange zest and cake mix by hand until combined. It will be very thick, but pliable like a soft dough. Using a spatula, press dough evenly into the bottom of the foiled pan. Evenly sprinkle on ½ cup chocolate chips and press lightly into the batter with a spatula, but don't bury them.
3. Place remaining 8 ounces cream cheese, 2 eggs, powdered sugar, cocoa powder, and orange extract in a small bowl. Begin mixing on low speed until sugar and cocoa are incorporated. Increase to medium speed and beat until smooth, at least 3 minutes or longer if need be. Spread evenly over bottom layer. Sprinkle on remaining chocolate chips.
4. Bake for 45 minutes. Cool completely. Carefully remove from pan, peel off foil, and cut into squares to serve.

TOOLS YOU NEED

▶ To use the microwave to soften block cream cheese for mixing with other ingredients: Remove from the foil packaging and place on microwave-safe plate. Cook on 50 percent power for about 1 minute for an 8-ounce block or 30 seconds for a 3-ounce block. Let rest for 1 minute before using.

Raspberry Linzer Triangles
YIELDS 48

These layered bars have a hazelnut cookie bottom topped with raspberry sauce, chocolate chips, and cookie crumbles. Since they are made in a pan and cut into cookie triangles after baking, they are fast and easy to make. Perfect for parties, showers, or fancy teas. If you cannot handle the raspberry seeds, they may be strained out.

1½ cups all-purpose flour
1 cup sugar
½ cup hazelnuts, ground
½ teaspoon cinnamon
1 box (10 ounces) frozen raspberries in light syrup, thawed and undrained

¼ cup fresh orange juice (about 1 orange)
1 cup butter, at room temperature
1 tablespoon cornstarch
¼ cup confectioners' sugar
¾ cup miniature semisweet chocolate chips

1. Preheat oven to 350°F. Line a 9" × 13" baking pan with non-stick foil.
2. Whisk together flour, sugar, hazelnuts, and cinnamon until evenly mixed. Cut in butter with a dinner fork until mixture is the texture of large crumbs. Remove 1 cup and reserve for topping. Press remaining crumbs into the bottom of the prepared baking pan with a spatula or your fingers to make a smooth, even layer. Bake 15 minutes.
3. Meanwhile, place thawed raspberries with syrup and orange juice in a small saucepan. Add cornstarch and confectioners' sugar. Heat, stirring constantly, until bubbles begin to form around the edge. Cook for 1 minute, continuing to stir until thickened. (If you do not want seeds, strain now.) Let cool for 10 minutes.

Raspberry Linzer Triangles (continued)

4. Sprinkle miniature chocolate chips evenly over the bottom crust. Carefully spoon the raspberries evenly over the chocolate chips. Sprinkle reserved dough crumbles over the top. Bake an additional 20 minutes.
5. Cool to room temperature, then refrigerate for 1 hour to set chocolate. Cut into 24 squares, then cut each square corner to corner into triangles. Serve at room temperature.

ASK YOUR GUIDE

Why are hazelnuts called filberts?

▶ The most commonly accepted explanation is because hazelnuts mature on or around St. Philibert's Day, August 20. Other historians believe the term "filbert" derives from the German *vollbart* meaning "full beard," a reference to the appearance of the husked shell. Although the current definition of filbert tends to refer to commercially cultivated crops of hazelnuts, the terms "hazelnut" and "filbert" are generally used interchangeably.

Key Lime Meltaways
YIELDS 4 DOZEN

These lemon cooler-style cookies are perfect for gifts and ship well.

1 cup flour
½ cup cornstarch
1½ cups confectioners' sugar, divided use
¾ cup butter (1½ sticks), cut into cubes
1 teaspoon lime juice

1 teaspoon key lime zest, grated
½ teaspoon orange zest, grated
1 cup white chocolate chips

1. Line cookie sheets with parchment paper or Silpat baking pad. In a small bowl, combine flour, cornstarch, and ½ cup confectioners' sugar. Set aside.
2. In a large bowl, cream butter, lime juice, key lime zest, and orange zest until smooth. Add flour mixture to butter mixture and begin mixing on low speed. Once mixture begins to get thick, increase speed to thoroughly mix until combined, scraping down sides. Scrape batter from beaters. Mix in white chocolate chips with a large spoon.
3. Refrigerate dough for 45 minutes to firm up. (It's important that the dough be very cold before going into the oven or it will spread.) Preheat oven to 350°F.
5. Roll dough into 1-inch balls. Place 1½ inches apart on lined baking sheet, and bake for 10 to 12 minutes until bottom edges just barely begin to turn brown. Do not overbake. Let cool on baking sheets for at least 5 minutes, then remove to racks to cool.
6. Pour remaining confectioners' sugar into a bowl. Roll key lime cookies in the sugar to cover. Store in an airtight container.

PB&J Cookies
YIELDS 3 DOZEN

Peanut butter and jelly sandwiches, the ultimate comfort food, become a fabulous cookie. Choose your favorite jelly, jam, or preserves for a more gourmet filling.

3 cups all-purpose flour
1 cup granulated white sugar
1 teaspoon baking soda
½ teaspoon salt
1½ cups smooth peanut butter
½ cup butter (1 stick), at room temperature
½ cup light corn syrup
2 tablespoons milk
½ cup grape jelly
1 cup roasted peanuts, chopped

1. Preheat oven to 375°F. Line two baking sheets with Silpat baking liners or parchment paper.
2. In a large bowl, combine flour, sugar, baking soda, and salt until evenly mixed. Add peanut butter and butter. Using a mixer, blend on medium speed until crumbly, about 3 minutes. Add corn syrup and milk. Mix until thoroughly combined. Mixture will be very thick.
3. Roll dough into balls about 1 inch in diameter. Using your thumb or finger, press an indentation into the center of each ball, and place 2 inches apart on baking sheet. Fill each cookie with jelly and sprinkle with chopped peanuts.
4. Bake 10 to 12 minutes, until edges are lightly browned. Let baked cookies cool 2 minutes, then remove to racks to cool completely. Store PB&J cookies in an airtight container.

ELSEWHERE ON THE WEB

▶ Did you ever wonder who had the brilliant idea to put together the long-standing combination of peanut butter and jelly? For the history of this famous sandwich, visit http://www.smuckers.com/fc/newsroom/archive/pbj0302_b.asp. And, for fun peanutty information, visit www.jif.com/aboutjif/aj_tidbits.asp.

Peanut Butter Crunch Candy Bars
YIELDS 48

No-bake peanut butter bars are easy to make and kids love them.

2 tablespoons butter
2 cups crunchy peanut butter
4 cups miniature marshmallows
1 cup crisp rice cereal
54 round butter-flavored cookies (1½ stacks, about 2 cups), crushed
1 cup semisweet chocolate chips
3 ounces semisweet chocolate bar, melted

1. Line a 9" × 13" baking pan with nonstick foil.
2. In a double boiler melt butter and peanut butter, stirring to avoid scorching, until combined. Mix in marshmallows, 2 cups at a time, until melted and smooth. Pour into a large bowl. Let cool for 5 minutes.
3. Stir in crisp rice cereal, crushed cookies, and chocolate chips. Pour into lined pan and smooth top. Let stand at room temperature for an hour to set.
4. Clean double boiler and dry thoroughly. (One drop of water will make the chocolate seize.) Gently melt chocolate bar stirring until smooth. You may melt chocolate in the microwave, if you wish, but be careful not to scorch it. Chocolate should be melted, but not hot. Pour melted chocolate into a zip-top bag, squeeze out all the air, and seal. Cut a small corner from the bag and use it as a pastry bag to drizzle chocolate in a zigzag pattern over the top of the candy bars.
5. Let cool and cut into squares. Store leftovers at room temperature in an airtight container.

S'mores Cups
YIELDS 4 DOZEN

Based on the old Girl Scout favorite, these are made with graham cracker crumbs, marshmallows, and chocolate. Although the marshmallows aren't toasted, there is toasted coconut on top. No-bake S'mores candy cups are easy to make and great for gifts.

½ cup butter (1 stick)
12 ounces special dark semisweet chocolate
   (2 giant 6-ounce bars), broken into chunks
1 cup graham cracker crumbs
2 cups miniature marshmallows
1 cup coconut, toasted and shredded

1. Line mini-muffin tins with muffin papers.
2. In a double boiler, melt butter and chocolate, stirring to avoid scorching, until combined. Remove from heat.
3. Spoon about ½ teaspoon of melted chocolate into each mini-muffin cup. Sprinkle with ½ teaspoon graham cracker crumbs while chocolate is still warm and liquid. Place 4 miniature marshmallows on top of graham cracker crumbs. Top marshmallows evenly with remaining chocolate (re-warm chocolate, if necessary).
4. When trays are full, tap gently on the counter to force chocolate down and around the marshmallows. Sprinkle coconut on top.
5. Chill at least two hours. Refrigerate leftovers.

ASK YOUR GUIDE

What are graham crackers?

▶ Graham crackers are really more of a not-too-sweet cookie made from graham flour in the shape of a cracker. Graham flour is a form of whole wheat flour. It is named for Sylvester Graham, a forerunner of the health food movement. Graham developed this form of flour in the 1830s in hopes of diverting people away from the less healthy refined white flour.

Get Linked

Here are some great links to my About.com site for more cookie, brownie, and candy recipes and related information.

CANDY RECIPES

From jelly chews to chocolate truffles to toffee bark, you'll find many different confections here.

http://about.com/homecooking/candy

COOKIE RECIPES

Here you will find recipes for many different kinds of cookies, including bar cookies, drop cookies, and rolled cookies.

http://about.com/homecooking/cookie

BROWNIE RECIPES

Every kind of brownie you need, including jalapeño(!), is in this index.

http://about.com/homecooking/brownie

Chapter 14

Cakes, Pies, and Muffins

About.

ASK YOUR GUIDE:

Does ginger have medicinal value?
▸PAGE **227**

Where did the cherry originate?
▸PAGE **236**

What can I do with the leftover vanilla bean pod after I scrape out the seeds?
▸PAGE **240**

Are blueberries healthier than other fruits?
▸PAGE **242**

Where do pecans come from?
▸PAGE **245**

Blueberry Sour Cream Coffee Cake

SERVES 12

Dried, frozen, or fresh fruit can be used in this rich coffee cake.

½ cup brown sugar
2 teaspoons cinnamon
3⅓ cups flour, divided use
4 tablespoons cold margarine
   (½ stick), cut into small pieces
¾ cup vegetable shortening
1½ cups sugar

3 eggs
2 teaspoons baking powder
1 teaspoon baking soda
½ teaspoon salt
1 cup sour cream
1 pint fresh blueberries

1. Preheat oven to 350°F.
2. Grease a Bundt pan and set aside.
3. Make streusel mixture by combining the brown sugar, cinnamon, ⅓ cup flour, and margarine with fingertips until crumbly. Set aside.
4. Cream together the vegetable shortening and sugar until fluffy.
5. Add eggs, one at a time, beating them in to form a smooth batter. Scrape down sides after each egg.
6. In a separate bowl, mix together 3 cups flour, baking powder, baking soda, and salt with a whisk.
7. Add flour mixture alternately with sour cream to the egg mixture until all is incorporated. Fold the blueberries into the batter.
8. Put half of the batter in the Bundt pan, sprinkle it with the streusel mixture, then layer the rest of the batter on top.
9. Bake 50 minutes, or until a toothpick inserted in the middle comes out clean.

▶ Blueberries are one of the few fruits native to North America. Native Americans used the berries, leaves, and roots for medicinal purposes. The fruit was used as a fabric dye and combined with meat into a nutritious dried jerky. Blueberries used to be picked by hand until the invention of the blueberry rake by Abijah Tabbutt of Maine in 1822—so it's no wonder that Maine's state berry is the blueberry.

Gingerbread

SERVES 9

Queen Elizabeth I of England is credited with the invention of the gingerbread man, which became a popular Christmas treat. This soft gingerbread need not be served only at Christmastime—it's a great treat year-round.

1 cup sugar
1 cup unsalted butter (2 sticks), softened
1 cup molasses
1 cup boiling water
2 teaspoons baking soda
1 tablespoon ground, dried ginger
½ teaspoon cinnamon
2½ cups flour
2 eggs, beaten
1 tablespoon fresh ginger, grated

1. Preheat oven to 350°F.
2. Spray a 9" × 9" × 2" baking pan with nonstick flour baking spray and set aside.
3. In a bowl, mix together the sugar, butter, molasses, and boiling water. Set aside.
4. In another bowl, mix together the baking soda, dried ginger, cinnamon, and flour.
5. Whisk the wet ingredients into the dry ingredients, then mix in the eggs and fresh ginger.
6. Pour the batter into the prepared pan and bake for one hour.

ASK YOUR GUIDE

Does ginger have medicinal value?

▶ Ginger tea has been recommended to alleviate nausea in chemotherapy patients primarily because its natural properties do not interact in a negative way with other medications. It is a safe remedy for morning sickness, since it will not harm the fetus. To make ginger tea: Slice some gingerroot, put it in a tea ball, and place in a teapot. Pour boiling water over the tea ball and let it sit for 10 minutes. Any medicinal use of ginger should be discussed with a physician.

Strawberry Banana Bread
SERVES 6

Bananas and strawberries just scream summer, and luckily they are available year-round, fresh or frozen. This taste-tempting combination is baked into a moist loaf for teatime or brunch.

½ cup sugar
½ cup brown sugar
¾ cup unsalted butter (1½ sticks), softened
2 eggs, beaten
1 teaspoon vanilla extract
3 very ripe bananas, mashed
½ cup strawberries, puréed
2 cups flour
1½ teaspoons baking soda
½ teaspoon salt

1. Preheat oven to 350°F.
2. Spray a 5" × 9" loaf pan with nonstick oil.
3. Combine sugar, brown sugar, and butter in a mixing bowl and beat with an electric mixer until fluffy and light yellow in color.
4. Add eggs and vanilla and mix well.
5. Add mashed bananas and puréed strawberries; mix well.
6. Combine flour, baking soda, and salt in a separate bowl and then add it to the batter, mixing well.
7. Scrape batter into the prepared loaf pan and bake for 1 hour 10 minutes, or until a wooden skewer inserted in the middle comes out clean. Cool on a rack.

TOOLS YOU NEED

▶ Bake this bread in mini loaf pans to give as host/ess gifts, wrapped in cellophane with a recipe attached so if they like it they can bake it themselves! To bake the mini loaves you will need to reduce the time to about 45 minutes. You should use the wooden skewer test to tell when they are done.

Caramel Banana Walnut Cake

SERVES 12

Banana cake is accented here with walnuts and covered in caramel frosting for a flavorful addition to any bake sale.

½ cup unsalted butter (1 stick), softened
1½ cups sugar
2 eggs
1 teaspoon vanilla
2 ripe bananas, mashed

2 cups flour
½ teaspoon baking soda
¼ cup buttermilk
2 cans caramel frosting
1 cup walnuts, chopped

1. Preheat oven to 350°F.
2. Spray 2 cake pans (9" each) with nonstick flour baking spray. Set aside.
3. In a mixing bowl, with an electric mixer, cream butter and sugar until fluffy.
4. Beat in the eggs one at a time, scraping down the bowl after each one.
5. Add the vanilla and bananas and combine until smooth.
6. In a separate bowl, combine flour and baking soda then add the flour mixture to the banana mixture in two parts, alternating with the buttermilk.
7. Pour the batter into the prepared cake pans.
8. Bake for 35 minutes, until a toothpick inserted in the middle comes out clean. Cool and remove cakes from pans. Cool cakes completely before frosting.
9. Frost both cakes with the caramel frosting and then stack one on top of the other. Frost the top and sides with the remaining frosting. Press the walnuts into the frosting around the sides of the cake.

WHAT'S HOT

▶ The yellow sweet banana was discovered in 1836 by Jamaican Jean Francois Poujot, who found one of his banana trees bearing yellow fruit rather than the usual green or red. Upon tasting the new discovery, he found it to be sweet in its raw state. He quickly began cultivating it. Once imported to America, they were considered such an exotic treat that they were eaten on a plate using a knife and fork. Learn more about cooking with bananas at http://about.com/homecooking/bananas.

Pumpkin Pie Cake with Cream Cheese Frosting
SERVES 24

It's everything you love about pumpkin pie all wrapped up in a dense, moist cake with irresistible cream cheese frosting. The texture is somewhere between a pie and a cake.

1⅔ cups cooked pumpkin purée (15 ounces)
1½ cups evaporated milk (12 ounces) (not condensed milk)
1 cup white granulated sugar
2 eggs, at room temperature
¼ cup butter, melted and cooled to room temperature
1 teaspoon pure vanilla extract
½ teaspoon salt
1½ tablespoons ground cinnamon
1½ teaspoons ground nutmeg
½ cup dried cranberries, pre-soaked in hot water for
   15 minutes
1 package yellow cake mix

CREAM CHEESE FROSTING:
8 ounces (1 package) cream cheese, at room temperature
1 cup powdered confectioners' sugar
1 teaspoon pure vanilla extract
1 tablespoon cream
½ cup pumpkin seeds (pepitas), toasted and shelled

1. Preheat oven to 350°F. Line a 9" × 13" baking pan with non-stick foil.
2. In a large bowl, beat pumpkin purée, evaporated milk, sugar, eggs, butter, vanilla extract, salt, cinnamon, and nutmeg until well combined.
3. Toss the cranberries in the cake mix, then add both to the wet ingredients. Stir only until combined. Pour into prepared pan.
4. Bake 50 to 55 minutes or until a toothpick inserted in the center of the cake comes out clean. Let cool to room temperature.
5. Cream cheese frosting: Blend cream cheese, confectioners' sugar, vanilla extract, and cream until smooth. Frost cooled cake. Sprinkle pumpkin seeds evenly on top.

ELSEWHERE ON THE WEB

▶ For more Halloween-themed recipes, visit www .razzledazzlerecipes.com/ halloween. Here you'll find recipes for what to do with that left-over Halloween candy, how to make delicious ghoulish treats, and much more.

Raspberry Fudge Cake
SERVES 10

This cake is so rich, moist, and easy, you'll want to bookmark it for reference. You can also make mini-muffins from this recipe—just fill mini-muffin tins lined with paper cups ⅔ full with the batter and bake 13 to 14 minutes. Feel free to experiment by using different-flavored chips or adding nuts.

> 1 package (about 18.25 ounces) devil's food cake mix
> 1 package(3 ounces) instant chocolate fudge pudding mix
> 1 cup sour cream
> 4 eggs
> ½ cup vegetable oil
> ½ cup water
> 1 bag (6 ounces) of semisweet chocolate chips, chilled
> 1 pint raspberries
> Powdered sugar, for garnish

1. Preheat oven to 350°F.
2. Grease and flour a Bundt or angel-food cake pan.
3. Beat together all ingredients except for chips, raspberries, and powdered sugar in a large bowl for 5 minutes at medium speed. Fold in chips and raspberries by hand.
4. Bake for 55 minutes.
5. Let cake cool completely on a rack, unmold, and then sift powdered sugar over the top.

Cornmeal Raisin Muffins
SERVES 12

Raisins have been around as long as grapes have been growing. We're all familiar with cakes, cookies, and sweet breads bursting with juicy raisins and these muffins are a delicious variation.

1½ cups flour
½ cup yellow cornmeal
⅔ cup sugar
1 tablespoon baking powder
½ teaspoon salt
2 eggs
1 cup milk
6 tablespoons corn oil
1 teaspoon vanilla
1 cup raisins

1. Preheat oven to 400°F.
2. Line a muffin tin with fluted paper cups.
3. Combine flour, cornmeal, sugar, baking powder, and salt in a large bowl using a whisk.
4. Combine eggs, milk, oil, and vanilla in another bowl using a whisk.
5. Stir the wet ingredients into the dry ingredients, fold in the raisins with a spatula, and then fill the muffin cups ¾ full with the batter.
6. Sprinkle the top of the batter with sugar.
7. Bake 15 minutes.

ELSEWHERE ON THE WEB

▶ Remember seeing those dancing raisins on TV? They were introduced in the 1980s by the California Raisin Association. For more information on the wonderful world of raisins, including raisin-related games for kids to play, visit www.calraisins.org.

Kitchen Sink Fruitcake
SERVES 24

Or rather, "everything but the kitchen sink" would be a more appropriate title. This delicious cake includes fruits, nuts, and vegetables all in one tasty package. It is moist and dense thanks to the carrots, pineapple, bananas, and cherries. Even carrot cake haters love this version. This is the best fruitcake you'll ever eat.

2 cups all-purpose flour
1 tablespoon ground cinnamon
¼ teaspoon ground nutmeg
2 teaspoons baking soda
½ teaspoon salt
1 cup vegetable oil
1 cup granulated white sugar
1 cup light brown sugar, firmly packed
4 large eggs
1½ cups carrots (about 2 large—see note, page 235), finely grated
½ cup canned crushed pineapple, drained
2 medium-size ripe bananas, mashed
½ cup walnuts, chopped
1 cup dried cherries, soaked in hot water for 30 minutes, then drained and patted dry

FROSTING:
8 ounces cream cheese, room temperature
1½ cups powdered sugar
¼ teaspoon cinnamon
1 teaspoon pure vanilla extract

Kitchen Sink Fruitcake (continued)

1. Preheat oven to 350°F. Line a 9" × 13" baking pan with non-stick foil or grease and flour pan.
2. In a medium bowl, whisk together flour, cinnamon, nutmeg, baking soda, and salt. Set aside.
3. In a large bowl, beat vegetable oil, white sugar, brown sugar, and eggs on medium speed until combined. Whisk in carrots, pineapple, and bananas.
4. Add dry ingredients to wet ingredients a third at a time until incorporated. Fold in walnuts and cherries.
5. Pour batter into prepared pan and spread evenly. Bake 40 to 45 minutes or until tester in center of cake comes out clean. Cool to room temperature.
6. Frosting: Beat cream cheese, powdered sugar, ¼ teaspoon cinnamon and vanilla in medium bowl until smooth. Spread frosting over cake.
7. Note: A microplane makes fast and easy work of grating carrots.

ELSEWHERE ON THE WEB

▶ Microplanes are used for various items such as nutmeg, Parmesan cheese, chocolate, citrus zest and ginger. They are available in different widths to accommodate the size of the item to be grated. They also come in fine, coarse, and medium so that you can grate anything to perfection. Visit your local kitchen store to explore the different types, and visit http://us.microplane.com for more information.

Chocolate Dump Cake
SERVES 10

This recipe is designed for kids to bake. It's incredibly easy with no mixing involved. Adults will also love this recipe.

1 can (20 ounces) crushed pineapple, undrained
1 can (21 ounces) cherry pie filling
1 teaspoon almond extract
1 box (18.25 ounces) devil's food cake mix
1 cup semisweet chocolate chips
2 sticks of butter (1 cup), each cut into 12 slices
¼ cup almonds, chopped
Powdered sugar, for garnish

1. Preheat oven to 350°F (325°F for glass baking dish). Have a 9" × 13" baking pan ready.
2. Dump undrained pineapple into the baking dish or pan and spread it out evenly.
3. Using a spoon, dump globs of cherry pie filling evenly on top of the pineapple. Sprinkle the almond extract over the cherries.
4. Sprinkle the cake mix evenly over the cherry and pineapple layers.
5. Scatter the chocolate chips over the cake mix.
6. Place the butter slices evenly over the chocolate chips and cake mix, then sprinkle almonds on top.
7. Bake for one hour. Remove from the oven and sprinkle with powdered sugar.
8. To serve, scoop cake out with a large spoon like a cobbler, and dump it on a nice plate. A scoop of vanilla ice cream is delicious with dump cake. Serve warm or cold.

Strawberry Rhubarb Pie
SERVES 8

Don't stop with strawberries: Rhubarb pie is also good with raspberries, blueberries, or sun-dried cherries.

2 pie crusts (unbaked)
3 cups rhubarb, chopped
2 cups strawberries, hulled and sliced
1 cup sugar
¼ cup cornstarch
Sugar, for garnish

1. Preheat oven to 350°F.
2. Line a pie pan with one of the pie crusts.
3. Mix rhubarb and strawberries together with sugar and cornstarch in a large bowl.
4. Fill the pie shell with the fruit mixture.
5. Cover the filling with the other pie dough circle, crimp the edges to seal, and cut slits in the top. Brush the top crust with water and then sprinkle it with sugar.
6. Bake for 50 minutes. Let pie cool completely before slicing.

WHAT'S HOT

▶ Strawberries are not only tasty, but are low in calories and very nutritious. They are high in vitamin C, which has been shown to be a deterrent to some forms of cancer and also helps prevent oxidation of LDL or bad cholesterol. They are a good source of fiber. But, most important, they are one of the few sources, along with grapes and cherries, of ellagic acid, a compound that has been shown to prevent carcinogens from turning healthy cells into cancerous ones.

Kentucky Derby Mint Julep Cake
SERVES 12 TO 18

With all of the elements of a Southern mint julep cocktail, this cake is perfect for Kentucky Derby Day. The rich pound cake has a chocolate ganache frosting with a light mint flavor to complement the bourbon butter sauce infused in the cake.

CAKE:
3 cups cake flour
2 cups white sugar
1 teaspoon salt
1 teaspoon baking powder
½ teaspoon baking soda
1 cup buttermilk
1 cup unsalted butter, melted
2 teaspoons vanilla extract
4 eggs

MINT FROSTING:
2 cups semisweet chocolate chips (12 ounces)
1 can sweetened condensed milk (14 ounces) (not evaporated milk)
½ teaspoon mint extract
Powdered sugar, for garnish

BOURBON BUTTER SAUCE:
½ cup confectioners' sugar
⅓ cup butter
3 tablespoons water
2 teaspoons bourbon whiskey

1. Preheat oven to 325°F. Grease and flour a 10" Bundt pan.
2. Whisk together flour, sugar, salt, baking powder, and baking soda in a large bowl. Make a well in the center.
3. In a separate smaller bowl, combine buttermilk, butter, vanilla extract, and eggs.

4. Add wet ingredients to flour mixture in the well. Beat at low speed for 1 minute, then increase to medium speed for 3 more minutes. Pour into prepared pan and smooth evenly around Bundt center.

5. Bake for 50 minutes or until toothpick inserted in the center comes out clean. Ten minutes before cake is done, prepare Bourbon Butter Sauce.

6. Bourbon Butter Sauce: In a saucepan over medium heat, combine ½ cup confectioners' sugar, ⅓ cup butter, and 3 tablespoons water. Stir until melted and combined. Do not boil. Remove from heat, continuing to stir for 2 minutes. Then stir in bourbon.

7. When cake is done and still warm from the oven, use a skewer to poke holes around the top of the cake. Pour bourbon butter sauce evenly over the top of the cake. Let cake cool to room temperature in the pan before removing.

8. Mint Frosting: Melt chocolate chips with sweetened condensed milk in heavy saucepan over low heat, stirring constantly until chips are melted. Remove from heat and stir in mint extract. Let cool for 10 minutes, then spread evenly over the cooled cake. Garnish with fresh mint leaves. Chill to set chocolate ganache. Take cake out of the refrigerator 30 minutes before cutting to serve. Sprinkle with powdered sugar.

WHAT'S HOT

▶ In the early part of the 1900s, both evaporated and sweetened condensed milk were used more than fresh milk because they were more shelf-stable and posed less of a health risk than fresh milk. The two are quite different and using the wrong one can ruin your recipe. To learn about the difference between the two, visit http://about .com/homecooking/canned milkinfo.

What can I do with the leftover vanilla bean pod after I scrape out the seeds?

▶ Make vanilla sugar by burying the empty pod in a jar of sugar and letting it sit for 3 months undisturbed. The resulting fragrant sugar can be used to flavor tea, coffee, and other beverages. It can also be sprinkled on cinnamon toast or pie crusts.

Vanilla Bundt Cake
SERVES 10

This cake has the dense texture of pound cake flavored with two different kinds of vanilla. The vanilla bean lends a delicate essence, and the vanilla extract adds depth for a layered effect on the palate.

1 cup sugar	3 eggs
1 cup unsalted butter (2 sticks), softened	2 cups flour
1 tablespoon vanilla extract	1 teaspoon salt
1 vanilla bean, split lengthwise and seeds scraped out and reserved	1 teaspoon baking soda
	2 teaspoons baking powder
	1 cup sour cream
	Confectioners' sugar, for garnish

1. Preheat oven to 350°F.
2. Spray a Bundt pan with baker's nonstick spray. Set aside.
3. Combine the sugar and butter with an electric mixer and beat until fluffy.
4. Add the vanilla and vanilla bean seeds and mix to incorporate.
5. Add the eggs one at a time, scraping down the sides between additions.
6. Combine the flour, salt, baking soda, and baking powder in another bowl, and then add half to the butter mixture and combine.
7. Add half the sour cream and mix well, then repeat with the remaining flour mixture and sour cream. Pour the batter into the prepared Bundt pan.
8. Bake for 45 minutes. Let cool 5 to 10 minutes then invert the pan to release the cake. Cool completely before cutting. Sprinkle with confectioners' sugar.

Cherry Almond Muffins

SERVES 12

One of the most beautiful signs of spring is the flowering of the cherry tree, promising luscious fruit in a matter of a short few months. When they're in the market, make these muffins for breakfast.

2 cups flour
⅔ cup sugar
1 tablespoon baking powder
½ teaspoon salt
2 eggs
1 cup milk
6 tablespoons butter, melted
1 teaspoon vanilla extract
1 cup dried cherries
¼ cup almonds, sliced

1. Preheat oven to 400°F.
2. Line a muffin tin with fluted paper cups.
3. Combine flour, sugar, baking powder, and salt in a large bowl using a whisk.
4. Combine eggs, milk, butter, and vanilla extract in another bowl using a whisk.
5. Stir the wet ingredients into the dry ingredients, fold in the dried cherries with a spatula, and then fill the muffin cups ¾ full with the batter.
6. Sprinkle the top of the batter with almonds.
7. Bake 15 minutes.

TOOLS YOU NEED

▶ There are basically two types of whisk: balloon and flat. Balloon whisks aerate whatever it is you're whipping, and flat whisks keep air bubbles to a minimum. So if you want whipped cream, use a balloon whisk; if you are making an omelet, use a flat whisk.

Patriotic Cupcakes
YIELDS 24

These red, white, and blue cupcakes are decorated for the Fourth of July, but you'll want to serve them year-round.

1 package yellow cake mix	8 ounces cream cheese
⅓ cup applesauce	(1 package), at room
3 egg whites	temperature
1¼ cups water	½ cup confectioners' sugar
3 cups fresh blueberries,	1 teaspoon vanilla extract
divided use	Red shoestring licorice

1. Preheat oven to 350°F. Line standard-size muffin tin with foil or paper muffin cups.
2. Combine cake mix with applesauce, egg whites, and water, mixing on low speed for 30 seconds. Increase to medium speed and beat another 2 minutes.
3. Divide batter evenly into 24 paper-lined muffin cups. Take one cup of the blueberries and distribute evenly on top of batter by dropping blueberries on top without mixing into the batter. Bake according to cake mix package directions. Cool to room temperature on wire racks before proceeding.
4. Beat cream cheese with confectioners' sugar and vanilla extract until smooth and creamy. Spread cream cheese frosting on tops of cooled cupcakes.
5. Cut the red shoestring licorice into 2-inch lengths. Place across one half of the cupcakes in rows (for stripes) over frosting. With the remaining blueberries, stud the remaining half of each cupcake in rows (for stars).

Golden Carrot Cake
SERVES 24

This may well be the ultimate carrot cake. The secret is in the microplaned carrots, which give moisture and natural sugar to the cake, and the spices that tickle the taste buds.

1¾ cups all-purpose flour
1 teaspoon baking soda
2 teaspoons baking powder
2 teaspoons cinnamon
½ teaspoon nutmeg
½ teaspoon salt
1½ cups brown sugar, firmly
  packed
1 cup vegetable oil
3 eggs

½ cup canned crushed pineapple (8 ounces) in juice,
  drained
1 cup golden raisins, soaked in
  water for 15 minutes, and
  drained
1 cup (about 2 large) finely
  grated carrots
½ cup coconut, grated
Confectioners' sugar, for garnish

TOOLS YOU NEED

▶ It's important that the carrots be finely grated. Most graters and/or food processors won't do the trick. This is the perfect job for a microplane grater/zester. If you want to add an extra kick, soak the raisins in rum. You can also use this batter to make miniature 3" × 6" loaves, miniature Bundt cakes, or large muffins. The baking time should be about 25 to 30 minutes.

1. Preheat oven to 350°F. Line a 9" × 13" baking pan with non-stick foil or grease with butter liberally.
2. In a large mixing bowl, whisk together flour, baking soda, baking powder, cinnamon, nutmeg, and salt. Set aside.
3. In a smaller bowl, beat brown sugar, vegetable oil, and eggs until well combined.
4. Add egg mixture to flour mixture and mix well. Stir in crushed pineapple, golden raisins, carrots, and coconut. Mix until evenly distributed.
5. Pour into prepared pan and bake about 30 minutes or until a toothpick inserted in the center comes out clean. Cool to room temperature.
6. Sprinkle the top of the cake with confectioners' sugar and cut into squares.

Orange Chocolate Cupcakes
SERVES 12

There's something magical about the combination of oranges and chocolate. The orange cream-cheese filling for these cupcakes may be made up to 3 days in advance and refrigerated.

ELSEWHERE ON THE WEB

▶ Halloween is the perfect time for these orange and black cupcakes with a ghostly white blob on top. For more spooky creations, visit www .halloweenkitchen.com. You'll find a recipe for bloody popcorn, witch's tea, and more.

1 package cream cheese (8 ounces), softened
2⅓ cup sugar, divided use
2 tablespoons orange zest, grated
1 egg
Pinch of salt
1 cup chocolate chips
3 cups flour

½ cup cocoa powder
2 teaspoons baking soda
1 teaspoon salt
2 cups cold water
⅔ cup vegetable oil
2 tablespoons distilled vinegar
2 teaspoons vanilla extract

1. Make the filling by combining the cream cheese, ⅓ cup sugar, and orange zest until well blended. Add the egg and salt and beat to incorporate. Fold in the chocolate chips and refrigerate until ready to use.
2. Preheat oven to 325°F. Place 12 fluted paper cups in a muffin tin and set aside.
3. Combine the flour, remaining 2 cups of sugar, cocoa powder, baking soda, and salt in a large mixing bowl.
4. In a medium bowl, combine the water, oil, vinegar, and vanilla. Pour the wet ingredients into the dry ingredients and beat with an electric mixer for 3 minutes.
5. Pour the batter into the prepared muffin tin, dividing evenly. Top each cupcake with 1 to 2 tablespoons of the orange cream cheese filling.
6. Bake for 25 to 30 minutes. Cool before serving.

Chocolate Pecan Pie
SERVES 8

Pecan pie is good enough as it is, but when you add chocolate it's even better. Enhance the flavor even more by adding a shot of bourbon or dark rum to the filling.

    1 prepared pie crust (unbaked)
    1½ cups pecans, chopped
    1 cup semisweet chocolate chips
    ½ cup brown sugar
    ½ cup sugar
    1 cup dark corn syrup
    6 tablespoons butter, melted
    3 eggs, slightly beaten
    1 teaspoon vanilla extract
    ½ teaspoon salt

1. Preheat oven to 350°F.
2. Line the empty pie crust with aluminum foil and then fill the foil with pie weights. (Dried beans work well.) Bake for 15 to 20 minutes. Remove from oven and let cool. Remove the weights and carefully peel away the foil.
3. Spread the pecans and chocolate chips out evenly in the pie crust.
4. Whisk together brown sugar, sugar, corn syrup, butter, eggs, vanilla, and salt to make filling.
5. Pour the filling into the crust over the pecans and chocolate.
6. Bake for 50 minutes. Let cool completely before cutting.

ASK YOUR GUIDE

Where do pecans come from?

▶ In 1846, a black slave gardener known only as Antoine developed the Centennial variety of pecan via grafting on Louisiana's Oak Alley plantation. Europeans had never even seen a pecan until the sixteenth century. Pecans were not exploited commercially until the middle of the nineteenth century. Pecan trees can grow to more than one hundred feet tall and live to be more than a thousand years old. Learn more about cooking with pecans at http://about.com/homecooking/pecans.

Get Linked

Here are some great links to my About.com site for more cake, pie, and muffin recipes and related information.

CAKE RECIPES

For cheesecakes, cakes, and fruitcakes, turn to this resource. You'll also find recipes using cake mix as an ingredient here.

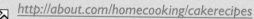 *http://about.com/homecooking/cakerecipes*

PIE RECIPES

All pies savory and sweet can be found at this link.

http://about.com/homecooking/pierecipes

MUFFIN AND QUICK BREAD RECIPES

All types of muffins and quick breads can be found at this link, using ingredients such as fruits, vegetables, chocolate, and nuts.

http://about.com/homecooking/muffinandquickbread

Chapter 15

Gifts from the Kitchen

ASK YOUR GUIDE:

What is the best way to include instructions with mixes?
▶**PAGE 252**

What's the best way to ship my glass jar gifts?
▶**PAGE 258**

Are there any homemade gifts that aren't labor intensive?
▶**PAGE 265**

Chocolate Graham Toffee Bark
YIELDS 1 POUND

These delicious toffee candies start with plain graham crackers and are topped with chocolate and toasted almonds.

½ box (approximate) graham crackers
½ pound butter (two sticks)
¼ cup brown sugar
¼ cup granulated white sugar
2 cups semisweet chocolate chips
1 cup almonds, chopped and toasted

1. Preheat oven to 350°F. Line a 10" × 15" jelly-roll pan with nonstick foil. Arrange whole graham crackers to fit the bottom of the pan in a single layer, breaking up the last few to fit the space.
2. Melt butter in a medium saucepan over medium heat. Add brown sugar and white sugar. Stir to combine. Bring mixture to a boil. Reduce heat and let the mixture gently bubble for 4 minutes. Remove from heat.
3. Carefully pour sugar/butter mixture evenly over the graham cracker layer. Spread to cover. Bake for 10 minutes.
4. When done, remove from oven and let rest until bubbling subsides. Sprinkle chocolate chips evenly over the top. Wait about 2 minutes for chocolate to melt, then use a spatula to gently spread chocolate chips into an even layer on top of the toffee graham crackers. Sprinkle with the chopped almonds, pressing down gently into the chocolate.
5. Cool to room temperature, then refrigerate for 2 hours. Peel foil from chilled bark. Break into 2-inch irregular pieces. Refrigerate any leftovers.

White Chocolate Cherry Mice
YIELDS 36

These white-chocolate and coconut-covered cherry mice are fun to create and make an adorable presentation for parties, bake sales, and of course, Halloween. Let the kids help by setting up a production line, and they will have a ball.

1 jar maraschino cherries with stems, drained and dried
6 ounces white chocolate
½ teaspoon butter
1 ounce paraffin, chopped

½ cup white chocolate chips
½ cup almonds, sliced
1 cup coconut, grated
1 tube red (clear) gel icing

1. Line a cookie sheet with waxed or parchment paper.
2. Rinse the maraschino cherries, drain thoroughly, and let dry on paper towels, turning often. The cherries must be completely dry or the chocolate will seize and get crumbly.
3. Gently melt white chocolate, butter, and paraffin in a double boiler until smooth, stirring often to prevent burning. Once melted, turn off heat but leave in the double boiler on the burner.
4. Dip dry cherries in melted chocolate to completely cover up to the stem. Place on lined cookie sheet. Immediately press a white chocolate chip, on its flat side, to the front of the dipped cherry, to form a head.
5. While chocolate is still warm, wedge two sliced almonds between chocolate chip and cherry to form ears.
6. Sprinkle coconut over the mice and let them cool to harden.
7. Use a toothpick to dab beady red eyes on either side of the chocolate chip with the red gel icing. Refrigerate to firmly set chocolate.

TOOLS YOU NEED

▶ If fresh sweet cherries are in season, by all means use them. Paraffin is sold in the canning supplies section, usually under the brand Gulf Wax. If your cherries are exceptionally large, you may wish to use white chocolate kisses for the heads. Check out the step-by-step instructions with photos of a dark chocolate version before you begin at http://about.com/homecooking/micestepbystep.

Raspberry Hot Chocolate Mix
YIELDS 9 PINT JARS

This makes a nice winter gift for the holidays. You can make other flavors by substituting mint extract, for example, for the raspberry flavoring.

1 box (4 quarts) powdered milk
1 jar (6 ounces) powdered creamer
1 cup powdered sugar
1 box (2 pounds) instant chocolate milk powder
2 teaspoons raspberry flavoring (extract)

1. Mix the powdered milk, creamer, sugar, and chocolate milk powder together in a large bowl.
2. Add the raspberry flavoring and knead well into the powdered mixture with your fingertips.
3. Pack the hot chocolate mix in pint jars with lids.
4. Make a label for the mix with instructions on how to use it: 4 tablespoons of mix to ¾ cup boiling water.

Chocolate Coconut Butter Brickle

YIELDS APPROXIMATELY 4 POUNDS

This delicious candy is suitable not just for the holidays, but for year-long gift-giving on any special occasion. It's also good to give to yourself.

> 1 package saltine crackers (1 sleeve from a box of 4)
> 1 cup brown sugar
> 1 cup butter
> 4 cups chocolate chips
> 1 cup coconut, toasted
> 1 cup macadamia nuts, chopped

1. Preheat oven to 400°F.
2. Line a 12" × 18" × 1" cookie sheet with aluminum foil. Spread crackers side by side, one layer thick. Fold up sides of foil to the edge of the crackers to keep them in place.
3. Combine sugar and butter in a 2-quart saucepan. Bring to boil for 3 minutes. Pour boiling sugar and butter mixture over crackers. Spread to cover evenly. Bake at 400°F for 5 minutes.
4. Remove from oven and let rest about 5 minutes, rearranging crackers back into a single layer if need be. Be careful. It will be very hot and bubbly.
5. In a microwave-safe glass bowl, melt chocolate chips by cooking on high for about three minutes, stirring at one-minute intervals, or until melted. Gently fold in toasted coconut.
6. Spread chocolate mix evenly over the top of the brickle cracker layer. Sprinkle with nuts and let cool to room temperature, then refrigerate for 1 hour. Break into pieces and store in airtight container in the refrigerator.

TOOLS YOU NEED

▶ If you've taken the time to cook up something special, you want it to look as scrumptious as it tastes. Metal tins are available in many shapes, colors, patterns, and sizes. Lidded clear plastic containers are not quite as common, but they are very inexpensive. Dress them up by gluing a fabric or paper skirt around the bottom and coordinating insert into the outer indentation of the lid. A bow on top completes the package.

What is the best way to include instructions with mixes?

▶ Make a gift card with baking instructions to attach as follows: To make Chocolate Chip Cookie Bars: Empty contents of jar into medium bowl. Stir in ½ cup (1 stick) melted butter or margarine; 1 large egg; and 1 teaspoon vanilla. Press into an 8" × 8" × 2" baking pan coated with cooking spray. Bake at 350°F for 18 to 22 minutes or until bars are light golden brown and center is almost set. Makes 16 bars.

Chocolate Chip Cookie Bar Mix in a Jar
YIELDS 16 BARS

This is a way to give the gift of cookies without having to bake them yourself! Try mixing and matching different-flavored chips and nuts.

> ½ cup semisweet chocolate chips
> ½ cup pecans, coarsely chopped, toasted, and cooled completely
> ½ cup light brown sugar, packed
> 2 cups buttermilk biscuit and baking mix, divided use
> ½ cup dark brown sugar, packed

1. In 1-quart wide-mouth glass jar, gently layer and pack ingredients in the order listed, beginning with chocolate chips. Save the second cup of baking mix and add it last.
2. If there is any space left after adding the second half of the baking mix, add more chips or pecans to fill the jar. Place lid on top.
3. Cut an 8-inch circle of fabric to cover lid. Place fabric over lid; secure in place with ribbon or raffia. Decorate as desired.

Marshmallow Surprise Popcorn Balls
YIELDS 15

These delicious popcorn balls have a surprise marshmallow tucked inside. Tie colorful ribbons on the wrappers to give as gifts.

    1 package (14 ounces) caramels
    ¼ cup corn syrup
    2 tablespoons water
    2½ quarts popped popcorn (keep warm in low oven)
    15 large marshmallows

1. Unwrap and melt the caramels in a bowl set over simmering water or a double boiler.
2. Add the corn syrup and water and mix until smooth.
3. Pour the melted caramel mixture over the popcorn in a large bowl or pan. Stir with a wooden spoon or spatula to mix well.
4. With oiled hands, shape the mixture into balls, tucking a marshmallow in the middle of each one before rounding them off.
5. Let the balls cool and dry completely before wrapping in wax paper, plastic wrap, or cellophane bags.

WHAT'S HOT

▶ Gift bags abound and are very inexpensive. Most are plastic-coated, making them a good choice for moist foods. You can easily make a "peek" window in these pretty bags by cutting out a square or shape from the side of the bag and gluing or taping cellophane or plastic wrap to cover the opening. Staple bags shut, tack on a bow, and voila!

Bloody Mary Mix

YIELDS 1 GALLON

This is a variation of a recipe that I picked up many years ago from a bartender friend who was renowned for his Bloody Marys. I think the beef bouillon gives it an added dimension in flavor. It is also a great addition to soups, and a non-alcoholic refreshing tonic.

2 46-ounce cans tomato juice
1 can (10 ounces) beef bouillon
1 teaspoon fresh black pepper, coarsely ground
1 teaspoon celery salt
1 tablespoon fresh horseradish, grated
½ cup lemon juice
1 bottle (5 ounces) Worcestershire sauce
Cayenne pepper sauce, to taste

1. Combine tomato juice, beef bouillon, pepper, celery salt, horseradish, lemon juice, Worcestershire sauce, and cayenne pepper sauce.
2. Mix thoroughly and refrigerate.

Chocolate Candy Cane Bark

YIELDS 1 POUND

This is a wonderful way to give someone the gift of winter holiday flavors. It is also a tasty way to use up an abundance of candy canes.

2 cups good quality semisweet chocolate, chopped
1 tablespoon paraffin, shaved
1 cup crushed candy canes

1. Melt the chocolate and paraffin in a double boiler.
2. Remove chocolate from the heat and stir in the crushed candy canes to coat.
3. Spread evenly on a baking sheet pan lined with a Silpat or foil. Let harden, approximately 1 hour.
4. Break into pieces and store in an airtight container at room temperature.

TOOLS YOU NEED

▶ Pick up orphan plates and platters at yard sales, flea markets, thrift stores, or store bargain bins to use for giving cookies and cakes. Oversized coffee mugs and soup mugs also make good reusable containers for food gifts. For this candy cane bark recipe, fill a mug so that there is a bit overflowing the brim. Place mug on the center of a large piece of colored cellophane, gather the ends at the top and secure with a ribbon.

Fruitcake Cookies with Cream Cheese Glaze
YIELDS 4 DOZEN

These personal-sized "fruitcakes" are topped with a creamy, rich glaze for a tastefully indulgent old-time treat.

FRUITCAKE:
- ⅓ cup unsalted butter, softened
- 1⅓ cups sugar
- 2 eggs
- 1 cup canned solid-pack pumpkin
- 1 teaspoon rum flavoring
- 1 teaspoon orange zest, finely grated
- 2½ cups flour
- 4 teaspoons baking powder
- 1 teaspoon salt
- ¼ teaspoon ground allspice
- 1 teaspoon ground nutmeg
- 1 teaspoon ground cinnamon
- 1 cup dried cherries
- 1 cup dried pineapple, chopped
- 1 cup dried apricots, chopped
- ½ cup pecans, chopped

GLAZE:
- 6 tablespoons cream cheese, softened
- 3 tablespoons fresh lemon juice
- 2 cups powdered sugar
- ¾ cup heavy cream
- 2 teaspoons vanilla extract

TOOLS YOU NEED

▶ A myriad of wonderfully shaped jars, cruets, and bottles are readily available and relatively inexpensive to add to the presentation of your gift. For canning jars, cut out a circle of pretty paper or fabric 2 inches in circumference larger than your jar lid. Secure them with bright yarn or ribbon. Purchase pretty labels to clearly mark your gift with the contents, usage, and recommended shelf life. Adding a recipe for usage of the gift is an appreciated touch.

Fruitcake Cookies with Cream Cheese Glaze (continued)

1. Preheat oven to 400°F.
2. In a large mixing bowl, beat together the butter and sugar until light and fluffy.
3. Beat in the eggs, one at a time, and then beat in the pumpkin, rum flavoring, and orange zest.
4. In a separate bowl mix together the flour, baking powder, salt, allspice, nutmeg, and cinnamon. Stir into the pumpkin mixture.
5. Stir in the cherries, pineapple, apricots, and pecans. Drop the batter by teaspoonfuls onto Silpat-lined baking sheets.
6. Bake 15 minutes, or until lightly browned.
7. Glaze: Beat together the softened cream cheese and lemon juice in a medium bowl until smooth.
8. Add powdered sugar and beat to combine. Beat in heavy cream and vanilla until blended and smooth.
9. Spoon the glaze over the cookies after they cool. (Thin with whole milk if necessary.)

WHAT'S HOT

▶ Those who don't like fruitcake generally point the finger at the candied citron or fruits used in the cake. Candied citron is made from the thick peel of the citrus fruit of the same name. If you don't like it, don't use it. Use dried fruits you like, and you may find fruitcake, and fruitcake derivatives, to your liking after all.

What's the best way to ship my glass jar gifts?

▶ When shipping more fragile bottles and jars, make sure they are tightly sealed. Place inside a plastic zip-top bag, leaving it full of air for added cushioning. Further protect the bottles by wrapping in bubble wrap. Once all individual items are tightly sealed, place into a sturdy carton for shipping. Use popped corn, wadded-up newspaper, bubble-wrap, or Styrofoam or cornstarch pellets to pack completely around any glass items.

Blueberry Butter
YIELDS 4 HALF PINTS

Apple butter gets a twist with this beautiful blueberry version that will dazzle your gift recipients.

> 4 cups apples, peeled and chopped
> 4 cups blueberries
> 1½ cups brown sugar
> 1½ cups sugar
> 1 teaspoon cinnamon
> ½ teaspoon nutmeg
> ¼ teaspoon allspice

1. Put apples, blueberries, sugars, and spices in a large pot, stir, and cook over medium heat until the sugar dissolves.
2. Bring to a boil then reduce heat and simmer 45 minutes, stirring occasionally.
3. Pour into hot sterilized jars, filling to ¼-inch from the top. Wipe jar rims. Cover at once with metal lids and screw-on bands. Process in boiling water bath for 10 minutes.

Mango Chutney

YIELDS 3 CUPS

Purchased mango chutney is good in a pinch, but this homemade version will knock your socks off.

2 cups mangoes, peeled and diced
¾ cup brown sugar, packed
½ cup currants
1 garlic clove, minced
½ cup apples, chopped
¼ cup green pepper, chopped
½ cup sweet onion, chopped
½ cup water
2 tablespoons fresh gingerroot, grated
¼ cup cider vinegar
¼ teaspoon ground cloves

1. In a nonreactive 3-quart saucepan, combine mangoes, brown sugar, currants, garlic, apples, green pepper, onion, water, ginger, vinegar, and cloves.
2. Heat to boiling over high heat. Reduce heat and simmer, stirring occasionally, for 15 minutes.
3. Cool and store covered in the refrigerator for up to one week.

ELSEWHERE ON THE WEB

▶ Do not mail highly perishable foods such as soft cheeses or meats. Cured dry sausages and hard aged cheeses are fine. Firm baked goods are best, such as cookies, candies, flavored nuts, fudge, breads, unfrosted cakes, and muffins, chutneys, and preserves. For more information and tips on shipping, visit the United States Postal Service Web site at www.usps.com.

▶ Save empty potato chip cans (such as Pringles and Stax). Wash the insides and let them dry thoroughly. Use decorative contact paper or glue on gift-wrapping paper to cover the outside of the can. Stack cookies or fill with spiced nuts or candies, seal, and top with a fancy bow.

Crunchy Rainforest Nuts

YIELDS 3 CUPS

Put these candied nuts in a decorative tin to give for Christmas presents or for any other holiday. For a variation of this recipe, try a mixture of different nuts if you don't care for these. They are easy to make, so don't delay.

2 egg whites, at room temperature
1 cup brown sugar, packed
¼ cup (½ stick) butter, melted and cooled to room temperature
1 pound Brazil nuts
½ pound cashews

1. Preheat oven to 275°F. Have an ungreased 15½" × 10½" jelly-roll pan ready.
2. Using an electric mixer, place egg whites in a bowl big enough to accommodate the nuts. Beat until the whites form soft peaks when beaters are lifted.
3. Add brown sugar ¼ cup at a time, beating well after each addition until mixture is stiff and glossy.
4. With a large spatula, stir in melted butter. Gently fold nuts into meringue mixture until they are evenly coated, taking care not to break nuts.
5. Spread coated nuts evenly on ungreased jelly-roll pan. Bake about 1 hour, stirring every 15 minutes to keep nuts separate, until meringue is dry and nuts are crunchy. Let cool in pan, stirring occasionally to keep separate.
6. Pour cooled nuts into covered containers and store up to 2 months at room temperature.

Bread and Butter Pickles
YIELDS 5 PINTS

These pickles are sweet and sour and they make a marvelous-looking gift. Add red bell peppers for extra color.

8 cups medium cucumbers, sliced ⅛-inch thick
2 cups small onions, sliced ⅛-inch thick
¼ cup kosher salt
½ cup water
1½ cups sugar
2 cups white vinegar
1 teaspoon turmeric
1 teaspoon mustard seed
½ teaspoon celery seed
5 whole cloves

1. Sprinkle the cucumbers and onions with salt and then soak them in ice water for 2 to 3 hours.
2. Combine the water, sugar, vinegar, and spices in a large pot and bring to a boil.
3. Drain the cucumbers and onions, then add them to the vinegar mixture and bring the whole pot back to a boil.
4. Remove from heat and ladle the pickles into sterilized pint jars and seal the lids in a water bath.

WHAT'S HOT

▶ Looking for something different but useful to give to your favorite cook? The following suggestions are a little off the beaten path, but are sure to be appreciated. These ideas are useful as stocking stuffers or for year-round gift-giving, and prices range from inexpensive to indulgent. Try giving an adjust-a-cup measuring cup, a heat resistant silicon spatula, or Silpat baking sheets to a budding pastry chef. Any cook will appreciate a garlic-peeler tube, microplane zester, or immersion blender.

Colorful Caramel Corn

YIELDS 8 CUPS

You can use any flavor gelatin you want for this recipe. Make several different flavors and combine them for a rainbow gift.

8 cups popped corn
¼ cup butter
3 tablespoons corn syrup
½ cup sugar
1 small box grape gelatin

1. Put popcorn in a large bowl.
2. Preheat oven to 300°F. Line a baking sheet pan with foil.
3. Heat the butter and corn syrup in a saucepan over low heat. Add the sugar and gelatin, stir, raise the heat to medium and bring the mixture to a boil.
4. When mixture comes to a boil, reduce the heat to low and simmer for 5 minutes.
5. Remove the syrup from the heat and immediately pour it over the popcorn. Toss the popcorn to coat it well and then spread it out on the foil.
6. Bake the coated popcorn for 10 minutes. Cool and break up into smaller pieces.

Silly Strawberries
YIELDS 75

These whimsical sweet treats make a nice addition to a petit four plate, cookie platter, or buffet.

    2 packages (7 ounces each) shredded coconut
    2 small boxes strawberry gelatin, divided use
    1 can sweetened condensed milk (not evaporated)
    ½ teaspoon almond extract
    5 drops red food coloring
    Paper candy cups (optional)

1. In a bowl, mix together coconut and 1 box of gelatin. Set aside.
2. In another bowl, combine the sweetened condensed milk, almond extract, and food coloring.
3. Pour the sweetened condensed-milk mixture over the coconut mixture and combine well.
4. Put the second box of gelatin in a bowl.
5. Shape coconut mixture into small strawberries and roll them in the dry gelatin. Shape again then let dry on a baking sheet.
6. Put each strawberry in a paper candy cup if desired.

ELSEWHERE ON THE WEB

▶ Miniature kitchen tools are cute, functional, and make great package decorations. Pick up some smidgen measuring spoons or mini egg whisks to dress up your kitchen gift. Another fun package decoration is a cookie cutter. Pick one that goes with the theme of the present. For a large supply of cookie cutters, including those hard-to-find shapes, visit www.cookiecutter.com.

▶ Here are some ideas for a nice hostess gift: Purchase a small Styrofoam cone. Using toothpicks to attach, cover the cone with fresh cranberries. Use whole clove studs interspersed and leftover pine clippings or fresh herbs as a decorative base. Or, purchase a salt mill or pepper grinder and package with gourmet salt or peppercorns. Lastly, you could line a large, heavy oven mitt with colored cellophane, fill with gourmet jellybeans or nuts, and tie with a bright ribbon.

Festive Snack Mix
YIELDS 14 CUPS

This takes snack mix a step further than the usual savory version with honey, spices, dried fruit, and chocolate.

3 cups crispy rice squares cereal
3 cups corn squares cereal
3 cups oat rings cereal
1 cup pretzel sticks
1 cup pecans
6 tablespoons butter, melted
2 tablespoons Worcestershire sauce

1 tablespoon honey
1 teaspoon seasoning salt
Pinch of cinnamon
1 cup honey-roasted peanuts
1 cup multicolored candy-coated chocolate pieces
1 cup Cheddar goldfish-shaped crackers
½ cup dried cranberries

1. Preheat oven to 250°F.
2. Combine cereals, pretzels, and pecans in a large roasting pan.
3. Combine melted butter, Worcestershire sauce, honey, seasoning salt, and cinnamon in a small bowl.
4. Drizzle the butter mixture over the cereal mixture and toss to distribute.
5. Bake in the oven for 20 minutes. Stir. Bake for another 20 minutes. Remove from oven, spread mix out on baking sheets, and let cool.
6. Toss the cooled mix with the peanuts, candy-coated chocolate pieces, crackers, and dried cranberries. Package the mix in cellophane bags or jars to give as gifts.

Butterscotch Porcupines
YIELDS 3 DOZEN

These crunchy butterscotch and chocolate candies are easy to create for parties, bake sales, gifts, and Halloween. The salty pretzels are a tantalizing offset to the sweetness of the combined butterscotch and chocolate. Be sure to let the kids help.

1 cup butterscotch chips
1 cup semisweet chocolate chips
1 can (14 ounces) sweetened condensed milk
2 cups pretzel sticks, broken into ½-inch pieces
1 cup honey-roasted peanuts
½ cup miniature candy-coated chocolate bits

1. Melt butterscotch, chocolate chips, and sweetened condensed milk in a heavy saucepan over low heat. Stir constantly until melted and smooth. Do not let it boil. Remove from heat and let rest for 5 minutes.
2. In a large bowl, toss pretzel sticks, peanuts, and chocolate bits until evenly combined. Gently fold in melted butterscotch/chocolate mixture.
3. Working quickly, drop mixture by the tablespoon onto wax paper-lined baking sheets. Refrigerate at least two hours, until firm.

ASK YOUR GUIDE

Are there any homemade gifts that aren't labor intensive?

▶ Try these: For families with children, fill a cookie jar with cookie-decorating accessories such as small bottles of neon food coloring, colored sugars, candy sprinkles, and jimmies. Or, purchase a Bundt pan with a hole in the center. Make a small nosegay of silk flowers in an inexpensive miniature bud vase and place in the center. Wrap with colored cellophane and a bow. Lastly, you can gather up treasured family recipes and copy them into a colorful purchased journal.

Get Linked

Here are some great links to my About.com site for more recipes and ideas for gifts from the kitchen.

MARMALADE RECIPES

There are many recipes for various marmalades here, as well as recipes using marmalade as an ingredient.

 http://about.com/homecooking/marmalade

GIFTS FROM THE KITCHEN RECIPES

Jams and jellies, cookies, and more are in this index of recipes suitable for gift-giving.

 http://about.com/homecooking/gifts

Appendix A: Glossary

Anchovies and anchovy paste   Tiny little fish that are filleted or not, salted, and packed in oil. The paste is a mash of the fishes. Both forms are used as flavorings, particularly in the famous classic Caesar salad dressing and Worcestershire sauce. There is generally no fishy flavor imparted when used in recipes.

Bake   Cook by dry heat in the oven.

Balsamic vinegar   A dark red, flavorful vinegar made from white grapes. It is aged for years and has a slightly sweet, robust flavor. It is more expensive because of the aging process, but well worth it.

Baste   Brush or spoon liquid over food while roasting.

Blanch   Partially boil and then stop the cooking in ice water.

Boil   1. To heat to a temperature of 212°F. The liquid is boiling when bubbles rise to the surface. A rolling boil is when the liquid continues to bubble, even when stirred. 2. To cook in hot, bubbling liquid.

Braise   Bake, covered, in a small amount of liquid.

Broil   Cook with the flame or heat source directly above the food.

Broth   The liquid derived from cooking foods in water, often referred to as bouillon.

Brown   Fry food in a small amount of oil briefly, just until the food turns brown on the outside.

Brown sugar   White sugar mixed with molasses. Brown sugar is more moist than granulated white sugar. Light brown sugar has less molasses and a more delicate flavor than dark brown sugar. Most recipes specifying brown sugar require that the sugar be firmly packed into the measuring cup.

Caramelize   Sauté until natural sugar (or added sugar) in food turns brown.

Chives   Not to be confused with scallions, chives are an herb with green, thin, tubular stems. As a member of the onion family, they have a faint onion flavor. Chives are used as a condiment, garnish, and ingredient when a strong onion presence is not desirable.

Chop   Coarsely cut into bite-sized or smaller pieces.

Cilantro   The green leaves and stems of the coriander plant, used as an herb most commonly in Latin American, Asian, and Caribbean dishes. This herb is also referred to as Chinese parsley and coriander. Although cilantro leaves are available dried, they lose much of their flavor and aroma during the drying process, so use fresh if at all possible.

Colander   A perforated, bowl-shaped container used to strain liquids from foods.

Condiment   A sauce, relish, chutney, or spice mixture served as an accompaniment to foods as a flavor enhancer. The two most popular condiments in the United States are mustard and ketchup.

Confectioners' sugar   Granulated sugar that has been ground into a fine powder. It is also commonly called powdered sugar. This fine sugar melts more quickly than granulated sugar and is often used in candies and frostings or as a decorative dusting on cakes, cookies, muffins, and pastries. Confectioners' sugar contains a small amount of cornstarch to prevent clumping.

Cumin or cumino   A seed from a plant in the parsley family. The seed is often ground into an aromatic powder used in Asian, Mexican, Mediterranean, and Middle Eastern dishes and commonly used in curries and chili powder mixtures.

Curdle or curdled   A term usually applied to dairy mixtures. When mixed with an acid or enzyme, the dairy product will coagulate into clumps in the liquid like extremely soured milk.

Curry powder   An Indian mixture of up to twenty different spices blended together. Most curry mixes are spicy hot, with the hotter commercial variety usually being labeled as Madras curry powder.

Deglaze   Loosen browned flavor bits from a pan with a liquid.

Dice   Cut julienne strips into squares.

Fold   A technique used to combine a light and airy ingredient with a heavier ingredient. A spatula is used to gently incorporate the bottom ingredient to the top in a circular motion, turning the bowl one-quarter turn with each rotation of the spoon until the lighter ingredient is completely incorporated. This gentle process helps retain the air bubbles in the lighter ingredient.

Food processor   A kitchen appliance that can chop, dice, shred, slice, grind, and purée most foods. Most are also able to knead simple dough mixtures if you take care not to over-process. High-end models can perform other functions as well, such as making pasta.

Fry   Cook in hot fat.

Grill   Cook with the flame or heat source directly under the food.

Horseradish   A root vegetable prized for its pungent, spicy heat. Horseradish is usually grated and preserved in vinegar to be used as a condiment. It is also used in sauces. Horseradish is quite strong and spicy when first grated but loses its punch with time.

Jalapeño   A popular chili pepper named for the city of Jalapa in Mexico. It is green in color and averages about two inches long and about one inch in diameter. On a scale of one to ten, the japaleño ranks at four on the Scoville chart for heat level. Removal of the veins and seeds will reduce the heat factor. Use gloves when handling chili peppers and avoid touching your eyes or body.

Margarine   A butter-like spread made from vegetable oil. Also referred to as "oleo" or "oleomargarine." Butter may be substituted for margarine in most cases.

Marinate   To soak foods in an acidic, enzymatic, or spiced mixture to tenderize and/or infuse flavor. The liquid is known as marinade. The most common ingredients in marinades are pineapple, papaya, ginger, kiwifruit, figs, citrus fruits, mango, wine, vinegar, beer, tomatoes, yogurt, and buttermilk. Foods may also be marinated in spice and herb mixtures

Mince   Chop very fine, finer than dice.

Mustard   Mustard seeds are ground into a paste and often combined with seasonings and/or wine. Mustard is used as a condiment and ingredient in sauces and salad dressings. Dry (powdered) mustard is used as a spice. Mustard greens are the edible leaves of the plant.

Paprika   A seasoning made from ground pimiento sweet red peppers. The finest is said to be Hungarian sweet paprika. Hot varieties are also available. Paprika is often used for a dash of color on such favorites as deviled eggs and casseroles. Dishes made with large amounts of paprika are referred to as paprikash.

Pimento or pimiento A variety of sweet red pepper which is said to be sweeter, juicier, and more aromatic than the standard red bell pepper. They are widely available in canned and bottled form. Green olives are often stuffed with pimentos.

Pipe A process of forcing a mixture into the hollow of another food, usually by use of a pastry bag with a metal tip that may or may not be decorative. If you do not have a pastry bag, a zip-top bag is usually a serviceable substitute. Just fill the bag with the food to be piped, seal, and snip off one corner.

Preserves Gelled fruit or vegetables that contain chunks or pieces rather than being puréed and smooth like jellies.

Press To push food through a sieve, ricer, or slots. This term is often applied to garlic, which is pushed through a tool called a garlic press, which reduces the garlic to small bits and juice. It is also applied to cookies where the dough is pushed through a die to form specific uniform shapes. The term is also used when applying pressure by way of heavy weights on top of foods while cooking, as in pressed duck or chicken, or when cooking bacon to keep it from curling.

Puff pastry A dough made by a process of placing pats of butter in between sheets of dough, then rolling and folding the dough until it consists of hundreds of layers. As it bakes, the moisture from the butter causes the dough to puff and separate into flaky layers.

Pulse This term is commonly used in reference to the use of a food processor or blender. To pulse is to allow the machine to run in one-second increments until the desired consistency of the food is obtained.

Reduce Simmer to thicken by evaporation.

Roast Bake in dry heat, usually meat or vegetables.

Roux A paste formed by cooking butter and flour together, used for thickening sauces, gravies, soups, and stews.

Sauté A method by which food is cooked quickly in very little oil or fat, usually in a skillet over direct heat. The pan used for sautéing is called a sauté pan and generally has high, rounded sides and a long handle.

Serrated knife A knife with an edge much like a saw. These knives are used with a sawing motion and work well for breads, tomatoes, and steaks.

Simmer Cook in liquid that is barely boiling.

Steam Cook in a basket or on a rack set over boiling water.

Stiff peaks This term is applies to whipping cream or cream mixtures. The cream is beaten until firm points stay upright when the beater is lifted from the mixture. If the peaks fall over when the beater is lifted, this is known as soft peaks.

Sweat Sauté on low heat until translucent (as in onions) and tender.

Vegetable spray Vegetable or olive oil that is commercially packaged in an aerosol can under pressure. You can also purchase oil misters and use your own oil.

Whisk A utensil made of looped wires in the shape of a teardrop used to combine and aerate mixtures. The term is also used as a verb, e.g., to whisk ingredients together by use of the utensil.

Worcestershire sauce A dark, piquant sauce used as a seasoning or table condiment. The sauce is made by many companies but usually includes tamarind, garlic, onions, molasses, lime, soy sauce, anchovies, vinegar, and other seasonings.

Appendix B
Suggested Menus

Bistro Fare
Brandy Peppercorn Filet Mignon (page 74)
Creamed Parsley Potatoes (page 43)
Broiled Tomato Halves (page 50)
Mint-Chocolate Mousse Bars (page 212)
Pinot Noir

Cuban Menu
Mango Mojo Pork Chops (page 88)
Coconut Rice (page 63)
Refried Black Beans (page 67)
Caramel Banana Walnut Cake (page 229)
Mojitos

Diner Dinner
1950s-Style Meatloaf (page 75)
Herbed Roasted Garlic Mashed Potatoes (page 47)
Shallot Green Beans Almandine (page 45)
Strawberry Rhubarb Pie (page 237)
Chocolate Kahlúa Malts

Football Cookout
Texas Brisket (page 71)
Ranch House Beans (page 65)
Red, White, and Blue Potato Salad (page 14)
S'mores Cups (page 223)
Lemonade and Beer

French Cafe
Nutty Parmesan Sole (page 130)
Savory Lemon Couscous (page 66)
Leek Gratin (page 44)
Chocolate Raspberry Meringue Cookies (page 207)
Sauvignon Blanc

Harvest Dinner
Roasted Herbed Turkey Breast (page 114)
Oyster and Rice Dressing (page 62)
Cranberry Acorn Squash (page 39)
Pumpkin Pie Cake with Cream Cheese Frosting (page 230)
Merlot

Italian Trattoria
Artichoke Hazelnut Soup (page 145)
Capri Salad (page 8)
Easy Chicken Piccata (page 108)
Gnocchi with Blue Cheese and Bacon (page 54)
Pinot Grigio and Chianti

LA Restaurant
Vegetable Soup with Pesto (page 157)
Mushroom Lasagna (page 55)
Caesar Salad Dressing (page 182)
Golden Carrot Cake (page 243)
Chardonnay

Mediterranean Meal
Olive Tapénade (page 191)
Pomegranate Lamb (page 81)
Apricot Scallion Rice Pilaf (page 56)
Champagne Vinaigrette on Mixed Greens (page 180)
Sangria

Summertime Patio Meal
Teriyaki Flank Steak (page 70)
Blue Cheese and Bacon Twice-Baked Potatoes (page 38)
Zucchini Tomato Casserole (page 51)
Orange Chocolate Cupcakes (page 244)
Iced Tea and Margaritas

Valentine Dinner
Onion Tart (page 48)
Pork Loin with Cherry Sauce (page 86)
Herbed Rice (page 61)
Mustard-Glazed Carrots (page 41)
Raspberry Fudge Cake (page 232)
Champagne

Appendix C:
Other Sites and Further Reading

Other Sites

About Southern U.S. Cuisine

Diana Rattray has amassed thousands of recipes covering good ol' Southern food featuring everything from classic soul food to French-influenced Cajun fare. The collection of slow-cooker recipes are a bonus for busy cooks.

http://southernfood.about.com

The Cook's Thesaurus

The most extensive online food dictionary, this site includes definitions, photos, cooking tips, substitutions, and more. If you don't know what an ingredient is, check here for a description, photo, and possible substitutions.

http://www.foodsubs.com

Paula Deen's Home Cooking

Paula Deen is the epitome of old-fashioned home cooking. Her recipes usually include lots of forbidden but yummy butter and mayonnaise, right out of the '50s and '60s. You just have to love her sense of humor.

http://www.foodnetwork.com/food/show_pa

Taste of Home

This popular magazine is based on recipe submissions from home cooks around the country. The Web site has a good catalog of free recipes from the magazine available for download.

http://www.tasteofhome.com

RecipeSource

RecipeSource is the original *SOAR*, the Searchable Online Archive of Recipes. It dates back to the early days of recipe sharing online, even before the Web, and still contains some great tried-and-true recipes from cooks around the nation and the world.

http://www.recipesource.com

Further Reading

The New Doubleday Cookbook by Jean Anderson and Elaine Hanna

Every kitchen needs a good all-around cookbook, and this is one I recommend. It contains more than 4,000 recipes from traditional American favorites to international delights. The recipes also contain basic nutritional statistics as well as suggested variations and reference charts.

The New Food Lover's Companion by Sharon Tyler Herbst

> With more than 6,000 entries, this culinary dictionary is a must-have food-reference tool for any kitchen. The entries explain all manner of foods, cooking techniques, kitchen utensils, measurements, substitutions, and other cooking terminology.

The New Food Lover's Tiptionary by Sharon Tyler Herbst

> This is an accompaniment to the *Food Lover's Companion* that includes more in-depth cooking tips, hints, shortcuts, and substitutions for the individual food entries. This is an excellent resource for novice and experienced cooks alike.

The Food Substitutions Bible by David Joachim

> This book lives up to its name with more than 5,000 substitutions for almost any kind of food, including exotic and unusual ingredients. Also included are healthier options, flavoring suggestions, altitude baking adjustments, and kitchen equipment measurement equivalents.

Ball Complete Book of Home Preserving by Judi Kingry and Lauren Devine

> For canning and preserving enthusiasts, this is the bible of canning resources with more than 400 recipes as well as comprehensive directions, equipment information, and tips.

Index

▶ IT'S **About** INFORMATION DELIVERED IN A REVOLUTIONARY NEW WAY.

The Internet. Books. Experts. This is how—and where—we get our information today. And now, the best of these resources are available together in a revolutionary new series of how-to guides from **About.com** and Adams Media.

**The About.com Guide to
Acoustic Guitar**
ISBN 10: 1-59869-098-1
ISBN 13: 978-1-59869-098-9

**The About.com Guide to
Baby Care**
ISBN 10: 1-59869-274-7
ISBN 13: 978-1-59869-274-7

**The About.com Guide to
Getting in Shape**
ISBN 10: 1-59869-278-X
ISBN 13: 978-1-59869-278-5

**The About.com Guide to
Having a Baby**
ISBN 10: 1-59869-095-7
ISBN 13: 978-1-59869-095-8

**The About.com Guide to
Job Searching**
ISBN 10: 1-59869-097-3
ISBN 13: 978-1-59869-097-2

**The About.com Guide to
Owning a Dog**
ISBN 10: 1-59869-279-8
ISBN 13: 978-1-59869-279-2

**The About.com Guide to
Shortcut Cooking**
ISBN 10: 1-59869-273-9
ISBN 13: 978-1-59869-273-0

**The About.com Guide to
Southern Cooking**
ISBN 10: 1-59869-096-5
ISBN 13: 978-1-59869-096-5

Available wherever books are sold! Or call us at 1-800-258-0929 or visit us at *www.adamsmedia.com*.